TOP TRAILS

Great Smoky Mountains National Park

50 MUST-DO HIKES FOR EVERYONE

SECOND EDITION

Written by
Johnny Molloy

 WILDERNESS PRESS ... *on the trail since 1967*

Top Trails Great Smoky Mountains National Park: 50 Must-Do Hikes for Everyone
Second edition, first printing

Copyright © 2017 by Johnny Molloy

Project editor: Ritchey Halphen
Maps and elevation profiles: Steve Jones and Johnny Molloy
Interior photos: copyright © 2017 by Johnny Molloy, except where noted
Cover design: Scott McGrew
Text design: Frances Baca Design; typesetting and layout: Annie Long and Miles Parsons
Proofreaders: Emily C. Beaumont, Rebecca Henderson
Indexer: Ann Weik Cassar/Cassar Technical Services

Library of Congress Cataloging-in-Publication Data

Names: Molloy, Johnny, 1961– author.
Title: Top Trails Great Smoky Mountains National Park : must-do hikes for everyone /
    written by Johnny Molloy.
Description: Second edition. | Birmingham, AL : Wilderness Press, [2017] | Series:
    The Top Trails Series | "1st EDITION 2012"—T.p. verso. | "Distributed by Publishers
    Group West"—T.p. verso. | Includes index.
Identifiers: LCCN 2016056649 | ISBN 978-0-89997-876-5 (paperback)
    ISBN 978-0-89997-877-2 (e-book)
Subjects: LCSH: Hiking—Great Smoky Mountains National Park (N.C. and Tenn.)—
    Guidebooks. | Trails—Great Smoky Mountains National Park (N.C. and Tenn.)—
    Guidebooks. | Great Smoky Mountains National Park (N.C. and Tenn.)—
    Guidebooks.
Classification: LCC GV199.42.G73 M648 2017 | DDC 796.5109768/89—dc23
LC record available at lccn.loc.gov/2016056649

Manufactured in the United States of America

Published by: **WILDERNESS PRESS**
    An imprint of AdventureKEEN
    2204 First Ave. S., Suite 102
    Birmingham, AL 35233
    800-443-7227, fax 205-326-1012

Visit wildernesspress.com for a complete list of our books and for ordering information.
Contact us at our website, at facebook.com/wildernesspress1967, or at twitter.com
/wilderness1967 with questions or comments. To find out more about who we are and
what we're doing, visit blog.wildernesspress.com.

Distributed by Publishers Group West

Cover photo: A view into North Carolina from the Smoky Mountain highlands; photo by
David Allen Photography/Shutterstock.com

Safety Notice Although Wilderness Press and the author have made every attempt to
ensure that the information in this book is accurate at press time, they are not responsible
for any loss, damage, injury, or inconvenience that may occur to anyone while using this
book. You are responsible for your own safety and health while in the wilderness. The fact
that a trail is described in this book does not mean that it will be safe for you. Be aware that
trail conditions can change from day to day. Always check local conditions, know your
own limitations, and consult a map.

The Top Trails Series

Wilderness Press

When Wilderness Press published *Sierra North* in 1967, no other trail guide like it existed for the Sierra backcountry. The first run of 2,800 copies sold out in less than two months, and its success heralded the beginning of Wilderness Press.

Since we were founded 50 years ago, we have expanded our territories to cover California, Alaska, Hawaii, the Southwest, the Pacific Northwest, New England, the Midwest, and Canada. Most recently, we have pushed our boundaries into the Southeast.

Wilderness Press continues to publish comprehensive, accurate, and readable outdoor books. Hikers, backpackers, kayakers, skiers, snowshoers, climbers, cyclists, and trail runners rely on Wilderness Press for accurate outdoor adventure information.

Top Trails

In its Top Trails guides, Wilderness Press has paid special attention to organization so that you can find the perfect hike each and every time. Whether you're looking for a steep trail to test yourself on or a walk in the park, a romantic waterfall or a distant view, Top Trails will lead you there.

Each Top Trails guide contains trails for everyone. The trails selected provide a sampling of the best that the region has to offer. These are the "must-do" hikes, walks, runs, and bike rides, with every feature of the area represented.

Every book in the Top Trails series offers the following:

- The Wilderness Press commitment to accuracy and reliability
- Ratings and rankings for each trail
- Distances and approximate times
- Easy-to-follow trail notes
- Map and permit information

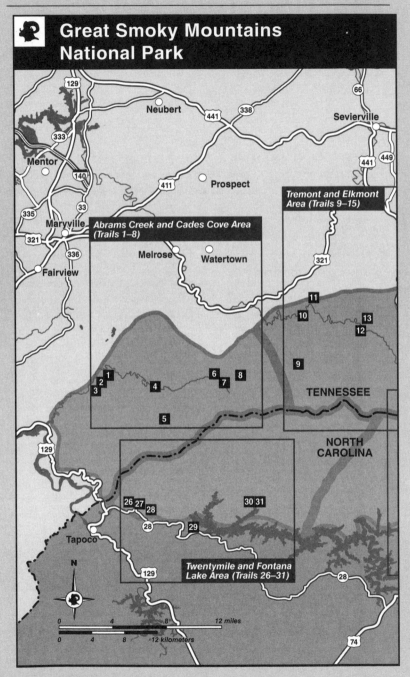

Great Smoky Mountains National Park

Neubert

Sevierville

Mentor

Prospect

Tremont and Elkmont Area (Trails 9–15)

Maryville

Melrose

Watertown

Abrams Creek and Cades Cove Area (Trails 1–8)

Fairview

TENNESSEE

NORTH CAROLINA

Tapoco

Twentymile and Fontana Lake Area (Trails 26–31)

N

0   4   8   12 miles

0   4   8   12 kilometers

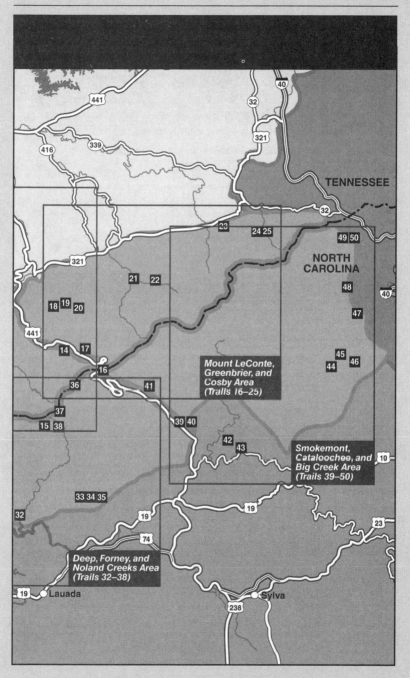

TENNESSEE

NORTH CAROLINA

Mount LeConte, Greenbrier, and Cosby Area (Trails 16–25)

Smokemont, Cataloochee, and Big Creek Area (Trails 39–50)

Deep, Forney, and Noland Creeks Area (Trails 32–38)

Lauada

Sylva

TRAIL FEATURES TABLE

Great Smoky Mountains National Park Trails

TRAIL NUMBER AND NAME	Page	Difficulty –12345+	Length in Miles	Type	Day Hiking	Backpacking	Horses	Child Friendly
1. Abrams Creek and Cades Cove Area								
1 Pine Mountain Loop	27	2–3	8.1	loop	✓	✓	✓	
2 Abrams Falls via Abrams Creek Ranger Station	33	3	11.0	↗	✓	✓		
3 Cane Creek Hike	39	4	9.8	↗	✓	✓	✓	
4 Abrams Falls via Cades Cove	45	2	5.0	↗	✓			
5 Gregory Bald via Gregory Ridge	49	4	11.0	↗	✓	✓		
6 Oliver Cabin via Rich Mountain Loop Trail	55	1–2	2.8	↗	✓		✓	✓
7 Spence Field and Russell Field Loop	61	4–5	13.0	loop	✓	✓	✓	
8 Rocky Top via Lead Cove	69	5	11.6	↗	✓	✓	✓	
2. Tremont and Elkmont Area								
9 Lynn Camp Prong Cascades	83	1	0.8	↗	✓			✓
10 Buckhorn Gap via Meigs Creek	89	2–3	6.8	↗	✓			
11 Walker Sisters Place via Little Greenbrier	95	2	5.0	↗	✓			
12 Cucumber Gap Loop	101	2–3	5.6	loop	✓			
13 Laurel Falls	107	2	2.6	↗	✓			
14 The Chimney Tops	113	3	4.0	↗	✓			
15 Silers Bald via Clingmans Dome	117	3	9.6	↗	✓	✓		
3. Mount Le Conte, Greenbrier, and Cosby Area								
16 Charlies Bunion	133	3–4	8.0	↗	✓	✓		
17 Alum Cave Bluff	139	2–3	4.6	↗	✓			
18 Rainbow Falls	145	2–3	5.4	↗	✓			
19 Baskins Falls	151	2	3.2	↗	✓			
20 Brushy Mountain via Grotto Falls	157	4	6.6	↗	✓			
21 Injun Creek from Greenbrier	163	2–3	6.4	↗	✓	✓		
22 Ramsey Cascades	169	4	8.0	↗	✓			
23 Albright Grove	173	3	6.7	loop	✓			
24 Maddron Bald Loop	179	4–5	17.3	loop		✓		
25 Mount Cammerer via Low Gap	187	5	11.2	↗	✓			

TRAIL FEATURES TABLE

	TERRAIN					FLORA & FAUNA					OTHER							
Summit	Ridgeline	Lake	Stream	Waterfall	Autumn Colors	Wildflowers	Wildlife	Spruce-Fir	Old-Growth	Great Views	Photo Opportunity	Backcountry Camping	Swimming	Secluded	Steep	Historical Interest	Geologic Interest

TRAIL FEATURES TABLE

Great Smoky Mountains National Park Trails

TRAIL NUMBER AND NAME	Page	Difficulty ~12345+	Length in Miles	Type	Day Hiking	Backpacking	Horses	Child Friendly
4. Twentymile and Fontana Lake Area								
26 Twentymile Loop	201	2	7.6	loop	✓	✓	✓	
27 Gregory Bald Loop	207	4	15.5	loop		✓	✓	
28 Shuckstack from Twentymile Ranger Station	215	3	11.0	point-to-point	✓	✓		
29 Lost Cove Loop	221	3–4	11.5	loop	✓	✓		
30 Fontana Lake Hike	227	3	13.3	out-and-back	✓	✓	✓	
31 Ruins of Proctor	235	1	2.0	point-to-point	✓	✓		✓
5. Deep, Forney, and Noland Creeks Area								
32 Goldmine Loop	251	2	3.2	loop	✓	✓	✓	
33 Indian Creek and Sunkota Ridge Loop	257	3	12.0	loop	✓	✓	✓	
34 Falls Loop of Deep Creek	263	1–2	2.4	loop	✓			✓
35 Newton Bald Loop	269	5	22.5	loop		✓	✓	
36 Fork Ridge Loop	277	5	20.1	loop		✓	✓	
37 Forney Creek Loop	285	5	19.4	loop		✓	✓	
38 Andrews Bald	293	2	3.6	point-to-point	✓			✓
6. Smokemont, Cataloochee, and Big Creek Area								
39 Smokemont Loop	309	2	6.0	loop	✓			
40 Cabin Flats Loop	315	4	17.4	loop		✓	✓	
41 Kephart Prong Shelter	321	2	4.0	point-to-point	✓	✓	✓	
42 Flat Creek Falls and Vista	327	2	3.8	point-to-point	✓			✓
43 Hemphill Bald Hike	333	3–4	9.6	point-to-point		✓		
44 Big Fork Ridge Loop	339	3	9.1	loop	✓	✓	✓	
45 Pretty Hollow Gap Loop	345	4–5	19.1	loop		✓	✓	
46 Boogerman Loop	351	3	7.5	loop	✓			
47 Little Cataloochee Church	357	2	4.0	point-to-point	✓		✓	
48 Mount Sterling via Mount Sterling Gap	363	3	5.4	point-to-point	✓	✓		
49 Low Gap Loop	369	5	17.2	loop	✓	✓		
50 Midnight Hole and Mouse Creek Falls	377	2	4.0	point-to-point	✓		✓	

TRAIL FEATURES TABLE

TERRAIN					FLORA & FAUNA					OTHER							
Summit	Ridgeline	Lake	Stream	Waterfall	Autumn Colors	Wildflowers	Wildlife	Spruce-Fir	Old-Growth	Great Views	Photo Opportunity	Backcountry Camping	Swimming	Secluded	Steep	Historical Interest	Geologic Interest
			✓	✓	✓	✓						✓	✓	✓			
✓	✓		✓	✓	✓	✓				✓	✓	✓	✓		✓		
✓	✓		✓	✓	✓	✓				✓	✓	✓	✓		✓		
✓	✓	✓	✓		✓	✓				✓	✓	✓	✓	✓	✓	✓	
	✓	✓	✓		✓	✓				✓		✓	✓			✓	
		✓	✓		✓	✓					✓	✓	✓			✓	
		✓	✓		✓	✓						✓	✓	✓		✓	
	✓		✓	✓	✓	✓						✓		✓		✓	
			✓	✓	✓	✓					✓		✓			✓	
	✓		✓	✓	✓	✓	✓					✓	✓	✓		✓	
	✓		✓		✓	✓		✓		✓		✓	✓	✓	✓		
	✓		✓	✓	✓	✓		✓		✓	✓	✓	✓		✓	✓	
✓	✓				✓	✓		✓		✓	✓						
✓	✓		✓		✓	✓								✓		✓	
	✓		✓	✓	✓	✓						✓	✓			✓	
			✓		✓	✓						✓				✓	
	✓		✓	✓	✓			✓		✓	✓						
	✓				✓	✓		✓		✓	✓			✓			
	✓		✓		✓	✓	✓		✓			✓	✓			✓	
	✓		✓		✓	✓	✓	✓		✓		✓		✓		✓	
	✓		✓		✓	✓			✓							✓	
			✓		✓	✓								✓		✓	
✓	✓				✓			✓		✓	✓	✓		✓			
	✓		✓	✓	✓	✓	✓			✓		✓				✓	
			✓	✓	✓	✓					✓	✓	✓				

Map Legend

Featured trail	▬ ▬ ▬ ▬ ▬ ▬ ▬	Appalachian Trail	◈
Alternate trail	─ ─ ─ ─ ─ ─	Bridge	⊃⊂
Cross-country trail	··················	Campground/campsite	▲
Interstate	━━━━━━	Cemetery	✝
Major road	────	Fire/lookout tower	🔭
Minor road	───	Gate	●━●
		General point of interest	•
		Interstate highway	(40)
Water body	◣◢	Mountain	▲
River/creek	~~~~	Overlook	⧊
		Parking	🅿
State boundary	─·─·─·─	Picnic area	🎋
		Ranger station	🏠
Park/forest	▒▒▒▒	Rapids/cascades	〰
		Restrooms	👫
		State highway	(28)
North indicator	N ⟶✦⟵	Trail shelter	⊏
		Tunnel	⌒
		US highway	(441)
		Vista point	⋈
		Waterfall	//

Contents

CHAPTER 1
Abrams Creek and Cades Cove Area

CHAPTER 2

Tremont and Elkmont Area

CHAPTER 3

Mount Le Conte, Greenbrier, and Cosby Area

CHAPTER 4

Twentymile and Fontana Lake Area

CHAPTER 5

Deep, Forney, and Noland Creeks Area

CHAPTER 6

Smokemont, Cataloochee, and Big Creek Area

Using Top Trails

Organization of Top Trails

Top Trails is designed to make identifying the perfect trail easy and enjoyable, and to make every outing a success and a pleasure. With this book you'll find it's a snap to find the right trail, whether you're planning a major hike or just a sociable stroll with friends.

The Region

Each Top Trails begins with an overview map (pages iv–v), displaying the entire area covered by the guide and providing a snapshot of its geography. The map is clearly marked to show which chapter covers which area.

After the overview map comes the master trails table (pages vi–ix), which lists every trail covered in the guide. Here you'll find a concise description, basic information, and highlighted features, all indispensable when planning an outing. A quick reading of the regional map and trails table will give you a good overview of the entire region covered by the book.

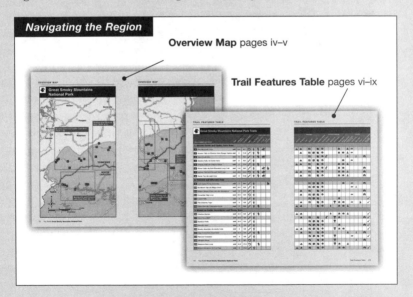

Navigating the Region

Overview Map pages iv–v

Trail Features Table pages vi–ix

The Areas

The region covered in each book is divided into areas, with each chapter corresponding to one area in the region. Each area chapter starts with information to help you choose and enjoy a trail every time out. Use the table of contents or the overview map to identify an area of interest; then turn to the area chapter to find the following:

- An overview of the area's parks and trails, including park and permit information
- An area map showing all trail locations
- A trail features table providing trail-by-trail details
- Trail summaries highlighting each trail's specific features

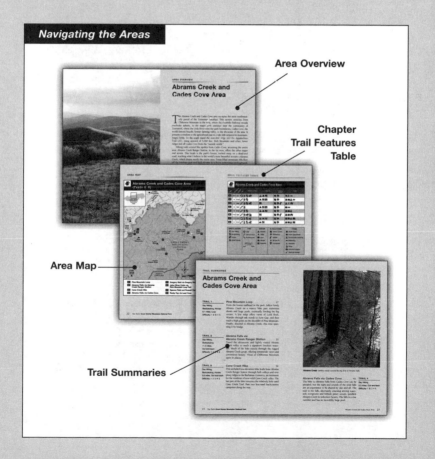

Navigating the Areas

Area Overview

Chapter Trail Features Table

Area Map

Trail Summaries

The Trails

The basic building block of the Top Trails guide is the trail entry. Each one is arranged to make finding and following the trail as simple as possible, with all pertinent information presented in this easy-to-follow format:

- A detailed trail map
- Trail descriptors covering difficulty, length, and other essential data
- A written trail description
- Trail milestones providing easy-to follow, turn-by-turn trail directions
- An elevation profile

Some trail descriptions offer additional information:

- Trail options
- Trail highlights

In the margins of the trail entries, keep your eyes open for graphic icons that signal features mentioned in the text.

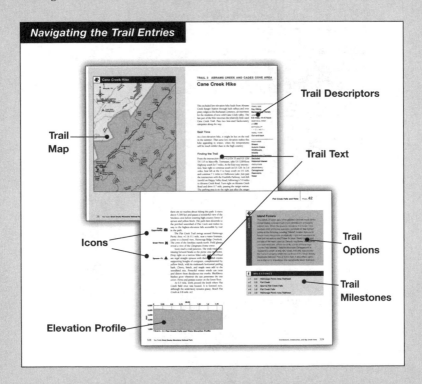

Choosing a Trail

Top Trails provides several different ways of choosing a trail, all presented in easy-to-read tables, charts, and maps.

Location

If you know in general where you want to go, Top Trails makes it easy to find the right trail in the right place. Each chapter begins with a large-scale map showing the starting point of every trail in that area.

Features

This guide describes the Top Trails of Great Smoky Mountains National Park. Each trail was chosen because it offers one or more features that make it appealing. Using the trail descriptors, summaries, and tables, you can quickly examine all the trails for the features they offer or seek a particular feature among the list of trails.

Best Time

Time of year and current conditions can be important factors in selecting the best trail. For example, an exposed low-elevation trail may be a riot of color in early spring but an oven-baked taste of hell in midsummer. Wherever relevant, Top Trails identifies the best and worst conditions for the trails you plan to hike.

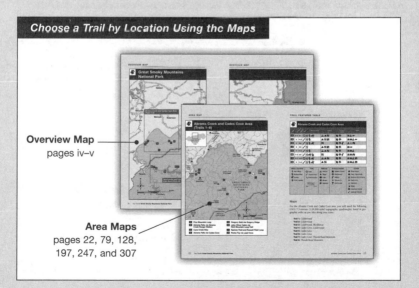

Choose a Trail by Location Using the Maps

Overview Map
pages iv–v

Area Maps
pages 22, 79, 128, 197, 247, and 307

Difficulty

Every trail has an overall difficulty rating on a scale of 1–5, which takes into consideration length, elevation change, exposure, trail quality, etc., to create one (admittedly subjective) rating. See the chart opposite for details.

The ratings assume that you are an able-bodied adult who is in reasonably good shape and using the trail for hiking. The ratings also assume clear, dry weather conditions.

Readers should make an honest assessment of their own abilities and adjust time estimates accordingly. Also, rain, snow, heat, wind, and poor visibility can all affect your pace on even the easiest of trails.

Vertical Feet

Every trail description contains the approximate trail length and the overall elevation gain and loss over the course of the trail. It's important to use this figure when considering a hike; on average, plan 1 hour for every 2 miles, and add an hour for every 1,000 feet you climb.

This important measurement is often underestimated by hikers when gauging the difficulty of a trail. The Top Trails measurement accounts for *all*

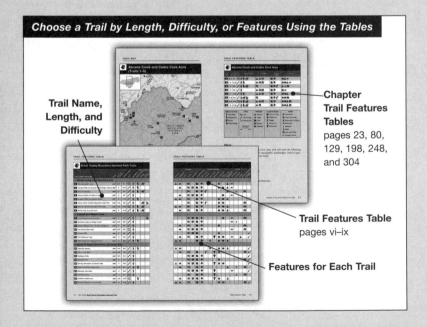

Choose a Trail by Length, Difficulty, or Features Using the Tables

Trail Name, Length, and Difficulty

Chapter Trail Features Tables
pages 23, 80, 129, 198, 248, and 304

Trail Features Table
pages vi–ix

Features for Each Trail

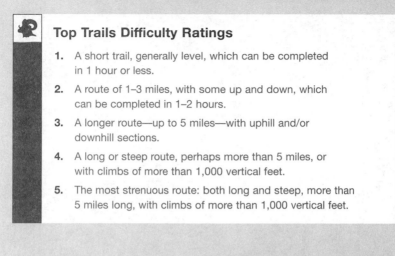

Top Trails Difficulty Ratings

1. A short trail, generally level, which can be completed in 1 hour or less.

2. A route of 1–3 miles, with some up and down, which can be completed in 1–2 hours.

3. A longer route—up to 5 miles—with uphill and/or downhill sections.

4. A long or steep route, perhaps more than 5 miles, or with climbs of more than 1,000 vertical feet.

5. The most strenuous route: both long and steep, more than 5 miles long, with climbs of more than 1,000 vertical feet.

elevation change—not simply the difference between the highest and lowest points, so that rolling terrain with lots of ups and downs will be identifiable.

The calculation of vertical feet in the Top Trails series is accomplished with a combination of trail measurement and computer-aided estimation. For routes that begin and end at the same spot—loops and out-and-backs— the vertical gain exactly matches the vertical descent. With point-to-point routes, the vertical gain and loss usually differ, in which case both figures are provided.

For one-way trips, the elevation gain (+) is listed first, and the loss (–) follows. Loops and out-and-back trips list a single measurement (±) of the elevation gain and loss for the entire trip.

Finally, each trail entry in this Top Trails guide has an elevation profile, an easy means of visualizing the topography of the route. The profile graphically depicts the elevation throughout the length of the trail.

Introduction to Great Smoky Mountains National Park

I have been hiking the Smokies since the early 1980s and have had a Smokies guide in print since 1995, with multiple updated and improved editions. Updating this guide for Wilderness Press gave me the chance to rehike all the trails and write a new guide to what I think is the most beautiful place on the planet. You will find this easy-access reference-type book a marked improvement. Though I've spent more than 800 nights backpacking in the Smokies and countless other times day hiking, any chance to return to the park lets me rediscover and appreciate the crown jewel of the Southern Appalachians. Writing this book meant more reasons to get back to the park where I cut my outdoor teeth.

And what a park it is: more than 800 miles of trails, 500,000 acres of land, and some of the largest stands of old-growth forest in the eastern US. The numbers of flora and fauna are just as impressive: 60 species of mammals, 50 species of fish, 200 species of birds, 1,600 species of flowering plants, 2,000 species of fungi, and more.

With the all-taxa biodiversity survey—an attempted cataloging of every living thing in the park—the sheer numbers and types of life cataloged keep rising. The park boasts numerous trees of record dimensions among the 130-plus species that grow here. The diversity of ecosystems found in the Smokies is unmatched in any other temperate climate. Perhaps this is the reason for its impressive designation as both a national park and an international biosphere reserve.

Choosing the Smokies as a place to spend your free time is a wise decision. And yet the Smokies can be intimidating, especially for the first-time visitor. Not only is there a lot of land to see, but with more than 9 million guests annually, Great Smoky Mountains National Park is the most visited national park in the American system—quite intimidating indeed. Thus, this book was conceived to make the majesty of the Smokies more accessible to visitors.

Smokemont Loop (Trail 39) *takes in the beauty of Bradley Fork.*

With so much land and so many people, discovering the beauty and solitude of this national park can be a hit-or-miss proposition. Where are the spectacular vistas? Where are the waterfalls and the old settlers' cabins? Where can I find solitude? Leaving it all to chance doesn't offer good odds for your all-too-brief vacation from the rat race. Weeks spent daydreaming of your fleeting slice of freedom could culminate in a 3-hour driving marathon or a noisy walk up a crowded trail. Fortunately, with this book, and a little bit of planning and forethought, you can make the most of your time in the Smokies.

This book presents a variety of hikes for you to choose from. The majority of the hikes steer you toward infrequently visited areas, giving you the opportunity to enjoy your time on the trail instead of behind someone's car. These hikes offer solitude to maximize your Smoky Mountains experience. However, as the subtitle of this book suggests, there are some "must-do" hikes that are popular. Consequently, portions of hikes traverse popular and potentially crowded areas. Each hike has a described "best time" that will help you manage the trails to your advantage.

The day hikes offered here fall into one of three categories: out-and-back, loop, or point-to-point (one-way). Out-and-back hikes take you to a particular rewarding destination and back on the same trail. The return trip allows you to see everything from the opposite vantage point. You may notice more minute features the second go-round, and retracing your steps at a different time of day can give the same trail a surprisingly different character.

To some, however, a return trip on the same trail isn't as enjoyable. Some hikers just can't stand the thought of covering the same ground twice, not with hundreds of untrodden Smokies miles awaiting them. Loops and point-to-point hikes avoid this—the ones in this book are generally longer than the out-and-back hikes, but a bigger challenge can reap bigger rewards.

Day hiking is the best and most popular way to break into the Smokies backcountry, but for those with the inclination, this book also offers some overnight hikes. There are 102 designated backcountry sites and shelters available for those who want to capture the changing moods of the mountains. The length of these hikes, three days and two nights, is perfect for the weekend backpacker. Longer trips are also available for those with more time.

A fee-based permit is required for overnight stays in the backcountry. Permits can be obtained through the official park website; visit smokies permits.nps.gov, and then click through the process. At this writing, backcountry reservation fees are $4 per person, per night, with a maximum fee of $20 per person; fees are nonrefundable. (Check the website for the most current prices.) Permits are good for seven nights, and changes to a permit may be made one time.

Reservations/permits may be obtained at any time up to 30 days in advance of the first night of your trip. They may also be obtained in person at the Sugarlands Visitor Center, near Gatlinburg, Tennessee. The Backcountry Office is available to answer questions at 865-436-1297.

Food-storage cables have been installed at backcountry campsites. Please use them—you get to keep your food, and they keep wild bears wild. Bears that get too used to human food often have to be put down.

When you visit the Smokies, it's a great temptation to remain in your car, in part because auto tours—including one end of the famed Blue Ridge Parkway—abound. While auto touring is a great way to get an overview of the park, it creates a barrier between you and the mountains. Windshield tourists, hoping for a glimpse of bears and other wildlife, often end up seeing the tail end of the car in front of them. And while roadside overlooks offer easy views, the drone of traffic and lack of effort in reaching the views can make them less than inspirational. The Smokies were made for *hiking*!

The wilderness experience can unleash your mind and body, allowing you to relax and find peace and quiet. It also enables you to catch glimpses of beauty and splendor: a deer crashing through the underbrush as it clambers up a mountainside, the cabin remnants of early settlers who scrabbled out a living among these woods, or a spectacular waterfall crashing above and below a trail. Out in these woods, you can let your mind roam free, go where it pleases. You can't do that from inside your car.

The Smokies are a wild and beautiful place. I hope you'll get out and enjoy what they have to offer.

Geography and Topography

The topography of the Great Smoky Mountains results from the weathering of one of the oldest mountain ranges in the world: the Appalachians. The Smokies, however, are the highest, wildest range in the entire chain, with more than 30 continuous miles above 5,000 feet, an outlying mountain massif unmatched anywhere east of the Mississippi. Elevations vary from 6,642 feet at Clingmans Dome (a scant 40 feet lower than Mount Mitchell, the highest point in the East) down to the mouth of Abrams Creek, less than 900 feet. This vertical variation is one of the reasons for the incredible diversity of life found within its boundaries.

From the Smokies emerges many a tributary for the Tennessee River. The Little River drains the high country directly into the Tennessee, while others, such the Oconaluftee River, feed bigger tributaries, namely the Pigeon and Little Tennessee Rivers, which in turn flow into the Tennessee River. The Little Tennessee River is dammed in a series of finger lakes—Fontana, Cheoah, and Calderwood—that form the Smokies' southern boundary.

The dominant landform is a high, continuous ridge extending east to west from one end of the Smokies to the other. In addition to dividing river drainages, it also forms the boundary line between North Carolina and Tennessee. Shoulder ridges, like ribs protruding from a backbone, extend from the state-line ridge and separate steep yet deeply wooded valleys cut by eons of precipitation. The Smokies boasts more than 2,100 miles of streams within its 800-square-mile confines.

Flora

The flora of the Smokies, from low to high, replicate a biological journey up the Appalachian Mountains from Georgia to Maine. Upward of 130 tree species are native to the park. But it's not just the beautiful trees and wildflowers that get attention; the Smokies also have amazing arrays of more humble yet biologically important plants from mosses to fungi.

The diverse plant mosaic blends and separates depending on elevation, precipitation, and exposure. In the park's lower reaches grow Southern temperate woodlands, an agglomeration of hardwoods from hickory, sourwood, and sassafras in drier areas to elm, maple, and ash in moister soils. Along the streams, towering white pines, black birch, and yellow birch reign over thickets of rhododendron. Eastern hemlocks have been all but wiped out by the nonnative hemlock woolly adelgid insect, save for specific areas where park personnel have treated specific trees. Forests are undergoing transition where hemlocks have died.

The great cove hardwood forests, where sheltered valleys harbor deep soils, are where tree giants can be found. Dominated by tulip trees, along with buckeye and basswood, the cove hardwoods rise to immense heights, creating a 150- to 200-foot canopy in cool moist hollows.

Drier, well-drained or south-facing ridges have xeric woods of Virginia pine, chestnut oak, and mountain laurel, along with a host of lesser oaks. Climbing higher, the vegetation morphs into northern hardwoods, such as yellow birch, beech, and cherry. Rise still higher, and you get into the spruce–fir woodlands, where evergreens form a mosaic of plant life found in New England or Canada. The forest cloaks the highest mantles of the park, and of that only around 13,000 acres of pure spruce–fir, a relic of a colder time. The last of the ice ages pushed this northern evergreen ecosystem south, and when the earth warmed again, the forest clung atop old Smoky in a climate still favorable for it. This has, in effect, created sky islands of plants and animals whose normal range is far removed from the rest of the South.

Together these forest types, blending and intermingling, make up arguably the most diverse biological life in Earth's temperate climes. But the trees are the most visible of the plants, for each of these forests has accompanying lesser known and seen plant forms that carpet the Smokies. The number of plant species is always rising as the well-researched park continually reveals new life forms. The all-taxa survey, an attempt to catalog every life form in the park, has resulted in an explosion of heretofore undocumented species.

Fauna

The area's rich vegetation and large amount of wild land support an impressive array of mammals: more than 60 species. The black bear thrives in the Smokies, with an estimated 1,500 specimens roaming within its boundaries: nearly 2 per square mile, arguably the densest concentration of bruins in North America. However, the population follows the yearly rise and fall of mast—berries, acorns, and the like. When the lower regions of the park were populated, unregulated hunting nearly drove the black bear from the Smokies, but the beasts hung on, and their numbers inside the park grew and stabilized. This park population of *Ursus americanus* creates a core from which surrounding lands also harbor plenty of bruins. Species management by wildlife agencies and people simply learning better how to live with bears has helped too. And because wild animals know no boundaries or borders, the greater populations outside the park keep the numbers of bears up throughout the Southern Appalachians. The state of Tennessee is thought to have more bears now than any time during the last century.

Extensive efforts have been made to keep black bears wild in the park. Gone are the days of roadside feedings. Education and bearproof garbage cans in the frontcountry and bearproof food-hanging cables in the backcountry have reduced unpleasant human–bear interactions.

Elk have been successfully reintroduced into the park, beginning in 2001, and their bugling can be heard in Cataloochee. The beasts will often be seen as well, grazing the meadows. The populations are reproducing, and the reintroduction is a resounding success. A red wolf reintroduction failed, but otters were successfully brought back and can now be found in many a Smokies stream. Peregrine falcons again soar above the slopes of Mount Le Conte after a park effort to restore this noble bird.

White-tailed deer are the animals you are most likely to see in the park. They can be found in woods and especially historically cleared areas such as Cades Cove. A quiet hiker may also witness turkeys on wooded hillsides or in clearings. Furtive bobcats can sometimes be spotted crossing trails. Raccoons are occasionally spotted in the wild and can be a nuisance at backcountry campsites. Coyotes are found throughout the park but will usually spot you before you spot them. A bounding tan tail disappearing into the distance will likely comprise a sighting of this critter, which effectively replaced the extirpated red wolf. Don't be surprised if you observe beavers or muskrats in Smokies streams. Beaver can be found in the lowermost, slowest park waters.

Critters in the Smokies reflect the varied forest types. In the high country, red squirrels will chatter at you from evergreen boughs. Overhead, birds, including pileated woodpeckers and red-tailed hawks, will ply the forest for food. The Eastern screech owl will emit its goose bump–raising calls. While hiking you may be startled by a ruffed grouse blasting from its camouflaged trailside locale. Songbirds native to the north and south find a home in the park. Other migrants come and go with the seasons. Birding is a popular pastime in the park and can add to a hike.

The main game fish in the Smokies is the coldwater trout, with the brook trout being the only fish native to the Smokies. Technically, the brook is not a true trout, but a char. Brooks prefer cold, clear waters and are primarily relegated to higher elevation streams, though the park service continues to restore brook habitat. Brook trout exclusively occupy 97 miles of trout streams in the park. Rainbow trout were introduced the park following logging, and have displaced native brook in many streams. Brown trout, a European native also introduced following logging, are found in quieter, stiller water, often in deep pools. Smallmouth bass and rock bass occupy the warmer, slower, and lower park streams. Beyond the game species, more than four dozen other fish species ply the Smokies waters. Some, such as the Smoky madtom, are quite rare, making the case for protecting the Smokies.

Interestingly, the Smokies may have more life mass in salamanders than any other vertebrate: at least 24 kinds have been found here. Biologists come from all over the world to study them. It is just one more example of how the life in these mountains lives up to its national park status.

When to Go

The Smokies have a somewhat undeserved reputation of being overcrowded. Yes, the roadways of the Smokies are crowded during summer, on warm season weekends, and on holidays. The roads are also busy during the October leaf-viewing season. However, get a quarter mile from a trailhead on a hiking trail, and you will experience solitude. Busy trails—and there are some—are noted in the narratives.

Great Smoky Mountains National Park is a four-season destination. Hikers with well-thought-out plans can easily execute their treks beyond the obvious busy times. Try to hike midweek and just before or after major holidays. Spring is a great time. Fall can be great, too, but avoid October weekends.

Solitude can be found anytime during winter. As far as busy trails, try to hike them early in the morning or later in the evening. Iffy weather, such as a 50-percent or more chance of rain, often keeps the crowds away. Avoid busy trails on nice weather weekends.

Weather and Seasons

The Smoky Mountains offer four distinct seasons for the hiker's enjoyment, but sometimes it seems all four are going on at once, depending on your location and elevation. Before your visit is over, you'll probably experience a little bit of everything.

The chart below lists the monthly average temperatures in degrees Fahrenheit at Gatlinburg, Tennessee, just outside the park. Expect temperatures in the higher portions of the park to be 10–15 degrees cooler than those listed here.

Average High and Low Temperature by Month: Gatlinburg, Tennessee						
	JAN	FEB	MAR	APR	MAY	JUNE
High	48°	52°	61°	69°	76°	82°
Low	25°	26°	33°	39°	49°	57°
	JULY	AUG	SEPT	OCT	NOV	DEC
High	85°	84°	79°	70°	60°	51°
Low	62°	60°	54°	42°	33°	28°

Be prepared for a wide range of temperatures and conditions, no matter the season. As a rule of thumb, the temperature decreases about three degrees with every 1,000 feet of elevation gained. The Smokies are also the wettest place in the South. The park's higher elevations can get upward of 90 inches of precipitation a year.

Spring, the most variable season, takes six weeks to reach the park's highest elevations. You may encounter both winter- and summerlike weather during April and May, often in the same day. As the weather warms, thunderstorms become more frequent. Summer days typically start clear, but as the day heats up, clouds build, often culminating in a heavy shower. Fall, the driest season, comes to the peaks in early September, working its way downhill, the reverse pattern of spring; warm days and cool nights are interspersed with less-frequent wet periods.

Winter presents the Smokies at their most challenging. Frontal systems sweep through the region, with alternately cloudy and sunny days, though cloudy days are most frequent. No permanent snowpack exists in the high country, though areas higher than 5,000 feet receive five feet of snow or more per year. The high country can see bitterly cold temperature readings during this time. When venturing in the Smokies, it's a good idea to carry clothes for all weather extremes.

Trail Selection

Four criteria were used during the selection of trails for this guide. Only the premier day hikes and overnight backpacking trips are included, based upon most beautiful scenery, unique Smoky Mountain features, ease of access, and diversity of experience. Some of the selected trails are very popular; others are used infrequently. If you are fortunate enough to complete all the hikes in this book, you will gain a comprehensive appreciation for the complex beauty of one of the world's most scenic and intact ecosystems in the temperate climate.

Key Features

Top Trails books contain information about features for each trail, such as old-growth trees, waterfalls, great views, and more. Great Smoky Mountains National Park is blessed with an incredible diversity of terrain and associated flora and fauna—no matter your interests, you're sure to find a trail to match them. Hikes range throughout the vast variety of ecosystems, from the spruce–fir high country to the old-growth forests to the verdant streams valleys where waterfalls tumble still deeper into the back of beyond. Those who love a view will find plenty of rock outcrops, balds, fire towers, and other vista points where rewarding views can be had. Photographers will be glad we live in the age of the digital camera, enabling them to shoot limitless shots of showy spring wildflowers and vibrant fall-color panoramas.

Campgrounds situated throughout the park make great bases for hikers; backcountry campsites allow hikers to extend their trips beyond day hiking. Anglers can toss a line in more than 2,000 miles of waters. Paddlers can ply the seasonal whitewater streams or enjoy the flat water of Fontana Lake. Swimming holes are abundant in the Smokies creeks. Wildlife can be seen in the meadows of Cades Cove and Cataloochee and other places between.

Multiple Uses

All of the trails described in this guide are suitable for hiking. Many of the trails can also be enjoyed by equestrians, though the number of horseback enthusiasts in the Smokies is far outstripped by hikers. Very few trails, except for dedicated horse paths used by park concessionaires, have more than sporadic equestrian use. Just a short stretch of the Deep Creek Trail is

Mountains rise *above the Hazel Creek embayment of Fontana Lake.*
(See Trail 31, Ruins of Proctor.)

open to bicycles. Two-wheel enthusiasts are otherwise relegated to sharing the roads, though Cades Cove Loop Road is closed to autos on certain days during the warm season. Paddlers and motorboaters are increasingly using watercraft to access the trails and campsites bordering Fontana Lake. Fishing is done along both park road streams and in the backcountry. A small number of cross-country-skiing enthusiasts use Clingmans Dome Road, closed during the winter, to enjoy the ample snow. (As in most national parks, pets are not allowed on backcountry trails.).

On the Trail

E very outing should begin with proper preparation, which usually takes only a few minutes. Even the easiest trail can turn up unexpected surprises. People seldom think about getting lost or injured, but unexpected things can and do happen. Simple precautions can make the difference between a good story and a dangerous situation.

Use the Top Trails ratings and descriptions to determine if a particular trail is a good match with your fitness and energy level, given current conditions and the time of year.

Have a Plan

Choose Wisely The first step to enjoying any trail is to match the trail to your abilities. It's no use overestimating your experience or fitness—know your abilities and limitations, and use the Top Trails difficulty rating that accompanies each trail.

Leave Word about Your Plans The most basic of precautions is leaving word of your intentions with friends or family. Many people will hike the backcountry their entire lives without ever relying on this safety net, but establishing this simple habit is free insurance.

It's best to leave specific information—the location, the trail name, and your intended time of travel—with a responsible person. If there is a registration process available, make use of it. If there is a ranger station, trail register, or park office, check in.

Review the Route Before embarking on any hike, read the entire description and study the map. It isn't necessary to memorize every detail, but it is

 Prepare and Plan

- Know your abilities and your limitations.
- Leave word about your plans with family and friends.
- Know the area and the route.

worthwhile to have a clear mental picture of the trail and the general area. If the trail or terrain are complex, augment the trail guide with a topographic map. Park maps, as well as current weather and trail condition information, are often available from local ranger and park stations.

Carry the Essentials

Proper preparation for any type of trail use includes gathering certain essential items to carry. Your trip checklist will vary according to trail choice and conditions.

Clothing When the weather is good, light, comfortable clothing is the obvious choice. It's easy to believe that very little spare clothing is needed, but a prepared hiker has something tucked away for any emergency from a surprise shower to an unexpected overnight in a remote area.

Clothing includes proper footwear, essential for hiking and running trails. As a trail becomes more demanding, you will need footwear that performs. Running shoes are fine for many trails. If you'll be carrying substantial weight or encountering sustained rugged terrain, step up to hiking boots.

The Smokies can be notoriously humid in summer. Hikers often sweat more than normal. Breathable, moisture-wicking clothes will help keep you cool and dry. In cooler weather, particularly when it's wet, carry waterproof outer garments and quick-drying undergarments (avoid cotton). The Smokies can be a rainy place. Unless the forecast calls for absolutely no chance of rain, bring a rain jacket or poncho. As general rule, whatever the conditions, bring layers that can be combined or removed to provide comfort and protection from the elements in a wide variety of conditions.

Water Never embark on a trail without carrying water. At all times, particularly in warm weather, adequate water is of key importance. Experts recommend at least two quarts of water per day, and when hiking in heat a gallon or more may be more appropriate. At the extreme, dehydration can be life threatening. More commonly, inadequate water brings fatigue and muscle aches.

For most outings, unless the day is very hot or the trail very long, you should plan to carry sufficient water for the entire trail. Unfortunately, in

Trail Essentials

- Dress to keep cool, but be ready for cold.
- Bring plenty of water and adequate food.

North America natural water sources are questionable, generally loaded with various risks: bacteria, viruses, and fertilizers.

Water Treatment If you find you need to make use of trailside water, you should filter or treat it. There are three methods for treating water: boiling, chemical treatment, and filtering. Boiling is best, but often impractical—it requires a heat source, a pot, and time. Chemical treatments, available in sporting goods stores, handle some problems, including the troublesome *Giardia* parasite, but will not combat many artificial chemical pollutants. The preferred method is filtration, which removes giardia and other contaminants and doesn't leave any unpleasant aftertaste.

If this hasn't convinced you to carry all the water you need, here's one final admonishment: be prepared for surprises. Water sources described in the text or on maps can change course or dry up completely. Never run your water bottle dry in expectation of the next source; fill up when water is available, and always keep a little in reserve.

Food

While not as critical as water, food is energy, and its importance shouldn't be underestimated. Avoid foods that are hard to digest, such as candy bars and potato chips. Carry high-energy, fast-digesting foods: nutrition bars, dehydrated fruit, trail mix, and jerky. Bring a little extra food—it's good protection against an outing that turns unexpectedly long, perhaps because of inclement weather or losing your way.

Useful but Less-Than-Essential Items

Map and Compass (and the Know-How to Use Them) Many trails don't require much navigation, meaning a map and compass aren't always as essential as water or food—but it can be a close call. If the trail is remote or infrequently visited, a map and compass should be considered necessities.

A handheld GPS receiver is also a useful trail companion, especially a unit with downloaded topographic maps—the drawback, of course, is batteries dying or the device otherwise becoming unusable. You could also make use of the GPS capabilities of your smartphone, although the same caveat regarding batteries applies. At the end of the day, neither a GPS nor a smartphone is a substitute for a paper map and a compass, so cover your bases and bring them all along.

Trail Checklist

- Leave no trace.
- Stay on the trail.
- Share the trail.
- Leave it there.

Phone Reception Some ridges and areas near Gatlinburg and Townsend and above Waynesville have some level of cellular coverage. But in many areas, especially in hollows and along streams, there is no phone service at all. In extreme circumstances, a cell phone can be a lifesaver, but don't depend on it; coverage is too unpredictable, and batteries run out. And be sure that the occasion warrants the phone call—a blister doesn't justify a call to search-and-rescue.

Gear Depending on the remoteness and rigor of the trail, you have many additional useful items to consider: pocketknife, flashlight, fire source (water-proof matches, light, or flint), and a first aid kit. Every member of your party should carry the appropriate essential items described above, as groups often split up or get separated along the trail. Solo hikers should be even more disciplined about preparation and carry more gear.

Trail Etiquette

The overriding rule on the trail is **"Leave No Trace."** Interest in visiting natural areas continues to increase in North America, even as the quantity of unspoiled natural areas continues to shrink. These pressures make it ever more critical that we leave no trace of our visits.

Never Litter If you carried it in, it's easy enough to carry it out. Leave the trail in the same, if not better condition than you find it. Try picking up any litter you encounter and packing it out—it's a great feeling! Pick up just one piece of garbage and you've made a difference.

Stay on the Trail Paths have been created, sometimes over many years, for many purposes: to protect the surrounding natural areas, to avoid dangers, and to provide the best route. Leaving the trail can cause damage that takes years to undo. Never cut switchbacks. Shortcutting rarely saves energy or time, and it takes a terrible toll on the land, trampling plant life and hastening erosion. Moreover, safety and consideration intersect on the trail. It's hard to get truly lost if you stay on the trail.

Share the Trail The best trails attract many visitors, and you should be prepared to share the trail with others. Do your part to minimize impact.

Commonly accepted trail etiquette dictates that **bike riders yield to both hikers and equestrians, hikers yield to horseback riders, downhill hikers yield to uphill hikers, and everyone stays to the right.** Not everyone knows these rules of the road, so let common sense and good humor be the final guide.

Leave It There Destroying or removing plants and animals or historical, prehistoric, or geological items is certainly unethical and almost always illegal.

Getting Lost If you become lost on the trail, stay on the trail. Stop and take stock of the situation. In many cases, a few minutes of calm reflection will yield a solution. Consider all the clues available; use the sun to identify directions if you don't have a compass. If you determine that you are indeed lost, stay on the main trail and stay put. You are more likely to encounter other people if you stay in one place.

Readers should make an honest assessment of their own abilities and adjust time estimates accordingly. Also, rain, snow, heat, and poor visibility can all affect the pace on even the easiest of trails.

Winter trims *the Appalachian Trail in white. (See Trail 15, Silers Bald via Clingmans Dome.)*

CHAPTER 1

Abrams Creek and Cades Cove Area

Abrams Creek and Cades Cove Area

The Abrams Creek and Cades Cove area occupies the most northwesterly parcel of the Tennessee Smokies. This section stretches from Chilhowee Mountain in the west, where the Foothills Parkway reveals overlooks aplenty, to the major park entrance near the community of Townsend, where the Little River exits the park boundaries. Cades Cove, the world-famous bucolic former farming valley, is the showcase of the area. It presents a window to the agricultural past in a vale still carpeted in mountain-ringed fields. To the south stand the state-line ridge and the Appalachian Trail (AT), rising upward of 5,000 feet. Rich Mountain and other, lower ridges seal off Cades Cove from the "outside world."

Hiking trails extend like spokes from Cades Cove, accessing the entire area. Abrams Creek Ranger Station, in the far west, offers the other major trail access. This locale is the park's lowest, tucked away on a dead-end road, reaching what I believe is the world's most beautiful stream—Abrams Creek, which drains nearly the entire area. Trout-filled mountain rills flow off the Smokies crest and feed Abrams as it flows, sometimes underground, through Cades Cove. At the cove's western end the stream begins cutting a gorge, making a popular waterfall. It picks up other major tributaries before flowing past Abrams Creek Campground and Ranger Station, then enters a final wild stretch before exiting the park at Chilhowee Lake. The mouth of Abrams Creek at Chilhowee Lake is, at 875 feet, the absolute lowest point in the entire park.

Area streams have both trout and smallmouth bass. Dense rhododendron and mountain laurel thickets border the waterways while black birch, tulip trees, and other moisture-loving trees shade the valleys. Regal white pines tower over creekside flats. Pine–oak forest complexes rise on drier sites. The forests transition to northern hardwoods up high, with beech, yellow birch, and cherry rising on the ridges.

Opposite and overleaf: *Looking west across the Smokies from Rocky Top (Trail 8)*

Entering Cades Cove is a trip back in time. Several preserved log cabins and homesteads dot the valley, which at one time had extensive agricultural operations; in contrast, most former Smokies denizens eked out a subsistence on small, rocky plots. Residents drove their cattle on what's left of mountaintop meadows that still bear their names: Spence Field, Russell Field, and Gregory Bald. Logging was never widespread in the area. In fact, the upper part of the mostly trailless valley of Panther Creek, a tributary of Abrams Creek, is now a forgotten haven of a large, fire-dependent pine–oak complex that barely saw an axe.

The trail system here is extensive. Cades Cove and its auto access, Laurel Creek Road, are the main jumping-off points. An 11-mile road circling Cades Cove not only accesses trailheads but is also popular with windshield tourists and bicyclers. Here, hikers can head to the high country and the AT along the state line, or they can wander the lesser mountains that form the park's north boundary. Rich Mountain Road reaches but one trailhead. The Abrams Creek access, where many loop hikes are possible, offers a quiet contrast to sometimes-busy Cades Cove. Cades Cove visitors can overnight at a convenient and large campground located in the heart of the action. The 159 reservable sites are open year-round. Campers hike, rent bikes, ride horses, or fish. Abrams Creek has a smaller first-come, first-served 16-site campground, generally open from mid-March through October. More-civilized accommodations are available in nearby Townsend.

The hikes described are both loops and out-and-back treks. Along the way you can see local highlights: Abrams Falls, Gregory Bald, Spence Field, the Oliver Cabin, and good ol' Rocky Top, heralded in the nearby University of Tennessee's fight song. Other treks travel less-trod trails, such as Pine Mountain and Cane Creek, where park beauty is subtler.

Permits

Permits are *not* required for day hiking. Backpackers must get a backcountry permit to stay at one of the 17 designated backcountry campsites and trail shelters in this area. All campsites require a reservation, which you can make online at smokiespermits.nps.gov, then print at home.

The author *at Cane Creek campsite #2 (Trail 3)*

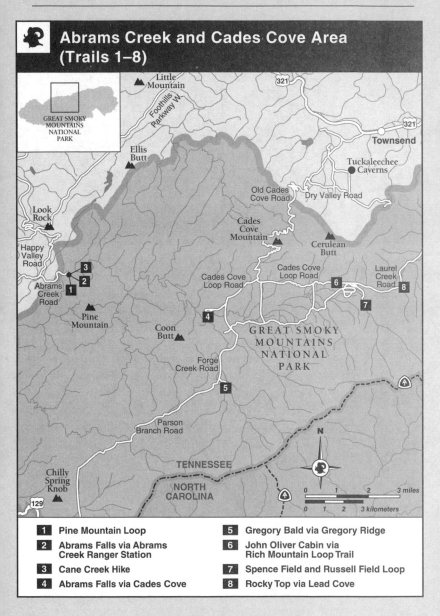

Abrams Creek and Cades Cove Area (Trails 1–8)

1 Pine Mountain Loop	**5** Gregory Bald via Gregory Ridge
2 Abrams Falls via Abrams Creek Ranger Station	**6** John Oliver Cabin via Rich Mountain Loop Trail
3 Cane Creek Hike	**7** Spence Field and Russell Field Loop
4 Abrams Falls via Cades Cove	**8** Rocky Top via Lead Cove

TRAIL FEATURES TABLE

Abrams Creek and Cades Cove Area

TRAIL	DIFFICULTY	LENGTH	TYPE	USES & ACCESS	TERRAIN	FLORA & FAUNA	OTHER
1	2–3	8.1	↻	🚶 🎒 🐎	▲ ▲ ▷	🍁 ❋	⋈ ▲ ⇌
2	3	11.0	✓	🚶 🎒	▲ ▷ ▌	🍁 ❋	⋈ 📷 ▲ ⇌
3	4	9.8	✓	🚶 🎒 🐎	▷	🍁 ❋ 🦌	▲ ↓ ⌂
4	2	5.0	✓	🚶	▲ ▷ ▌	🍁 ❋	📷 ⇌
5	4	11.0	✓	🚶 🎒	▲ ▲ ▷	🍁 ❋	⋈ 📷 ▲
6	1–2	2.8	✓	🚶 🐎 👥	▷	🍁 ❋ 🦌	⋈ 📷 ⌂
7	4–5	13.0	↻	🚶 🎒 🐎	▲ ▲ ▷	🍁 ❋	⋈ 📷 ▲ ⌂
8	5	11.6	✓	🚶 🎒 🐎	▲ ▷	🍁 ❋	⋈ 📷 ▲ ⌂

USES & ACCESS	TYPE	TERRAIN	FLORA & FAUNA	OTHER
🚶 Day Hiking	↻ Loop	▲ Summit	🍁 Autumn Colors	⋈ Great Views
🎒 Backpacking	✓ Out-and-back	▲ Ridge	❋ Wildflowers	📷 Photo Opportunity
🐎 Horses	＼ Point-to-point	〰 Lake	🌿 Wildlife	▲ Backcountry Camping
👥 Child Friendly		▷ Stream	⚘ Spruce–Fir	⇌ Swimming
	DIFFICULTY – 1 2 3 4 5 + less more	▌ Waterfall	⚑ Old-Growth	↓ Secluded
				≛ Steep
				⌂ Historical Interest
				↗ Geologic Interest

Maps

For the Abrams Creek and Cades Cove area, you will need the following USGS 7.5-minute (1:24,000-scale) topographic quadrangles, listed in geographic order as you hike along your route:

Trail 1: *Calderwood*
Trail 2: *Calderwood*
Trail 3: *Calderwood, Blockhouse*
Trail 4: *Cades Cove, Calderwood*
Trail 5: *Cades Cove*
Trail 6: *Cades Cove*
Trail 7: *Cades Cove, Thunderhead Mountain*
Trail 8: *Thunderhead Mountain*

Abrams Creek and Cades Cove Area

Abrams Creek *rambles noisily toward the big drop of Abrams Falls.*

Abrams Falls via Cades Cove........ 45

The hike to Abrams Falls from Cades Cove can be peopled, but the sight and sounds of the wide falls are an experience to be shared by one and all. The trail to the falls, alternately coursing among waterside evergreens and hillside piney woods, parallels Abrams Creek in unbroken beauty. The falls is a true rumbler and has an incredibly large pool.

TRAIL 4

Day Hiking
5.0 miles, Out-and-back
Difficulty: 1 **2** 3 4 5

Pine Mountain Loop

From the lowest trailhead in the park, follow lovely Abrams Creek on a watery hike past numerous shoals and huge pools, eventually fording the big stream. A low ridge offers views of Look Rock. Wander through oak woods to Scott Gap, and then reach a high point on the shoulder of Pine Mountain. Finally, descend to Abrams Creek, this time spanning it by bridge.

Best Time

This hike requires making what is the biggest ford in the park: across lower Abrams Creek. With that in mind, midsummer through late fall offers the lowest water for fording. Outside that, winter offers great solitude, and the low elevations make this hike doable when the high country is frigid. In May, the mountain laurel blooms in the Abrams Creek watershed can be spectacular.

Finding the Trail

From the intersection of US 411/TN 33 and US 129/TN 115 in Maryville, Tennessee, take US 129/Alcoa Highway south for 7 miles. At the four-way intersection, bear right to continue south on US 129. In 3.6 miles, bear left at the T to keep south on US 129, and continue 7.1 miles to Chilhowee Lake. Just past the intersection with the Foothills Parkway, turn left (north) on Happy Valley Road, following it 5.9 miles to Abrams Creek Road. Turn right on Abrams Creek Road and drive 0.7 mile, passing the ranger station. The parking area is on the right just after the ranger

TRAIL USE
Day Hiking,
Backpacking, Horses
LENGTH
8.1 miles, 4–5½ hours
VERTICAL FEET
±1,000
DIFFICULTY
– 1 **2 3** 4 5 +
TRAIL TYPE
Loop

FEATURES
Summit
Ridgeline
Stream
Autumn Colors
Wildflowers
Great Views
Backcountry Camping
Swimming
FACILITIES
(SEASONAL)
Campground
Restrooms
Water

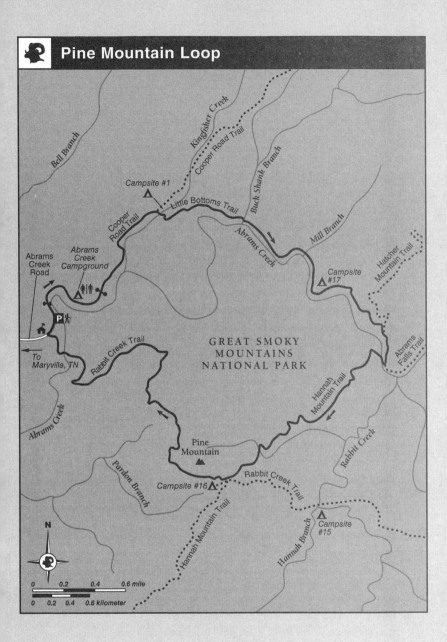

Pine Mountain Loop

Bell Branch

Kingfisher Creek

Cooper Road Trail

Buck Shank Branch

Campsite #1

Cooper Road Trail

Little Bottoms Trail

Mill Branch

Hatcher Mountain Trail

Abrams Creek

Abrams Creek Road

Abrams Creek Campground

Campsite #17

P

Abrams Falls Trail

GREAT SMOKY MOUNTAINS NATIONAL PARK

To Maryville, TN

Rabbit Creek Trail

Hannah Mountain Trail

Abrams Creek

Rabbit Creek

Pine Mountain

Pardon Branch

Campsite #16

Rabbit Creek Trail

Campsite #15

Hannah Mountain Trail

Hannah Branch

N

0   0.2   0.4   0.6 mile

0   0.2   0.4   0.6 kilometer

station. The Cooper Road Trail starts at the rear of
Abrams Creek Campground.

Park your car in the designated area near the
ranger station. *Do not park in the campground, which
is gated during the cold season.*

Trail Description

This hike would be rated less difficult if it weren't
for the ford of Abrams Creek, widely regarded as the
most troublesome in the park. But don't let the ford
discourage you from taking this scenic loop hike.
A drive-up campground and three backcountry
campsites along the route make trailside overnighting easy. First you'll leave Abrams Creek Ranger
Station, tracing a gravel park road to Abrams Creek
Campground. Join Cooper Road Trail, rambling
along Abrams Creek to meet small Kingfisher Creek.
Surmount a ridge with views to enter the rugged
Abrams Creek gorge, passing Little Bottoms campsite #17.

Wander through a past burn on an open rocky
mountainside before reaching that potentially troublesome ford. Beyond here, it's uphill through quiet
pine–oak woods to make Scott Gap. Join an old jeep
road to skirt the western shoulder of Pine Mountain.
Descend via switchbacks on the thickly wooded
north side of Pine Mountain to reach Abrams Creek
yet again, this time near old homesites. A footlog
avails a safe ending to the hike.

Leave the parking area, ▶1 walking the gravel
road upstream along Abrams Creek. Reach quaint
16-site Abrams Creek Campground at 0.4 mile. Pass
around a pole gate, joining Cooper Road Trail ▶2 as
it traverses a streamside flat over which tower tall
white pines. Beech, maple, and holly are scattered
in the understory. Surmount a small bluff, then
come to Kingfisher Branch at 0.9 mile. The trail and
stream become one for a short distance, then divide.

Backcountry Camping Reach a trail junction at 1.3 miles. ▶3 Cooper Road backcountry campsite #1 is just a short ways farther on Cooper Road Trail, but this hike turns right on Little Bottoms Trail, crossing Kingfisher Branch a final time. Pass the cool waters of small Herndon Spring, located at the base of a dead hemlock, just before climbing a ridge. The 200-foot ascent leads through scrubby woodlands, recovering from fire. Look left for northwesterly views of Chilhowee Mountain and the tower at Look Rock.

Great Views

Descend from a gap in the ridge. The rumbles of Abrams Creek return. The slender singletrack path winds along the gorge slope, finding Abrams Creek at 2.0 miles. Here, Buck Shank Branch—one of the Smokies' all-time great names—flows into Abrams Creek. Now you hike directly along the rock-strewn waterway, bordered by alder. Mountain laurel flanks the path.

Stream

At 2.5 miles, step over Mill Branch (a common Smokies name) and enter Little Bottoms, a now-wooded flat, once a settlers' home and farm. The hiking is easy here. Pass the official spur trail to Little Bottoms backcountry campsite #17, at 2.9 miles. ▶4

Backcountry Camping

The scenery changes as the gorge closes and the path rises to a steep slope, scarred by past fires and storms. Open onto a rocky, treeless incline with

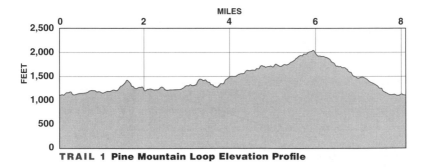

TRAIL 1 Pine Mountain Loop Elevation Profile

A backpacker *feels her way across Abrams Creek.*

Abrams Creek crashing below. Westerly views of Chilhowee Mountain open here, too. The slender path meets Hatcher Mountain Trail at 3.6 miles. ▶5 Stay right and downhill, now on Hatcher Mountain Trail, to reach another trail junction in a streamside rhododendron thicket at 3.8 miles. ▶6 Stay right with the Hannah Mountain Trail, immediately fording Abrams Creek. Use your trekking poles or grab a stick to aid your crossing of the irregular depths. Avoid the ultraslippery flat rock slabs. In late summer or fall, the crossing will be a minor nuisance, but in winter or early spring use good judgment as to whether or not to ford.

Climb from Abrams Creek, turning up a dark rhododendron hollow. Other greenery includes galax, white pine, and holly. At 4.4 miles, split a gap. Cruise piney south-facing slopes on a nearly level, needle-carpeted track. Reach clear Scott Gap Branch at 5.1 miles. Make Scott Gap and a five-way trail junction at 5.4 miles. ▶7 Backcountry campsite #16 is down the least-used path and has a small spring.

Stream

Explore the park's pine and oak–forested western end in a less-peopled setting.

Our loop turns right on the wide, rocky double-track Rabbit Creek Trail, heading away from Rabbit Creek and up the shoulder of Pine Mountain, where views of the ridges and hollows of the lower Abrams Creek valley open. Dogwood, sourwood, sassafras, and pine provide colorful fall displays.

Wildflowers

Summit ▲

Reach the loop's high point, 2,050 feet, at 6.0 miles. ▶8 The ensuing descent off the mountain's north slope is mostly gentle. Here is where a tornado back in 2011 downed an amazing number of trees. The forest is now regenerating on its own schedule. Make hard switchbacks at 6.4 and 6.8 miles, as the wide wooded trail winds downhill. Another switchback at 7.5 miles opens a view of Abrams Creek. Soon you reach the stream bottoms, passing a pair of homesites.

At 7.8 miles, bridge Abrams Creek on an ingenious footlog. ▶9 The side you are on is set on a concrete footing designed to let the footlog slide off in flood. The other side is chained to a big boulder, allowing it to turn downstream in high water yet not float away. After floods, the unchained side of the log is restored. Turn upstream beyond the crossing. Soon reach Abrams Creek Ranger Station, completing your hike at 8.1 miles. ▶10

🚶	**MILESTONES**	
▶1	0.0	Abrams Creek parking area
▶2	0.4	Cooper Road Trail at Abrams Creek Campground
▶3	1.3	Little Bottoms Trail
▶4	2.9	Campsite #17 spur
▶5	3.6	Hatcher Mountain Trail
▶6	3.8	Hannah Mountain Trail and Abrams Creek ford
▶7	5.4	Scott Gap
▶8	6.0	Pine Mountain high point
▶9	7.8	Abrams Creek
▶10	8.1	Abrams Creek parking area

Abrams Falls via Abrams Creek Ranger Station

Travel ultrascenic and lightly visited Abrams Creek valley to reach a signature Smokies waterfall. Much of the hike travels through the rugged Abrams Creek gorge, offering streamside views and continuous beauty. Vistas of Chilhowee Mountain open in places.

Best Time

Abrams Falls will be its boldest during winter and spring. You will also enjoy solitude and relatively mild winter temperatures on this lowland trek that never rises above 1,600 feet of elevation. May has the added benefit of trailside mountain laurel blooms. Summer brings crowds to the falls, the vast majority coming from Cades Cove.

Finding the Trail

From the intersection of US 411/TN 33 and US 129/TN 115 in Maryville, Tennessee, take US 129/Alcoa Highway south for 7 miles. At the four-way intersection, bear right to continue south on US 129. In 3.6 miles, bear left at the T to keep south on US 129, and continue 7.1 miles to Chilhowee Lake. Just past the intersection with the Foothills Parkway, turn left (north) on Happy Valley Road, following it 5.9 miles to Abrams Creek Road. Turn right on Abrams Creek Road and drive 0.7 mile, passing the ranger station. The parking area is on the right just after the ranger station. The Cooper Road Trail starts at the rear of Abrams Creek Campground.

Park your car in the designated area near the ranger station. *Do not park in the campground, which is gated during the cold season.*

TRAIL USE
Day Hiking,
Backpacking
LENGTH
11.0 miles, 6 hours
VERTICAL FEET
±500
DIFFICULTY
− 1 2 **3** 4 5 +
TRAIL TYPE
Out-and-back

FEATURES
Ridgeline
Stream
Waterfall
Autumn Colors
Wildflowers
Great Views
Photo Opportunity
Backcountry Camping
Swimming
FACILITIES
(SEASONAL)
Campground
Restrooms
Water

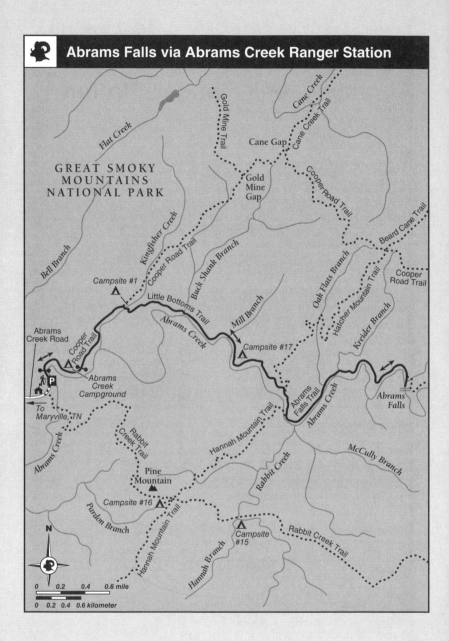

Abrams Falls via Abrams Creek Ranger Station

GREAT SMOKY
MOUNTAINS
NATIONAL PARK

Flat Creek

Gold Mine Trail

Cane Creek

Cane Creek Trail

Cane Gap

Gold Mine Gap

Cooper Road Trail

Kingfisher Creek

Cooper Road Trail

Beard Cane Trail

Bell Branch

Buck Shank Branch

Oak Flats Branch

Hatcher Mountain Trail

Cooper Road Trail

Campsite #1

Little Bottoms Trail

Mill Branch

Kreider Branch

Abrams Creek Road

Cooper Road Trail

Abrams Creek

Campsite #17

Abrams Falls Trail

Abrams Creek

Abrams Falls

P

Abrams Creek Campground

To Maryville, TN

Abrams Creek

Rabbit Creek Trail

Hannah Mountain Trail

Rabbit Creek

McCully Branch

Pine Mountain

Campsite #16

Hannah Mountain Trail

Pardon Branch

Campsite #15

Rabbit Creek Trail

Hannah Branch

N

0   0.2   0.4   0.6 mile

0   0.2   0.4   0.6 kilometer

Trail Description

This great hike, which explores lower Abrams Creek—my favorite waterway in the entire park—includes a visit to a powerful cataract, coupled with hillside views. While Abrams Falls is a popular destination, you'll be taking the back way, which is longer but avails much more solitude. The hills are ample enough to challenge but not overwhelm. Since the hike starts near a drive-up campground and you pass two backcountry campsites along the way, combining an overnight experience with this hike is easy.

Your return trip is sure to add new sights. Make sure and stop along the way to absorb some Abrams Creek streamside scenery. You will have plenty of opportunities since the trail is near the creek at multiple junctures.

Leave the parking area, ▶1 walking the gravel road upstream along Abrams Creek. Anglers and swimmers wanting easy access will be seen here in the summer. Curve right to reach Abrams Creek Campground. The 16 sites are situated in a teardrop loop. Campers coming during the week are sure to get a site.

At 0.4 mile, walk around a pole gate, joining the Cooper Road Trail. ▶2 A regal forest of white pines shades smaller beech, maple, and holly. The path rises to a small bluff. Abrams Creek gurgles at the

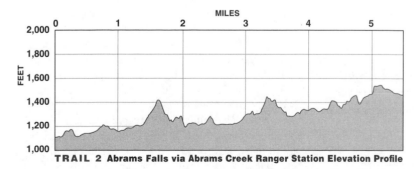

TRAIL 2 Abrams Falls via Abrams Creek Ranger Station Elevation Profile

Stream

Backcountry Camping

Great Views

Stream

Wildflowers

Backcountry Camping

bluff base. Descend to Kingfisher Branch at 0.9 mile. The trail and stream merge. You're sure to do a little rock-hopping here, depending on water levels.

Meet the Little Bottoms Trail at 1.3 miles. ▶3 Cooper Road backcountry campsite #1 is about 50 yards beyond on Cooper Road Trail, but the hike to Abrams Falls turns right and joins the Little Bottoms Trail. Immediately, rock-hop Kingfisher Branch.

As you continue, look for small Herndon Spring, at the base of a dead hemlock, just before the Little Bottoms starts to scale a ridge dividing Kingfisher Creek from Abrams Creek. Switchbacks moderate the 200-foot ascent. Walk among scrubby young trees that allow northwesterly views of Chilhowee Mountain and the tower at Look Rock.

Descend from a gap in the ridge. Abrams Creek bellows below. The slender singletrack path winds along the gorge slope, descending to the mouth of Buck Shank Branch. Alder and mountain laurel border the trail, running directly beside Abrams Creek.

At 2.5 miles, hop over Mill Branch and reach Little Bottoms, a now-wooded flat isolated within the Abrams Creek gorge. Curve around Little Bottoms. Spur paths lead left to Little Bottoms backcountry campsite #17, but you reach the official spur trail (with a signpost) at 2.9 miles. ▶4

The gorge closes and the trail angles onto a steep open slope laid bare after a rare tornado. The forest is now regenerating. Cruise along an open rock outcrop dropping sharply below. Look back, westerly, to see the ridge of Chilhowee Mountain. The slender path meets Hatcher Mountain Trail at 3.6 miles. Stay right and downhill, joining Hatcher Mountain Trail. ▶5 Reach a trail junction in rhododendron at 3.8 miles. Here, the Hannah Mountain Trail leaves right to ford Abrams Creek.

Stay left, joining the Abrams Falls Trail, ▶6 a little tamer than Little Bottoms Trail. Tunnel through thick woods and rhododendron. Abrams Creek is a little smaller. You are now upstream of

If you're unwilling to walk 5 miles one-way to worthy Abrams Falls, consider coming from Cades Cove.

its confluence with major tributary Rabbit Creek. The trail turns northeast, mimicking the wanderings of Abrams Creek. The foot trail is simply gorgeous here. Rise to meet Oak Flats Branch at 4.3 miles. ▶7 The path soon bisects Kreider Branch. The trail then climbs a dry slope well above the creek. Gain top-down views of singing rapids below. The creek turns away, and the trail bisects a bend in the creek.

Level off at 5.1 miles, ▶8 at the hike's high point of 1,550 feet, then cruise downhill to reach a trail junction at 5.5 miles. Here, a spur trail leads straight over a footlog spanning Wilson Branch while the Abrams Falls Trail leaves left for Cades Cove.

Beyond the bridge, you come to the massive pool below powerful Abrams Falls. Sitting rocks and logs abound. Abrams Falls roars in the distance. Walk to the base of the potent cataract. ▶9 The powerful cascade drops 20 feet over a rock berm.

▌ **Waterfall**

In summer, you may be surprised at the throngs who have walked 2.5 miles from Cades Cove while so few have hiked your route. The pool, one of the park's deepest, lures sweaty hikers trekking in the summer heat. With any luck, you'll have enough time to linger at the falls and stop a time or two on your way back as well.

◢● **Swimming**

🚶	**MILESTONES**	
▶1	0.0	Abrams Creek parking area
▶2	0.4	Cooper Road Trail at Abrams Creek Campground
▶3	1.3	Little Bottoms Trail
▶4	2.9	Campsite #17 spur
▶5	3.6	Hatcher Mountain Trail
▶6	3.8	Join Abrams Falls Trail
▶7	4.3	Oak Flats Branch
▶8	5.1	Hike high point
▶9	5.5	Abrams Falls

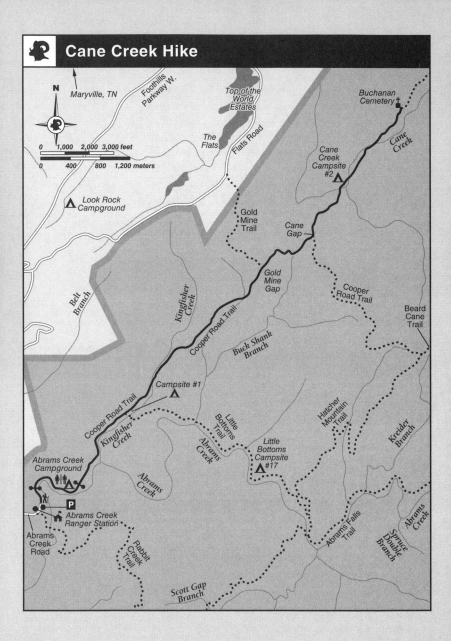

Cane Creek Hike

N Maryville, TN

Foothills Parkway W.

Top of the World Estates

Buchanan Cemetery †

The Flats

Flats Road

Cane Creek

Cane Creek Campsite #2

Gold Mine Trail

Look Rock Campground

Cane Gap

Cooper Road Trail

Gold Mine Gap

Beard Cane Trail

Belt Branch

Kingfisher Creek

Cooper Road Trail

Buck Shank Branch

Campsite #1

Little Bottoms Trail

Hatcher Mountain Trail

Kreider Branch

Cooper Road Trail

Kingfisher Creek

Abrams Creek

Little Bottoms Campsite #17

Abrams Creek Campground

Abrams Creek

Abrams Creek Ranger Station

Abrams Creek

Abrams Falls Trail

Spruce Double Branch

Abrams Creek Road

Rabbit Creek Trail

Scott Gap Branch

0 1,000 2,000 3,000 feet
0 400 800 1,200 meters

Cane Creek Hike

This secluded low-elevation hike leads from Abrams Creek Ranger Station through lush valleys and over piney ridges to the Buchanan Cemetery, an interment for the residents of now-wild Cane Creek valley. The last part of the hike traverses the relatively little-used Cane Creek Trail. Pass two less-used backcountry campsites along the way.

TRAIL USE
Day Hiking,
Backpacking, Horses

LENGTH
9.8 miles, 4½–6 hours

VERTICAL FEET
±1,080

DIFFICULTY
– 1 2 3 **4** 5 +

TRAIL TYPE
Out-and-back

FEATURES
Stream
Autumn Colors
Wildflowers
Wildlife
Backcountry Camping
Secluded
Historical Interest

FACILITIES
(SEASONAL)
Campground
Restrooms
Water

Best Time

As a low-elevation hike, it might be hot on the trail in the summer. That same low elevation makes this hike appealing in winter, when the temperatures will be much milder than in the high country.

Finding the Trail

From the intersection of US 411/TN 33 and US 129/TN 115 in Maryville, Tennessee, take US 129/Alcoa Highway south for 7 miles. At the four-way intersection, bear right to continue south on US 129. In 3.6 miles, bear left at the T to keep south on US 129, and continue 7.1 miles to Chilhowee Lake. Just past the intersection with the Foothills Parkway, turn left (north) on Happy Valley Road, following it 5.9 miles to Abrams Creek Road. Turn right on Abrams Creek Road and drive 0.7 mile, passing the ranger station. The parking area is on the right just after the ranger station. The Cooper Road Trail starts at the rear of Abrams Creek Campground.

Park your car in the designated area near the ranger station. *Do not park in the campground, which is gated during the cold season.*

Trail Description

Sometimes it can be difficult to find solitude along the trails of Great Smoky Mountains National Park, but you just need to know what trails to take—and that's what this guide is all about: helping you realize your desired Smoky Mountains hiking experience.

This hike takes place at the extreme northwestern part of the park, in the Abrams Creek area. Characterized by pine- and oak-covered ridges dividing small creeks that once harbored subsistence farms, the area has the Smokies' lowest elevations yet also some of its most remote locales. Despite being near civilization, the area contains vast swaths of trailless terrain—good habitat for the fauna of the park. Don't be surprised to see a deer, a turkey, or even a bear.

The hike follows the old Cooper Road, which once connected Happy Valley to Cades Cove. The road-turned-trail makes for easy walking as it travels by former habitations before rising to Gold Mine Gap, then heading to Cane Gap. Here, the hike follows yet another old road, descending to Cane Creek, a lovely little Smokies stream. A few crossings take you to the Buchanan Cemetery, a resting place for residents who made their home in the Cane Creek valley before it became a national park.

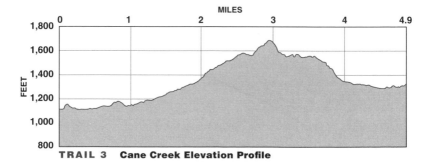

TRAIL 3   Cane Creek Elevation Profile

Buchanan Cemetery, *a peaceful resting place near Cane Creek*

The whole area exudes solitude, and it is certainly quieter here than in other parts of the park. The last part of the hike traverses the seldom-used Cane Creek Trail, which dead-ends at the park boundary. Along the way you pass two less-used backcountry campsites, the first- and third-lowest-elevation camps in the entire park. Consider incorporating a backcountry campout into your hike. If you prefer car camping, small Abrams Creek Campground is located at the trailhead.

Start your hike by leaving the Abrams Creek parking area, ▶1 then walking 0.4 mile along gorgeous Abrams Creek, which is my favorite stream in the entire park. Pass through Abrams Creek

Campground (*note:* no parking for day users) to reach a gate and the Cooper Road Trail. ▶2 The wide trail makes for easy hiking, allowing you to enjoy your surroundings. Gently roll through hills, then drop to cross Kingfisher Branch twice in a wet area. At 1.3 miles, ▶3 the Little Bottoms Trail leaves right, but you keep straight, walking by Cooper Road backcountry campsite #1, just ahead. Most hikers will have turned at Little Bottoms. Solitude lies ahead. The forest here was once fields of the old Myers Place nearby. The diverse woodland makes it hard to believe that rows of corn once spread across this flat.

Stream

Backcountry Camping ⚠

Keep gently rising along Kingfisher Creek and, at 2.1 miles, make an easy ford of the creek. Rise farther into a drier forest of sourwood, black gum, and pine. Step over a tributary of Buck Shank Branch at 2.7 miles, and keep climbing to make Gold Mine Gap and the hike's high point of 1,685 feet at 3.0 miles. Here, ▶4 the Gold Mine Gap Trail heads left 0.8 mile for Flats Road outside the park. This hike keeps straight, descending on red clay, rocky soil shaded by regal forest, though in moister areas the demise of the Eastern hemlock is leaving other wooded areas in transition.

Secluded

Autumn Colors 🍁

At 3.4 miles, come to Cane Gap and another intersection. Here, Cooper Road heads right past Rugels Rocks, so named for a former park superintendent who stopped park personnel from driving between Cades Cove and Abrams Creek by having boulders placed in the trail. Instead, we head left, joining the seldom-hiked Cane Creek Trail, ▶5 also an easy-walking doubletrack path. Keep dropping to step over Cane Creek at 4.0 miles, then quickly come ▶6 to Cane Creek backcountry campsite #2. I've camped at the small, shaded flat upwards of 20 nights and have had it to myself every time. I recommend the experience.

Backcountry Camping ⚠

The hike continues with a quick second crossing of Cane Creek. At higher water levels, expect to wet your feet; nimble rock-hoppers won't have a problem, however. Cross back over to the left bank at 4.5 miles. The trail passes a crumbled chimney in the woods before arriving at the short spur leading left to ▶7 Buchanan Cemetery at 4.9 miles. Here, a pair of bigger oaks shades the 20 or so graves, where local residents were interred from the late 1880s to the 1920s. A community once existed in the valley. The 1931 Department of the Interior–commissioned Smokies map shows Cane School hereabouts, a little down the valley. How differently the residents of Cane Creek lived compared with our rushed electronic-based lives!

Such things are worthy of deliberation on your return trip. ▶8 If you want to say you did the whole thing, the Cane Creek Trail continues a little over a half mile beyond the Buchanan Cemetery, dead-ending at private property and the park boundary.

 Stream

 Wildflowers

 Historical
Interest

🚶	**MILESTONES**	
▶1	0.0	Abrams Creek parking area
▶2	0.4	Cooper Road Trail at Abrams Creek Campground
▶3	1.3	Little Bottoms Trail
▶4	3.0	Gold Mine Gap
▶5	3.4	Cane Creek Trail
▶6	4.0	Cane Creek backcountry campsite #2
▶7	4.9	Buchanan Cemetery
▶8	9.8	Abrams Creek parking area

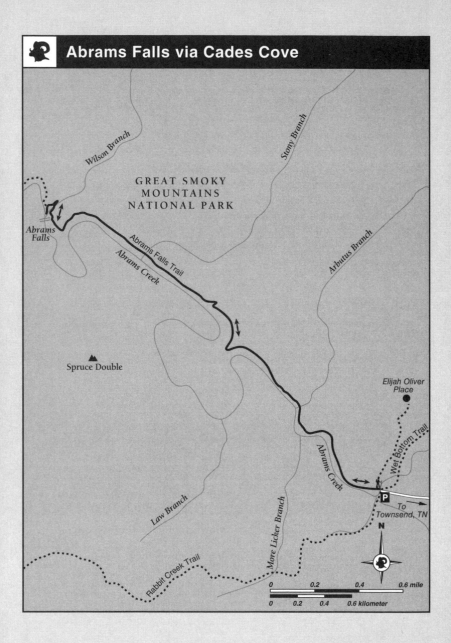

Abrams Falls via Cades Cove

Wilson Branch

Stony Branch

GREAT SMOKY
MOUNTAINS
NATIONAL PARK

Abrutus Branch

Abrams
Falls

Abrams Falls Trail

Abrams Creek

Spruce Double

Elijah Oliver
Place

Wet Bottom Trail

Abrams Creek

Law Branch

More Licker Branch

P

To
Townsend, TN

Rabbit Creek Trail

N

| 0 | 0.2 | 0.4 | 0.6 mile |

| 0 | 0.2 | 0.4 | 0.6 kilometer |

Abrams Falls via Cades Cove

The hike to Abrams Falls from Cades Cove can be heavily peopled, but the sight and sounds of the wide falls are an experience to be shared by one and all. The trail to the falls, alternately coursing among waterside evergreens and hillside piney woods, parallels Abrams Creek in unbroken beauty. The falls is a true rumbler and has an incredibly large pool.

Best Time

Winter offers the most solitude. The falls will be at its boldest then as well as in the spring. Summer can be hot and crowded but is good for swimming. Consider going early or late in the day during potentially busy times.

Finding the Trail

From the junction of US 321/TN 73 and East Lamar Alexander Parkway in Townsend, Tennessee, bear right on Lamar Alexander and take it 1.4 miles to the park entrance. Once in the park, drive 0.9 mile, turn right on Laurel Creek Road at the Townsend Wye swimming hole, and follow Laurel Creek for 7.4 miles to the beginning of Cades Cove Loop Road. Join one-way Cades Cove Loop Road for 5.1 miles, then turn right on the marked spur road for 0.4 mile to the Abrams Falls Trailhead.

Trail Description

The parking area can be busy and the trailhead confusing. ▶1 First-time hikers to Abrams Falls can

TRAIL USE
Day Hiking

LENGTH
5.0 miles, 2½–3 hours

VERTICAL FEET
±300

DIFFICULTY
– 1 **2** 3 4 5 +

TRAIL TYPE
Out-and-back

FEATURES
Ridgeline
Stream
Waterfall
Autumn Colors
Wildflowers
Photo Opportunity
Swimming

FACILITIES
None

From Arbutus Ridge, you can see Abrams Creek coming and going as it works around the horseshoe.

Even deer enjoy *hiking to Abrams Falls via Cades Cove.*

often surreptitiously follow others onto the correct path. You will see the Rabbit Creek Trail leaving left for Hannah Mountain—the Abrams Falls Trail goes straight, bridging Abrams Creek, while the Wet Bottom Trail leaves right for Cooper Road Trail. **Stream** Take the Abrams Falls Trail over Abrams Creek. Here, a trail leaves right; take it and, in a half mile, reach the Elijah Oliver Place, a potential historical addition to your trek. Ahead, you can see the inflow

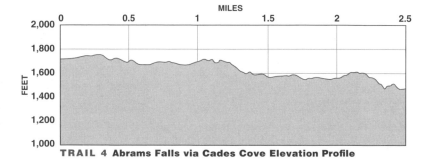

TRAIL 4 Abrams Falls via Cades Cove Elevation Profile

of Mill Creek, which adds significant water to Abrams Creek.

Begin tracing the crashing creek downstream. Shortly climb above the greenish watercourse, under pine, beech, birch, and oak. Rhododendron and mountain laurel border the track. Spur trails lead to the water. Be careful if you head to the creek, the underwater rocks are notoriously slick! Bridge Arbutus Branch on a footlog at 0.6 mile. ▶2 A favorable water access lies just beyond the span.

At 1.1 miles, after ascending a slaty hill on a rocky tread, the trail crosses Arbutus Ridge. ▶3 Meanwhile, Abrams Creek is working around the ridge, forming a horseshoe. Descend to Abrams Creek, crossing a creeklet at 1.4 miles. Alternately travel creekside and farther up the ridgeside to view the watercourse from different perspectives as well

🍁 **Autumn Colors**

❀ **Wildflowers**

▲ **Ridge**

A hiker poses *in front of crashing Abrams Falls.*

as work your muscles a bit. At 1.8 miles, cross Stony Branch on a footlog. ▶4. Climb another hill, and at 2.3 miles you can hear and partially see Abrams Falls. Descend to Wilson Branch, bridging it by footlog before returning to Abrams Creek. Cross back over Wilson Branch on another footlog and you are there. ▶5

Waterfall

Swimming

The wide plunge pool below the falls is nearly as impressive as the falls itself. Note the log jumble at the lower end of the pool. In the summer the pool is a popular swimming hole. The falls itself, wide and powerful, descends in a roar of power and mist—quite a sight.

🚶	**MILESTONES**	
▶1	0.0	Cades Cove Loop Road Trailhead
▶2	0.6	Cross Arbutus Branch
▶3	1.1	Arbutus Ridge
▶4	1.8	Bridge Stony Branch
▶5	2.5	Abrams Falls

Gregory Bald via Gregory Ridge

This classic hike takes you to a signature Smokies destination. Follow Forge Creek past big trees in a deep valley, then rise to Gregory Ridge, which leads to the state line. Take the Gregory Bald Trail to an open field with world-renowned wild azalea displays, berries in season, and a first-rate view of nearby Cades Cove, the state-line ridge, and waves of mountains beyond.

Best Time

Hike the trail in spring for streamside wildflowers and good views. June can be hazy, but that's when the world-famous wild azaleas bloom. Come in July and early August for blueberries. Views once again become far-reaching when fall cold fronts clear the skies. Winter can be very windy and cold atop the open parts of Gregory Bald.

Finding the Trail

From the junction of US 321/TN 73 and East Lamar Alexander Parkway in Townsend, Tennessee, bear right on Lamar Alexander and take it 1.4 miles to the park entrance. Once in the park, drive 0.9 mile, turn right on Laurel Creek Road at the Townsend Wye swimming hole, and follow Laurel Creek for 7.4 miles to the beginning of Cades Cove Loop Road. Join one-way Cades Cove Loop Road for 5.5 miles, then turn right on Forge Creek Road (this intersection is near the Cades Cove Visitor Center). Follow Forge Creek Road for 2.3 miles to the turn-around and the Gregory Ridge Trail.

TRAIL USE
Day Hiking, Backpacking

LENGTH
11.0 miles, 5½–7½ hours

VERTICAL FEET
±2,980

DIFFICULTY
– 1 2 3 **4** 5 +

TRAIL TYPE
Out-and-back

FEATURES
Summit
Ridgeline
Stream
Autumn Colors
Wildflowers
Great Views
Photo Opportunity
Backcountry Camping

FACILITIES
Restrooms at nearby Cades Cove Visitor Center

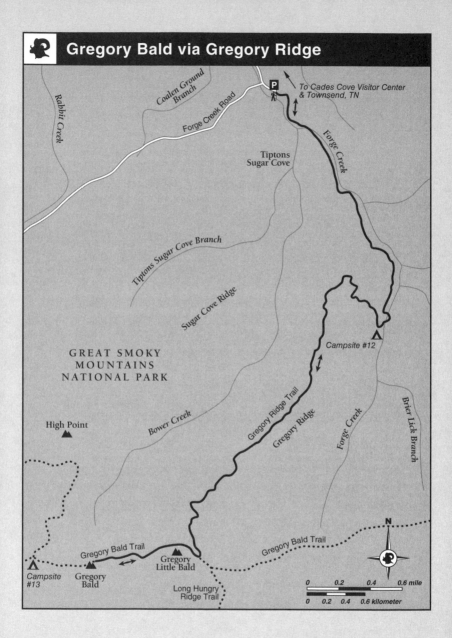

Gregory Bald via Gregory Ridge

To Cades Cove Visitor Center
& Townsend, TN

Coalen Ground Branch

Rabbit Creek

Forge Creek Road

Forge Creek

Tiptons Sugar Cove

Tiptons Sugar Cove Branch

Sugar Cove Ridge

GREAT SMOKY
MOUNTAINS
NATIONAL PARK

Campsite #12

Gregory Ridge Trail

Gregory Ridge

Brier Lick Branch

High Point

Bower Creek

Forge Creek

Gregory Bald Trail

Gregory Bald Trail

Campsite #13

Gregory Bald

Gregory Little Bald

Long Hungry Ridge Trail

N

0   0.2   0.4   0.6 mile

0   0.2   0.4   0.6 kilometer

Trail Description

This hike is packed with features to satisfy even the most demanding hiker. On the way to Gregory Bald pass a mountain stream bordered by old-growth woodland, and ascend a ridge. Take a side trip to historic Moore Spring, where an Appalachian Trail (AT) shelter once stood. It's a steady climb to the bald, but well worth it.

Make a short, quick ascent in pines upon leaving Forge Creek Road ▶1 to join up with Forge Creek proper, crossing it on a footbridge at 0.3 mile. ▶2 A little less than a mile into the hike, large tulip trees rise tall above the mountain scenery, along with smaller red maples, black birch, and rhododendron. Forge Creek gathers in pools, then dashes downstream amid rocks. Climb well above the creek onto a slope above the stream. At 1.5 miles, Ekaneetlee Branch spills into Forge Creek. A historic Indian trail once crossed the mountains at Ekaneetlee Gap, then followed Ekaneetlee Branch to the confluence below.

 Stream

Wildflowers

Head deeper into the Forge Creek valley. Footlogs help you cross a much smaller Forge Creek at 1.8 and 1.9 miles. ▶3 Just beyond the last crossing is Forge Creek backcountry campsite #12, ▶4 located on a hardwood knoll. Forge Creek makes a semicircle below. Fill up with water here, as the rest of the way is dry until the state line.

Backcountry Camping

Leave the valley behind, working up the east slope of Gregory Ridge, flanked by galax. Cut into a hollow at 2.3 miles, then emerge on a fire-scarred ridge with standing bleached tree skeletons towering over mountain laurel and young pines. The trail twists among exposed boulders. Look right (north) for views of Cades Cove below. ▶5

At 2.5 miles, the path turns south, aiming for the state line, now in a drier forest of chestnut oak, pine, and blueberries. You've worked hard to get here, but the ridge keeps on rising until 3.1 miles, where the

Ridge

Once 15 acres, Gregory Bald dwindled to less than half that by the mid-1980s. The park service returned it to the dimensions it was when grazing kept the forest from overtaking the grasses.

trail levels off at 3,400 feet. Grab a breather for 0.1 mile while tunneling through mountain laurel.

Slip over to the northwest side of Gregory Ridge, regaining the crest at 3.8 miles. In this upper section the path stays off the center of the ridge, away from the now-overgrown but still rutted cattle path that once connected the state line balds to Cades Cove farms below. In pre-park days, farmers drove the cattle to the balds for the summer, while they grew hay for winter in the fields below.

Break the 4,000-foot-elevation mark at 4.0 miles. Yellow birch trees become common in this chillier clime. At 4.7 miles, the trail slips over to the southeast side of the Gregory Ridge. Winter views of the Smokies crest open, keeping your spirits high. Saunter into Rich Gap and a trail junction, at mile 4.9. The Gregory Ridge Trail ends here. ▶6 To the left 0.1 mile, the Long Hungry Ridge Trail terminates from Twentymile Ranger Station. An unmarked path leads 0.3 mile straight ahead to Moore Spring, where an AT shelter once stood before the trail was rerouted over Fontana Dam in the 1940s. The spring, in a small clearing, is one of the Smokies' finest.

Turn right up the Gregory Bald Trail. Ascend into beech and yellow birch rising above a rock and grass understory. Level off at 5.2 miles, then rise

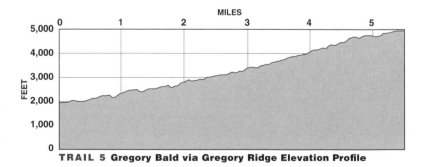

TRAIL 5 Gregory Bald via Gregory Ridge Elevation Profile

Looking down *on a prescribed fire in Cades Cove from Gregory Bald*

again, opening onto the bald. Note the wind-sculpted blueberry and azalea bushes where grasses are absent. Crest out on a field at 5.5 miles. ▶7 Note the USGS survey markers.

 Summit

Flame azalea bushes bloom in an eye-popping display of oranges and reds during June. A hungry hiker can sample the blueberries later in summer. Inclement weather excepted, Gregory Bald offers nearly a 360-degree view year-round. To the south are wave upon wave of mountains of the Nantahala National Forest. The crest of the Smokies rolls away to the east. To the north, the fields of Cades Cove lie below, with East Tennessee stretching to the horizon. Sheep Pen Gap backcountry campsite #13 lies a half mile beyond the bald on the Gregory Bald Trail.

🚶	**MILESTONES**

►1	0.0	Forge Creek Trailhead
►2	0.3	Bridge Forge Creek
►3	1.8	Bridge Forge Creek twice in short succession
►4	1.9	Forge Creek Campsite #12
►5	2.5	Gain crest of Gregory Ridge
►6	4.9	At Rich Gap, turn right on Gregory Bald Trail
►7	5.5	Top of Gregory Bald

John Oliver Cabin via Rich Mountain Loop Trail

Walk the edge of field and forest, drinking in views of Cades Cove and the mountains that rim it. Cross a few streams, then come to the historic John Oliver Cabin, built in 1820. Absorb a way of life that went on for nearly 120 years before the Smoky Mountains National Park came to be.

Best Time

Fall through spring are the best times to make this walk. In fall, the clear skies will allow for mountain and field panoramas. Also, you may spot deer then, too. Winter will offer solitude, and since it is a low-elevation hike, it will have better weather than the high country. In spring, the stream crossings may be a little high but shouldn't pose a problem under normal conditions.

Finding the Trail

From the junction of US 321/TN 73 and East Lamar Alexander Parkway in Townsend, Tennessee, bear right on Lamar Alexander and take it 1.4 miles to the park entrance. Once in the park, drive 0.9 mile, turn right on Laurel Creek Road at the Townsend Wye swimming hole, and follow Laurel Creek for 7.4 miles to the beginning of Cades Cove Loop Road. Park at the loop's beginning in the large parking area on the left.

To pick up the Rich Mountain Loop Trail, walk a short distance down the loop road, past the pole gate, to where the signed trail begins on your right. *Do not drive into one-way Cades Cove Loop Road*, lest

TRAIL USE
Day Hiking, Horses, Child Friendly

LENGTH
2.8 miles, 1½–2 hours

VERTICAL FEET
±90

DIFFICULTY
– **1 2** 3 4 5 +

TRAIL TYPE
Out-and-back

FEATURES
Stream
Autumn Colors
Wildflowers
Wildlife
Great Views
Photo Opportunity
Historical Interest

FACILITIES
Campground
Camp store *(seasonal)*
Picnic Area
Restrooms
Water

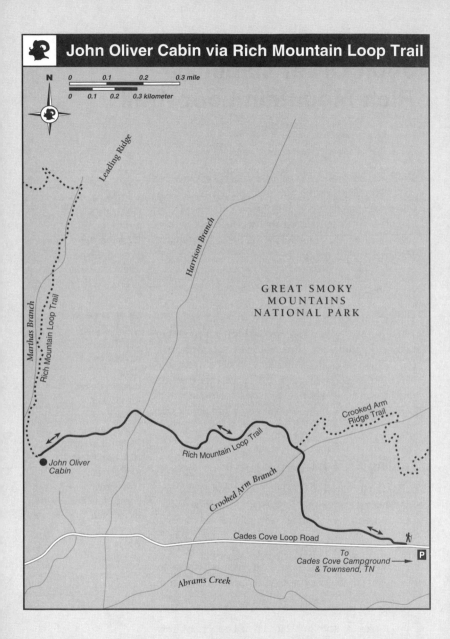

John Oliver Cabin via Rich Mountain Loop Trail

N

0   0.1   0.2   0.3 mile
0   0.1   0.2   0.3 kilometer

Leading Ridge

Harrison Branch

GREAT SMOKY
MOUNTAINS
NATIONAL PARK

Marthas Branch

Rich Mountain Loop Trail

Rich Mountain Loop Trail

Crooked Arm
Ridge Trail

John Oliver
Cabin

Crooked Arm Branch

Cades Cove Loop Road

To
Cades Cove Campground →
& Townsend, TN

P

Abrams Creek

you be forced to make the entire loop or shortcut on Sparks Lane.

Trail Description In the early 19th century, Cades Cove was wildland belonging to the Cherokees, but a treaty in 1819 opened this mountain-rimmed valley to settlement. It wasn't long after—and maybe even before 1819—when John Oliver put down roots in Cades Cove. Oliver had migrated south from northeast Tennessee, up Elizabethton way, where settlers were already pouring over the mountains. The former soldier, who had fought under fellow Tennessean Andrew Jackson, decided to stay a spell here in the shadow of the Smokies.

The settlers' simple agrarian way of life seems idyllic compared to the daily rush we face today. It was a time when families worked together, following the seasons to reap what they had sown, whether it be corn (the staple of the people of Cades Cove), butchering a pig when the first frost lay down, gathering wild blueberries and blackberries from the land, or harvesting apples from planted orchards.

Today you can slow yourself down and take the stroll along the foot of Rich Mountain. Gain views of the state line crest that loomed over Oliver and his fellow Cades Cove residents. In the foreground, enjoy the fields of Cades Cove. They are still kept open today, preserving this pastoral backwater. And when you reach the cabin of John Oliver, walk around inside and imagine yourself in his shoes two centuries ago, carving out a homestead and raising a family in a land that was to become a national park. It is these historic cabins that give a tangible link to a past way of life that has left us forever.

From the parking area at the beginning of Cades Cove Loop Road, ▶1 walk the loop road a short piece to join the Rich Mountain Loop Trail, a singletrack dirt-and-rock path leaving right. Cades Cove Loop Road is to your left and Crooked Arm Ridge rises to your right. White pines, oaks, and

Great Views

Wildlife

Stream

Stream

Historical Interest

tulip trees shade the nearly level path. By 0.3 mile, fields open to your left through tall trees that lined the former settler road. ▶2 Gain bucolic views through the trees of waving grasses with wooded mountains beyond, perhaps deer foraging in the fields. At 0.5 mile, rock-hop over seasonal Crooked Arm Branch, then come to a trail junction. ▶3

Here, the Crooked Arm Ridge Trail leaves right. Stay straight with the Rich Mountain Loop Trail as it rolls through slightly hilly wooded terrain heavy with shortleaf pines, indicating this was likely pasture or cropland in Cades Cove's heyday. Cross a small, unnamed rocky branch at 0.8 mile. ▶4 Keep a westerly course amid more pines and sourwood. At 1.0 mile, step over Harrison Branch, which can be completely dry in late summer or fall. ▶5

Wander more foothills then drift into a clearing and the John Oliver Cabin at 1.4 miles. ▶6 One legend has it that Oliver wandered into Cades Cove while hunting and then spent the night in an Indian hut. Since he found the area already beautiful and potentially productive, he built his home here. This is but one of many impressive log cabins within the cove. They serve as a link to East Tennessee's rural past. John Oliver and his offspring populated the cove and never left.

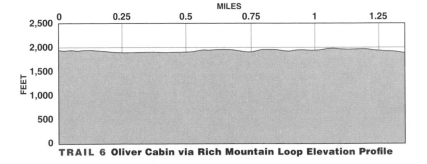

TRAIL 6 Oliver Cabin via Rich Mountain Loop Elevation Profile

This cabin *was one of the first homesteads in Cades Cove.*

Other visitors will be accessing the cabin from Cades Cove Loop Road. If bicycling, be apprised that the loop road is closed to autos on Wednesday and Saturday mornings until 10 a.m. during the warm season. Camp at Cades Cove Campground and enjoy an early start! Another option is to pedal the road under a full moon. Leave a little while before dusk and enjoy sunset and moonrise. (Note that you must have a flashlight if pedaling at night.)

Explore the rest of Cades Cove via the many hiking trails that lace the cove perimeter, by bicycling the 10-mile cove loop road, or by driving the cove loop road.

A backpacker treks *past the John Oliver Cabin in the rain.*

Spence Field and Russell Field Loop

This is a classic Smokies loop, done as either a day hike or overnight adventure. Leave Cades Cove along scenic Anthony Creek. Rise to Bote Mountain, reaching Spence Field and the Appalachian Trail (AT). Gain views from what is left of Spence Field. Take the AT to Russell Field trail shelter. From there, it is downhill on slender Ledbetter Ridge. Finally rejoin Anthony Creek for the return trip to Cades Cove.

Best Time

Cool off during summer along Anthony Creek, then get breezes while in the high country. Fall and spring offer better views in addition to colorful foliage and wildflowers.

Finding the Trail

From the junction of US 321/TN 73 and East Lamar Alexander Parkway in Townsend, Tennessee, bear right on Lamar Alexander and take it 1.4 miles to the park entrance. Once in the park, drive 0.9 mile, turn right on Laurel Creek Road at the Townsend Wye swimming hole, and follow Laurel Creek for 7.4 miles. Just before the beginning of the Cades Cove Loop Road, turn left toward Cades Cove Campground, then immediately turn left into the picnic area. The Anthony Creek Trail is on your right at the back of the picnic area. Parking can be limited in the picnic area.

If you are backpacking, be apprised that *overnight parking is prohibited* in the picnic area. Instead, either park in the long parking strip at the beginning

TRAIL USE
Day Hiking,
Backpacking, Horses
LENGTH
13.0 miles, 6–8 hours
VERTICAL FEET
±3,040
DIFFICULTY
– 1 2 3 **4 5** +
TRAIL TYPE
Loop

FEATURES
Summit
Ridgeline
Stream
Autumn Colors
Wildflowers
Great Views
Photo Opportunity
Backcountry Camping
Historical Interest
FACILITIES
Campground
Picnic Tables
Restrooms near
trailhead

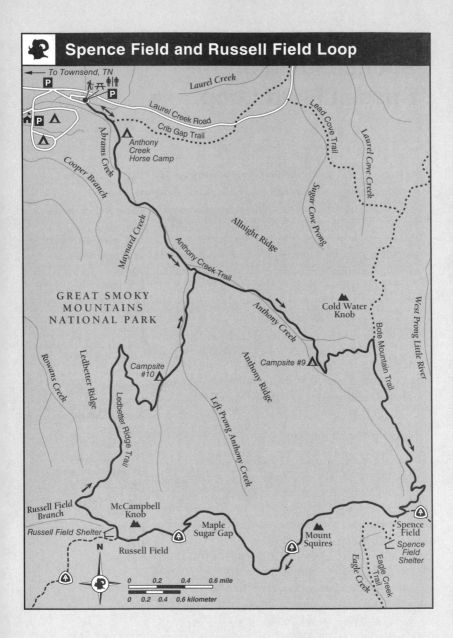

Spence Field and Russell Field Loop

To Townsend, TN

Laurel Creek

Laurel Creek Road

Crib Gap Trail

Anthony Creek Horse Camp

Lead Cove Trail

Laurel Cove Creek

Sugar Cove Prong

Abrams Creek

Cooper Branch

Maynard Creek

Allnight Ridge

Anthony Creek Trail

GREAT SMOKY MOUNTAINS NATIONAL PARK

Cold Water Knob

Anthony Creek

West Prong Little River

Rowans Creek

Ledbetter Ridge

Campsite #10

Ledbetter Ridge Trail

Anthony Ridge

Campsite #9

Bote Mountain Trail

Left Prong Anthony Creek

Russell Field Branch

McCampbell Knob

Maple Sugar Gap

Mount Squires

Spence Field

Russell Field Shelter

Russell Field

Spence Field Shelter

Eagle Creek Trail

Eagle Creek

N

| 0 | 0.2 | 0.4 | 0.6 mile |

| 0 | 0.2 | 0.4 | 0.6 kilometer |

of Cades Cove Loop Road or return toward the campground and park in the lot beside the campground office and camp store.

Trail Description

This strenuous all-day hike or satisfying overnight backpack provides ample reward to those who want to see the Smokies from bottom to top. Starting in Cades Cove, you will climb along a deeply forested, crashing mountain stream. Intersect the famed AT at the Smokies crest. Once on the AT, outstanding views open at Spence Field. Return to Cades Cove via Russell Field Trail with its section of old-growth trees. You pass four backcountry camping options along the way.

Pick up the double-track Anthony Creek Trail, ►1 leaving the picnic area in preserved hemlock, tulip trees, sycamore, and rhododendron. Upper Abrams Creek crashes to your right. At 0.2 mile, the Crib Gap Trail leaves left for Turkeypen Ridge. ►2 Continue straight and dip to pass through Anthony Creek Horse Camp. ►3 The trail narrows beyond the camp. Bridge Abrams Creek at 0.6 mile in a once-settled area. Look for leveled areas as well as old roadbeds.

 Stream

At 0.9 mile, span Abrams Creek on a footlog. Bridge it again at 1.1 miles. Note the rock walls on trail right at 1.4 miles, indicating another settled area, now returned to the bears. Bridge Left Prong Anthony Creek at 1.6 miles, then come to a trail junction. Stay left with the Anthony Creek Trail. Ledbetter Ridge Trail leaves right and is your return route. ►4

Historical Interest

Watch for an old chimney on your left at 1.7 miles. At 2.0 miles, bridge Anthony Creek. Keep ascending on a rocky tread. Tulip trees make up a significant part of a majestic hardwood forest towering overhead. At 2.6 miles, step over a tributary of Anthony Creek. Continuing to climb,

Backcountry Camping ⚠

As you climb Spence Field, look back for views of Thunderhead Mountain and *the* Rocky Top that inspired the University of Tennessee Volunteers signature fight song.

the trail passes the Anthony Creek backcountry campsite #9, on your right at 2.8 miles. ▶5 It is set in a series of somewhat tiered flats. Turn away from the campsite, leaving Anthony Creek for Bote Mountain, rising in viney cove hardwoods nestled on a north-facing slope. Wintertime views of Cades Cove open below.

Intersect Bote Mountain Trail at 3.5 miles. ▶6 Turn right on the former Cherokee-built toll road. When building the turnpike from the lowlands to the Smokies crest, the Cherokee chose the route that should be taken, "voting" for this ridge, which ended up being called "Bote Mountain," since the natives had a hard time with the letter *v*. The next ridge east, not chosen, became known as Defeat Ridge.

Herders later used the wide track to drive their cattle to Spence Field for the summer. Reach an old jeep turnaround at 3.8 miles. This is where the trail narrows and becomes a deeply rutted, rocky path, bordered by moss, galax, and rhododendron. Occasional brief level sections allow a breather. Watch for a hollowed-out rock on the right at 4.6 miles. Settlers would set out salt licks for their cattle using hollowed rocks or logs. The path can be rocky or muddy. Step over a spring branch, then make your final assault on Spence Field using switchbacks that

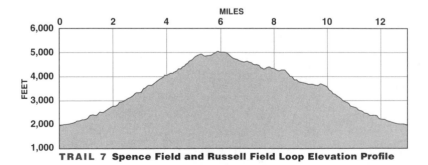

TRAIL 7 Spence Field and Russell Field Loop Elevation Profile

"Rocky Top, *you'll always be home sweet home to me . . ."*

take you through buckeye, beech, and yellow birch forest. Pass a piped spring at 5.0 miles. A final push takes you up to the lower reaches of Spence Field and the AT at 5.2 miles. ▶7

Take time to explore this former pasture that still has broken fields, continually shrinking as tree cover advances. It is an ideal spot to have a snack and rest before you turn west on the AT toward Russell Field. Before leaving Spence Field, the AT passes the Eagle Creek Trail, where a backcountry shelter and spring are located 0.2 mile distant. Leave what is left of Spence Field and reenter beech woods. Dip to a gap at 5.6 miles, then skirt around the north side of

 Great Views

Backcountry Camping

Barren haw trees *and tawny grasses characterize Spence Field in winter.*

Summit Mount Squires. Reach the high point of your hike, breaking the 5,000-foot mark at 5.9 miles. ►8 It's mostly downhill from here.

Slip over to the south side of the state-line ridge, passing through sporadic rhododendron thickets amid hardwoods. Wintertime views into the Tar Heel State open. Step over a spring branch at 6.6 miles. Pass through Maple Sugar Gap at 7.0 miles, ►9 and continue a downgrade. A pair of switchbacks at 7.3 miles takes you lower still. Reach McCampbell Gap at 7.7 miles, ►10 then make a brief ascent around McCampbell Knob.

Backcountry Camping At 8.0 miles, reach Russell Field Shelter, ►11 a trail junction and your departure from the AT. Turn right, northbound, on the Ledbetter Ridge Trail. Pass an evergreen-bordered spring, the headwaters of Russell Field Branch, before coming beside Russell

Field at 8.4 miles. Spur trails lead right to a small relic meadow bordered by white pines.

Descend a north-facing slope, joining slender Ledbetter Ridge at 8.9 miles. The path runs nearly level in pines, oaks, mountain laurel, and maples. Make a sharp turn at 9.7 miles, ►12 descending for a tributary of Left Prong Anthony Creek. Between the ridge and Ledbetter Ridge backcountry campsite #10, at mile 10.6, ►13 look for sizeable tulip trees. The Ledbetter Ridge Trail crosses the tributary just below the campsite.

 Backcountry Camping

Span Left Prong Anthony Creek on a footbridge at 10.8 miles. At 11.4 miles, come again to the Anthony Creek Trail, completing the loop portion of the hike. ►14 Retrace your steps down the Anthony Creek Trail to arrive at the Cades Cove Picnic Area at 13.0 miles. ►15

🚶 MILESTONES

►1	0.0	Anthony Creek Trailhead at Cades Cove Picnic Area
►2	0.2	Crib Gap Trail leaves left
►3	0.3	Anthony Creek Horse Camp
►4	1.6	Ledbetter Ridge Trail leaves left
►5	2.8	Anthony Creek backcountry campsite #9
►6	3.5	Right on Bote Mountain Trail
►7	5.2	At Spence Field, turn right on Appalachian Trail
►8	5.9	Mount Squires
►9	7.0	Maple Sugar Gap
►10	7.7	McCampbell Gap
►11	8.0	At Russell Field Shelter, turn right on Ledbetter Ridge Trail
►12	9.7	Leave Ledbetter Ridge
►13	10.6	Ledbetter Ridge backcountry campsite #10
►14	11.4	Left on Anthony Creek Trail and backtrack
►15	13.0	Anthony Creek Trailhead at Cades Cove Picnic Area

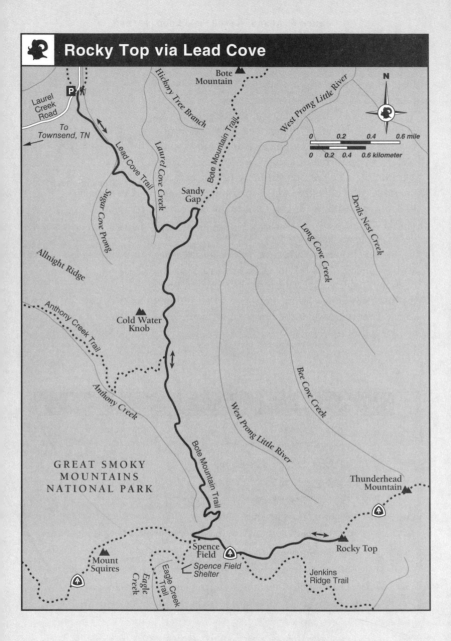

Rocky Top via Lead Cove

Laurel Creek Road

To Townsend, TN

Lead Cove Trail

Hickory Tree Branch

Bote Mountain

Laurel Cove Creek

Bote Mountain Trail

West Prong Little River

N

0   0.2   0.4   0.6 mile

0   0.2   0.4   0.6 kilometer

Sandy Gap

Sugar Cove Prong

Devils Nest Creek

Allnight Ridge

Long Cove Creek

Anthony Creek Trail

Cold Water Knob

Anthony Creek

Bee Cove Creek

West Prong Little River

GREAT SMOKY MOUNTAINS NATIONAL PARK

Bote Mountain Trail

Thunderhead Mountain

Mount Squires

Spence Field

Spence Field Shelter

Eagle Creek

Eagle Creek Trail

Rocky Top

Jenkins Ridge Trail

Rocky Top via Lead Cove

This hike is the epitome of the adage "You reap what you sow." You'll burn a lot of calories on this climb with views as good as they come. Travel Lead Cove to intersect Bote Mountain Trail. Join the Appalachian Trail (AT), passing through Spence Field, climbing farther still to the storied Rocky Top.

Best Time

This hike covers a lot of ecological zones as it climbs and therefore offers year-round beauty. Practically speaking, the warmer season will avail snow-free conditions up high. Fall and spring will have clear skies and the best vistas.

Finding the Trail

From the junction of US 321/TN 73 and East Lamar Alexander Parkway in Townsend, Tennessee, bear right on Lamar Alexander and take it 1.4 miles to the park entrance. Once in the park, drive 0.9 mile, turn right on Laurel Creek Road at the Townsend Wye swimming hole, and follow Laurel Creek for 5.6 miles. The Lead Cove Trail is on your left, just beyond a small parking area that extends on both sides of the road.

Trail Description

Leave Laurel Creek Road behind ▶1 and step into history on the Lead Cove Trail, for what is a hike in the Smokies without a little human history? One theory states Lead Cove derived its name from ore

TRAIL USE
Day Hiking,
Backpacking, Horses
LENGTH
11.6 miles, 6–8 hours
VERTICAL FEET
±3,500
DIFFICULTY
– 1 2 3 4 **5** +
TRAIL TYPE
Out-and-back

FEATURES
Ridgeline
Stream
Autumn Colors
Wildflowers
Great Views
Photo Opportunity
Backcountry Camping
Historical Interest
FACILITIES
None

that was extracted in the 1800s. If that was so, the operation was so small-scale as to be unseen today. Soon you pass an old homesite that lingers in the cool forest of the cove, bordered by Sugar Cove Branch. Keep climbing and the hollow narrows, then you pass an unlikely chimney from a homesite at 0.5 mile.

Historical Interest

At 0.7 mile, the hike turns away from Sugar Cove Branch. Slice through a ridgetop gap at 0.9 mile, then drift to Lead Cove Branch at 1.2 miles. Leave the water behind to arrive at Sandy Gap and the Bote Mountain Trail at mile 1.7. ▶2

Stream

Turn right on the ridge to follow the former jeep trail of Bote Mountain. Ascend steadily through the fairly open pine–oak forest, slipping over to the east side of Coldwater Knob. Intermittent views of Defeat Ridge open to your left. At mile 2.9, pass through the Anthony Creek Trail junction. ▶3 Come to a jeep turnaround at mile 3.2. ▶4 The trail, dug out by generations of cows, horses, and people traveling a seemingly continuous rhododendron tunnel, becomes furrowed and narrow. Wind through a few switchbacks, passing trickling springs, to make a saddle on Spence Field at mile 4.6.

Ridge

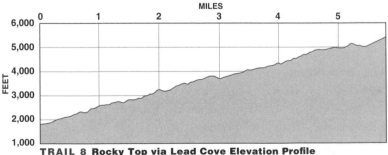

TRAIL 8 Rocky Top via Lead Cove Elevation Profile

A classic Smokies vista *from Rocky Top*

Rocky Top *delivers another inspirational panorama.*

Backcountry Camping

Turn left on the storied AT, ►5 northbound, skirting Spence Field's eastern flank. The Spence Field backcountry shelter is right, a short distance away, on a spur trail. The trek to Rocky Top continues along the formerly large grassy meadow, now crowding in with haw, other trees, and rhododendron. Pass the Jenkins Ridge Trail, leaving right into North Carolina, at mile 4.9. ►6

Great Views

Descend briefly only to begin the final 0.7-mile irregular climb to Rocky Top, 5,440 feet, and its rousing 360-degree view. ►7 Sandstone rock emerges from the soil and points toward the sky.

Once on top, you'll understand why the view inspired a famed country song called "Rocky Top," which has become the fight song for the Volunteers of the University of Tennessee, a mere 30 miles away and visible on a clear day. To your west, the meadows of Spence Field and the western crest of the Smokies all the way to Shuckstack Mountain stand out in bold relief. The views into Tennessee and North Carolina stretch to the horizon. To your east the prominent peak with the imposing name "Thunderhead" competes with the sky. Embrace the view from this rock outcrop just as others have for generations. And maybe belt out a verse or two of "Rocky Top" before you leave.

 Autumn Colors

🚶	**MILESTONES**	
►1	0.0	Lead Cove Trailhead
►2	1.7	Right on Bote Mountain Trail
►3	2.9	Pass Anthony Creek Trail
►4	3.2	Old jeep turnaround
►5	4.6	Left on Appalachian Trail
►6	4.9	Pass Jenkins Ridge Trail
►7	5.8	Rocky Top

CHAPTER 2

Tremont and Elkmont Area

Tremont and Elkmont Area

T remont and Elkmont form the heart of the Tennessee Smokies. The hikes here are as varied as the elevation and include not only natural beauty but also historical destinations. Both day hikes and overnight treks are represented. Major highlights include fantastic vistas from the Appalachian Trail (AT) between Clingmans Dome and Silers Bald, the classic Smokies trek to The Chimney Tops, visits to waterfalls, and off-the-beaten-path getaways where nature reigns supreme.

Little River, easily one of the most scenic and largest watercourses in the Smokies, drains this diverse swath of Volunteer State mountain land. The headwaters of Little River flow north from Clingmans Dome and the state-line crest, gathering volume from innumerable rills and branches. The biggest tributaries, Lynn Camp Prong and Middle Prong Little River, drain the Tremont area. The Tennessee and North Carolina state line forms the southern boundary. It is also where the AT runs, presenting some of the finest high-country hiking in the Southeast. Newfound Gap Road splits the area to the east. The north side of the Little River Valley, cleaving the park from Wear Valley, encases Tremont and Elkmont.

The most extensive road and trailhead access in the Smokies and a huge biodiversity-creating elevation variation—from 6,642 feet at Clingmans Dome to 1,100 feet along the Little River are upsides of the trail system here. Up high, spruce–fir forest adorns the crest from Newfound Gap westward to Silers Bald and along the highest spur ridges. Northern hardwoods prevail below the Canadian-esque evergreens, descending to reach the significant streams, which take on a more temperate vegetation as they crash deeper and lower. Here, notoriously dense forests rise, making the Smokies what they are. It is these temperate jungles that lead to the saying, "If it ain't movin', something's growin' on it." Pines and hardwoods such as oak thrive on south-facing xeric sites.

Opposite and overleaf: *Hikers rest and regroup at Laurel Falls (Trail 13).*

Auto-access points start up top with seasonally open Clingmans Dome Road. Newfound Gap Road connects the high country to the Sugarlands Visitor Center, offering information, maps, books, and more. Little River Road heads west from the Sugarlands. First, it reaches Elkmont, a campground and major trailhead, before winding through the Little River gorge, connecting to Tremont. A separate, short motorway links Little River Road with Wear Valley. A dead-end road enters Tremont and provides more remote trail access. Two towns, Gatlinburg and Townsend, are conveniently situated nearby, but their proximity can be problematic during peak windshield-tourist seasons, such as summer holidays and fall weekends.

Historically speaking, this former Cherokee hunting ground gave way to settlers working their way deeper and deeper into the mountains, up the Little River Valley, residing at simple farms and rude shacks. Settlement was never as thick as at places like Cades Cove, though one John Walker attempted to singlehandedly colonize Tremont with his multiple wives and scores of children. Some of the last residents of the Smokies, holdovers with lifetime leases, lived out their days here. The last man standing, Ol' Lem Ownby, lived into the 1980s along Jakes Creek above what is now Elkmont Campground. The Walker sisters also lived their days out in the Smokies; their preserved cabin is a hiking destination described here. It became a tourist stop so popular that they wished for solitude late in life.

But large-scale logging ran Elkmont and Tremont settlers out before the park did. One W. B. Townsend, for whom the nearby town is named, began a railroad-based logging operation that nearly denuded Elkmont and Tremont. Eventually, Townsend sold his land to the park, but only with the agreement that he could continue logging for another 15 years. The amazing recuperative powers of nature are on display here, as verdant forests have risen to once again carpet the mountains. Later, Elkmont became a resort and summer-home community, with some unoccupied houses still standing.

Today, Elkmont is a major Smokies jumping-off point for tubers, anglers, campers, and equestrians. The Great Smoky Mountains Institute at Tremont adds an educational aspect to the area. Elkmont Campground is the major in-park overnight destination, though many area visitors lodge in Gatlinburg and Townsend. You might say that Elkmont and Tremont aren't just in the heart of the Tennessee side of the Smokies but are the pulse of the entire park.

Permits

Permits are *not* required for day hiking. Backpackers, however, must get a permit to stay at one of the nine designated backcountry campsites and four trail shelters located here. All campsites require a reservation, which you can make online at smokiespermits.nps.gov, then print at home.

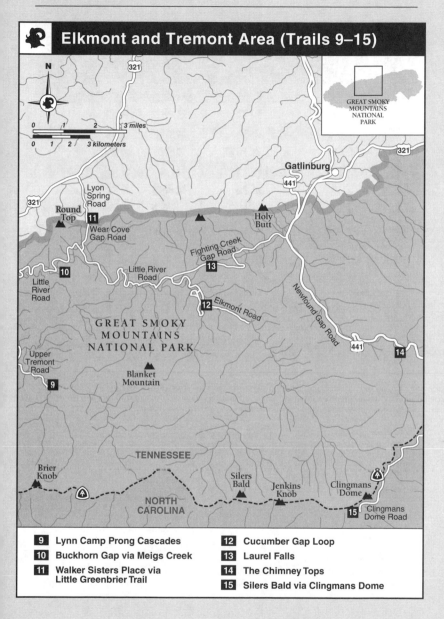

Elkmont and Tremont Area (Trails 9–15)

GREAT SMOKY MOUNTAINS NATIONAL PARK

321

Gatlinburg

441

Lyon Spring Road

321

Round Top

11

Wear Cove Gap Road

Fighting Creek Gap Road

13

Holy Butt

10

Little River Road

Little River Road

12 Elkmont Road

Newfound Gap Road

441

14

GREAT SMOKY MOUNTAINS NATIONAL PARK

Upper Tremont Road

9

Blanket Mountain

TENNESSEE

Brier Knob

Silers Bald

Jenkins Knob

Clingmans Dome

15 Clingmans Dome Road

NORTH CAROLINA

9 Lynn Camp Prong Cascades	**12**	Cucumber Gap Loop
10 Buckhorn Gap via Meigs Creek	**13**	Laurel Falls
11 Walker Sisters Place via Little Greenbrier Trail	**14**	The Chimney Tops
	15	Silers Bald via Clingmans Dome

Tremont and Elkmont Area

TRAIL	DIFFICULTY	LENGTH	TYPE	USES & ACCESS	TERRAIN	FLORA & FAUNA	OTHER
9	1	0.8	↗	👟 👪	📷🏞	🌺✿	📷➤🏠
10	2–3	6.8	↗	👟	📷🏞	🌺✿	➤⚲
11	2	5.0	↗	👟	🔺📷	🌺✿	⛰🏠
12	2–3	5.6	↺	👟	🔺📷🏞	🌺✿	➤🏠
13	2	2.6	↗	👟	📷🏞	🌺	⛰✏
14	3	4.0	↗	👟	🔺📷	🌺✿🌲	⛰📷➤⚲✏
15	3	9.6	↗	👟👣	🔺🔺	🌺✿🌲	⛰📷🔺

USES & ACCESS	TYPE	TERRAIN	FLORA & FAUNA	OTHER
👟 Day Hiking	↺ Loop	🔺 Summit	🌺 Autumn Colors	⛰ Great Views
👣 Backpacking	↗ Out-and-back	🔺 Ridge	✿ Wildflowers	📷 Photo Opportunity
🐎 Horses	↘ Point-to-point	🌊 Lake	🐾 Wildlife	🔺 Backcountry Camping
👪 Child Friendly		📷 Stream	🌲 Spruce–Fir	➤ Swimming
	DIFFICULTY	🏞 Waterfall	🌳 Old-Growth	⚲ Secluded
	– 1 2 3 4 5 +			⚿ Steep
	less more			🏠 Historical Interest
				✏ Geologic Interest

Maps

For the Tremont and Elkmont area, here are the USGS 7.5-minute (1:24,000-scale) topographic quadrangles you'll need, listed in geographic order as you hike along your route.

Trail 9: *Thunderhead Mountain*
Trail 10: *Wear Cove*
Trail 11: *Wear Cove*
Trail 12: *Gatlinburg*
Trail 13: *Gatlinburg*
Trail 14: *Mount Le Conte, Clingmans Dome*
Trail 15: *Clingmans Dome, Silers Bald*

Tremont and Elkmont Area

Lynn Camp Prong Cascades 83

This easy family stroll follows a quintessential mountain stream. Take a wide and easy track along scenic Lynn Camp Prong. Enjoy a forest montage of a valley that was once the site of a logging community. Reach an observation bench with a straight-on view of the cataract. The falls can be accessed from here or a little farther up the trail.

TRAIL 9

Day Hiking,
Child Friendly
0.8 mile, Out-and-back
Difficulty: **1** 2 3 4 5

Buckhorn Gap via Meigs Creek 89

From the popular waterfall and swimming area of the Sinks on the Little River, take the quiet Meigs Creek Trail over a ridge with views. Join Meigs Creek to view a waterfall. Numerous creek crossings of Meigs Creek and its tributaries lead through a gorgeous and secluded valley to wooded Buckhorn Gap.

TRAIL 10

Day Hiking
6.8 miles, Out-and-back
Difficulty: 1 **2** 3 4 5

Walker Sisters Place via Little Greenbrier Trail 95

Soak up some views and then visit one of the last working pioneer homesteads in the Smokies. Trace the Little Greenbrier Trail as it straddles the national park boundary. Vistas are numerous from a pine-cloaked mountainside before reaching a gap. Descend a hollow and reach the Walker Sisters Place, occupied by spinster siblings until 1964.

TRAIL 11

Day Hiking
5.0 miles, Out-and-back
Difficulty: 1 **2** 3 4 5

Lynn Camp Prong Cascades

This easy family stroll follows a quintessential mountain stream. Take a wide and easy track along scenic Lynn Camp Prong. Enjoy a forest montage of a valley that was once the site of a logging community. Reach an observation bench with a straight-on view of the cataract. The falls can be accessed from here or a little farther up the trail.

Best Time

This short hike is good for all seasons. Spring wildflowers will be rife in the valley, and the stream will be at its boldest. In summer, the stream will avail an ideal cooling place. In winter you will best see evidence of the former logging community.

Finding the Trail

From the junction of US 321/TN 73 and East Lamar Alexander Parkway in Townsend, Tennessee, bear right on Lamar Alexander and take it 1.4 miles to the park entrance. Once in the park, drive 0.9 mile, turn right on Laurel Creek Road at the Townsend Wye swimming hole, follow it for 0.2 mile, and then turn left on Tremont Road at the second intersection, just across the river. Follow Tremont Road past the Great Smoky Mountains Institute at Tremont, where the road turns to gravel, to its dead end after 5.1 miles. The Middle Prong Trail starts at the upper end of the parking area.

TRAIL USE
Day Hiking,
Child Friendly
LENGTH
0.8 mile, 1 hour
VERTICAL FEET
±150
DIFFICULTY
– 1 2 3 4 5 +
TRAIL TYPE
Out-and-back

FEATURES
Stream
Waterfall
Autumn Colors
Wildflowers
Photo Opportunity
Swimming
Historical Interest
FACILITIES
None

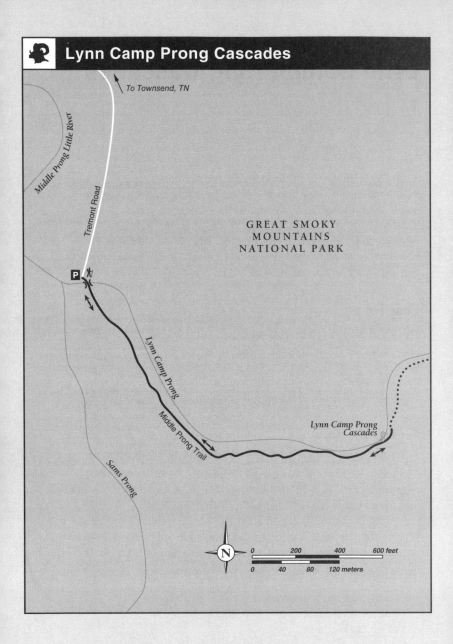

Lynn Camp Prong Cascades

To Townsend, TN

Middle Prong Little River

Tremont Road

GREAT SMOKY
MOUNTAINS
NATIONAL PARK

P

Lynn Camp Prong

Middle Prong Trail

Sams Prong

Lynn Camp Prong
Cascades

N

| 0 | 200 | 400 | 600 feet |
| 0 | 40 | 80 | 120 meters |

Trail Description

When visiting the Smokies, we see the park in its current state. Sometimes it is hard to imagine what it once was. Along this hike you could envision the time when the Middle Prong Little River was the forest primeval—a place where uncut giants stretched for the mountaintops; where nature's hand placed a dizzying array of trees and lesser flora just so; where bear, elk, bison, and red wolves vied for supremacy. Or you could imagine a place where John Walker and his numerous wives—as well as his numerous offspring—populated this valley that came to be known as Tremont. Picture rudimentary log cabins in sunlit clearings, where a stone chimney pushed smoke above a plot of overturned soil, waiting for spring to begin. Or you could conceive what took place just before this locale became part of the Great Smoky Mountains National Park—one of the first railroad-driven, massive-scale, no-holds-barred logging operations in the South, undertaken from the late 1920s to the late 1930s, an operation so complete and efficient for the time that it shocked and stunned even those involved.

On this trek you'll see nature's beauty standing the test of time and the amazing recuperative powers of these Tennessee woods. You will also see remnants of the Little River Lumber Company and its push up the valley in a quest for some of the largest uncut forests in the country.

The access road to the trailhead and the trail itself follow the old logging rail originally graded by the lumber company. Northern timber interests had perfected railroad-based, steam engine–powered logging and set their sights on the uncut verdant forests of the Smokies. And they came in using not only the latest machinery but also a new efficiency that moved men and their families wherever the cutting was to be done. The trailhead was once the community of Tremont.

After parking, walk around and picture a simple community building that functioned as the school, the church, and movie theater—the center of group events. The employees lived in portable shacks that were moved by the railroad and offloaded by steam shovels. These steam-powered machines were used primarily to load cut logs onto the railcars. There was a railroad siding area, where cars were taken on and off the train. The movable homes were located in the flat. A water-powered generator provided electricity to the community.

Now, begin your walk, ▶1 crossing the arched steel bridge over Lynn Camp Prong, just above its confluence with Sams Prong. Together they form the Middle Prong Little River. Just across the bridge was another part of the community. Here stood the company store, where employees paid their bills in scrip, a unit of value issued by the company for employees to buy supplies. The post office was in the store as well. A rudimentary doctor's office stood near Lynn Camp Prong.

Historical Interest 🏠

Rail lines went up Sams Prong and Lynn Camp Prong. Your hike goes left here, up Lynn Camp Prong. The grade is steep for a train. Only gear-driven locomotives were used to push the cars up

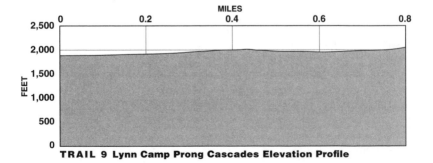

TRAIL 9 Lynn Camp Prong Cascades Elevation Profile

Lynn Camp Prong *crashes in a white froth over a rock face.*

empty and slowly work them back down to the sawmill in Townsend.

Imagine what a noisy, rumbling place this would've been. But even amid the logging chaos, the Smokies' splendor was undeniable. In the flat across the river, the Tremont Hotel was established. Originally for employees of the logging outfit, it later offered tourists lodging and hot meals. The hotel was dismantled with the coming of the park and is now just a picture and a memory.

Leave the logging world behind, continuing on up the trail. The forest is once again magnificent and should continue to flourish. The moist valley is an ideal wildflower habitat. The wide track allows hikers to trek side-by-side in conversation while appreciating the scenery. At 0.4 mile, you come to a contemplation bench facing Lynn Camp Prong Cascades. ▶2

The cataract leaves an upstream pool, then fills a rock-lined channel, building up energy. It then is unleashed, tumbling down a stone face in white

 Wildflowers

 Waterfall

froth. A jumble of rocks, left over from blasting the rail line, lie between you and the falls, but hikers make it to the base of the falls for an up-close view of Lynn Camp Prong. Others continue along the trail, and reach the upper end of the falls and the stone face over which it tumbles. This upper vantage complements the view from the bench.

Photo Opportunity

You will also see more cascades upstream of the main falls—together they're more than 80 feet tall! When you add together the ceaseless waterfall flowing through all the changes of Tremont, the rising forests making a national park–level comeback, and the pioneer lives led in this neck of the woods, followed by the loggers and their portable world, this locale really is a place for contemplation.

MILESTONES

▶1   0.0   Middle Prong Trailhead
▶2   0.4   Lynn Camp Prong Cascades

Buckhorn Gap via Meigs Creek

From the popular waterfall and swimming area of the Sinks on the Little River, take the quiet Meigs Creek Trail over a ridge with views. Join Meigs Creek to view a waterfall. Numerous creek crossings of Meigs Creek and its tributaries lead through a gorgeous and secluded valley to wooded Buckhorn Gap.

TRAIL USE
Day Hiking
LENGTH
6.8 miles, 3½–4½ hours
VERTICAL FEET
±980
DIFFICULTY
– 1 **2** 3 4 5 +
TRAIL TYPE
Out-and-back

FEATURES
Stream
Waterfall
Autumn Colors
Wildflowers
Swimming
Secluded
FACILITIES
None

Best Time

You will have to make nearly 20 rock-hop crossings of Meigs Creek and its tributaries on this trek. Late summer and fall offer the lowest water and easiest crossings. However, the waterfall of the Sinks and Meigs Creek Falls is less spectacular then. Consider coming during early summer when you can wet your feet without penalty and enjoy bolder cascades. During spring, the Meigs Creek valley can be a wildflower wonderland.

Finding the Trail

From the junction of US 321/TN 73 and East Lamar Alexander Parkway in Townsend, Tennessee, bear right on Lamar Alexander and take it 1.4 miles to the park entrance. Once in the park, drive 0.9 mile, turn left on Little River Gorge Road at the Townsend Wye swimming hole, and follow it east for 5.7 miles to the Sinks parking area, just across the Little River on your right. The Meigs Creek Trail starts at the rear of the parking area.

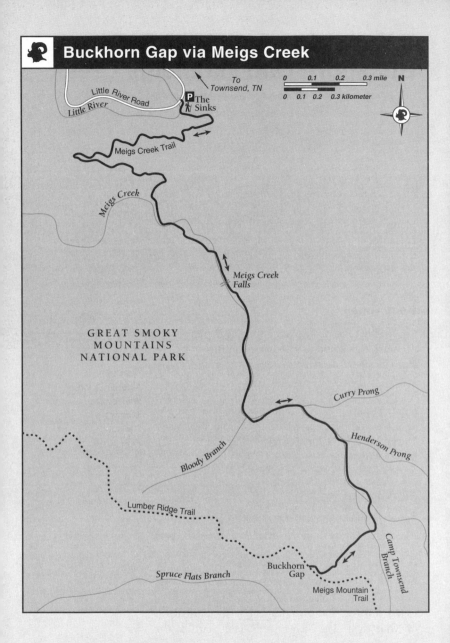

Buckhorn Gap via Meigs Creek

To Townsend, TN

Little River Road

Little River

The Sinks

Meigs Creek Trail

Meigs Creek

Meigs Creek Falls

GREAT SMOKY
MOUNTAINS
NATIONAL PARK

Curry Prong

Henderson Prong

Bloody Branch

Lumber Ridge Trail

Spruce Flats Branch

Buckhorn Gap

Meigs Mountain Trail

Camp Townsend Branch

0   0.1   0.2   0.3 mile
0   0.1   0.2   0.3 kilometer

N

Meigs Creek Falls *feeds the Sinks, a popular swimming hole.*

Trail Description

After leaving the crowds at the Sinks behind, you'll probably have this intimate slice of the Smokies to yourself. The smaller subtle features of a Southern Appalachian mountain valley stand out on this trail. Meigs Creek will surely catch your eye, as you cross it nearly 20 times. Not to worry though, as most crossings are not difficult in times of normal water flow.

Leave the Sinks parking area, ►1 leading to a wide path and a viewing platform overlooking the falls feeding the Sinks, a large pool popular with swimmers. The signed Meigs Creek Trail begins on stone steps beyond the platform. Pass a natural rock promontory overlooking the Sinks. Once on the Meigs Creek Trail, drop into a boggy area, unusual for the Smokies. Black birch, white pine, and tulip trees grow tall and lush. A slender path rises past rock outcrops as it winds into small tributaries.

Waterfall

Ascend onto a dry, piney ridge, leveling off at 0.9 mile ▶2 amid sassafras, sourwood, and oaks, a forest change from the Little River Valley. In winter, views of Meigs Creek open to the south. Wind back down to finally encounter the trail's namesake, Meigs Creek, at 1.4 miles. ▶3

Here begin the crossings, as the creek and trail merge amid a dark green forest interspersed with crashing cascades that flow beneath tunnels of rhododendron above which rise black birch. Rock-hop your way across the stream. At 1.7 miles, a particularly comely cascade, Meigs Creek Falls, announces its presence on your right. It spills over a sheer stone face 15 feet into a pool. Beyond the falls, continue fording. While crossing, notice the clarity of the stream.

At 2.0 miles, on trail left, look for the first of two huge beech trees. ▶4 Buckeyes grow tall in this valley, which also once harbored massive hemlocks. Selective loggers left these hemlock trees behind. They were not considered commercially valuable in the early 20th century and were left to become the giants of the forest they are today, ultimately to fall prey to the hemlock woolly adelgid. As you continue a moderate uptick, Meigs Creek and the side creeks that feed it shrink, but still display an array

Great Views

Stream

Waterfall

The people who settled these isolated coves revered their moving water and couldn't cotton to drinking "still" well water after they left their highland homes.

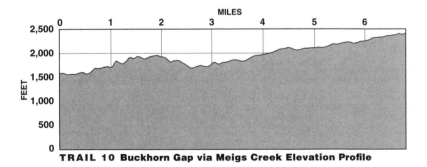

TRAIL 10 Buckhorn Gap via Meigs Creek Elevation Profile

of scenic shoals, slides, and pools amid mossy logs, gray boulders, and overhanging rhododendron.

Rock-hop tributaries in the upper valley. The final climb at 3.3 miles signals your impending arrival at Buckhorn Gap. ▶5 Once at the gap, you intersect the Meigs Mountain Trail, which goes left to Elkmont, and the Lumber Ridge Trail, which goes to Tremont. Take a seat at the gap and listen to the sounds of the Smokies before returning to the busy Sinks.

🚶	**MILESTONES**	
▶1	0.0	The Sinks parking area
▶2	0.9	Ridgetop with views
▶3	1.4	First crossing of Meigs Creek
▶4	2.0	Huge beech trees
▶5	3.4	Buckhorn Gap

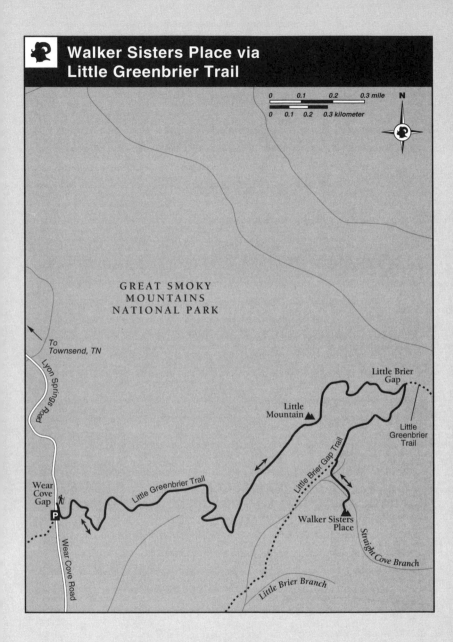

Walker Sisters Place via Little Greenbrier Trail

0   0.1   0.2   0.3 mile

0   0.1   0.2   0.3 kilometer

N

GREAT SMOKY
MOUNTAINS
NATIONAL PARK

To
Townsend, TN

Lyon Springs Road

Little Brier Gap

Little Mountain

Little Greenbrier Trail

Wear Cove Gap

P

Little Greenbrier Trail

Little Brier Gap Trail

Walker Sisters Place

Wear Cove Road

Little Brier Branch

Straight Cove Branch

Walker Sisters Place via Little Greenbrier Trail

Soak up some views and then visit one of the last working pioneer homesteads in the Smokies. Trace the Little Greenbrier Trail as it straddles the national park boundary. Vistas are numerous from a pine-cloaked mountainside before reaching a gap. Descend a hollow and reach the Walker Sisters Place, occupied by spinster siblings until 1964.

TRAIL USE
Day Hiking
LENGTH
5.0 miles, 3 hours
VERTICAL FEET
±400
DIFFICULTY
– 1 **2** 3 4 5 +
TRAIL TYPE
Out-and-back

Best Time

Because this is a relatively low-elevation hike, winter is favorable. Spring is also a good choice, when Little Brier Branch comes alive with wildflowers. Fall brings clear skies and dry trails.

FEATURES
Ridgeline
Stream
Autumn Colors
Wildflowers
Great Views
Historical Interest
FACILITIES
None

Finding the Trail

From the junction of US 321/TN 73 and East Lamar Alexander Parkway in Townsend, Tennessee, bear right on Lamar Alexander and take it 1.4 miles to the park entrance. Once in the park, drive 0.9 mile, turn left on Little River Gorge Road at the Townsend Wye swimming hole, and follow it east 7.7 miles. Turn left into the Metcalf Bottoms Picnic Area and cross the Little River on a bridge; then turn immediately left on Wear Cove Gap Road. Keep north on the road for 1.3 miles to the park border, where the Little Greenbrier Trail starts on the right. There is parking here for only one car directly by the trail; another parking area is located just over the hill from the trailhead.

Trail Description

This hike travels a ridgeline that seemingly divides time periods in East Tennessee. On one side there is Great Smoky Mountains National Park, where the preserved Walker Sisters Cabin, your destination, exemplifies a simpler time, when the Smokies were truly the "back of beyond," where homesteaders would spend a lifetime and never get more than 100 miles from home. On the other side of the ridge, modern "homesteaders" stake vacation homes in Wear Valley to be near the beauty that is the national park, changing Wear Valley from a land of the forgotten to an urban outpost. Your mind may contemplate such things while you wander the ridge known as Little Mountain, the northern border of the Smokies.

Begin this hike at Wear Cove Gap on the Little Greenbrier Trail. ▶1 Climb through archetypal pine, oak, and mountain laurel forest on a narrow pathway. Blueberries are abundant in sunnier locales. This path skirts the park border in several places; you will see boundary signs here and there. Also, observe elaborate stonework by trail makers that keeps the path from sliding down the mountainside. **Great Views** 🔭 Views open north beyond the park, especially at a gap at 0.5 mile. ▶2

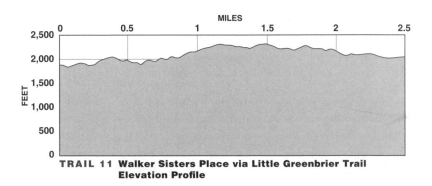

TRAIL 11 Walker Sisters Place via Little Greenbrier Trail Elevation Profile

Hike more up than down then curve around the south side of Little Mountain at 1.0 mile. Listen for flowing water in the lowlands below. Enjoy peering into the park's heart. Numerous dead pine snags are the result of natural relationships between pines and the native pine beetle; the snags are now falling and younger trees are taking their place. The walking is easy, allowing you to enjoy more views into Wear Cove and Cove Mountain to the east. Descend the ridge of Little Mountain to reach

 Ridge

 Great Views

The Walker Sisters Place *is one of the better preserved homesteads in the park.*

Autumn Colors

Wildflowers

Stream

Little Brier Gap and a trail junction at mile 1.9. ▶3 Turn right here, joining the Little Brier Gap Trail, descending into the moist cove of Little Brier Branch. Tulip trees join the forest.

The V-shaped hollow widens. Little Brier Branch gains flow from tributaries. Reach a signed trail junction at 2.3 miles. ▶4 The Little Brier Gap Trail continues as a gravel road while a spur track leads left to the Walker Sisters Place. Turn left along tiny Straight Cove Branch. The preponderance of tulip trees and shortleaf pines indicates former fields. Imagine these trailside flats growing corn and other vegetables, perhaps as pasture, back when this was an active homestead. Come to an open area at 2.5 miles and reach the Walker Sisters Place in a grassy clearing. ▶5 This cove was occupied for 150 years, with the Walker sisters remaining after the national park was established, thanks to a lifetime lease agreement. After they passed away, the park preserved their homestead. Now, the springhouse, main home, and small barn remain.

Historical Interest

Notice the notched-log construction of the buildings and the nonnative ornamental bushes. Walk inside. The low roof required less construction material and also made the home easier to heat. The white stuff on the walls is old pieces of newspaper that the sisters used to brighten and insulate the cabin. A ladder leads to the sleeping loft. The large fireplace warmed the home, and heat rising up the rock "chimbley" kept loft sleepers a little toastier. The springhouse kept critters from fouling the water and also helped milk and butter stay cool in the summertime. The barn is a smaller version of the cantilever-type popular in East Tennessee a century and more ago. Note the farm implements on the wall.

Walk the perimeter of the yard, and you will see other relics, including old car tires, which the Walker Sisters likely regarded as junk. Remember to leave all artifacts so others can enjoy and discover them. If you are further interested in the area's history, continue down the Little Brier Gap Trail for 1.1 more miles to the Little Greenbrier Schoolhouse before returning to Wear Cove Gap.

🚶	**MILESTONES**	
▶1	0.0	Little Greenbrier Trailhead
▶2	0.5	Gap with views
▶3	1.9	Right on Little Brier Gap Trail
▶4	2.3	Left on spur to Walker Sisters Place
▶5	2.5	Walker Sisters Place

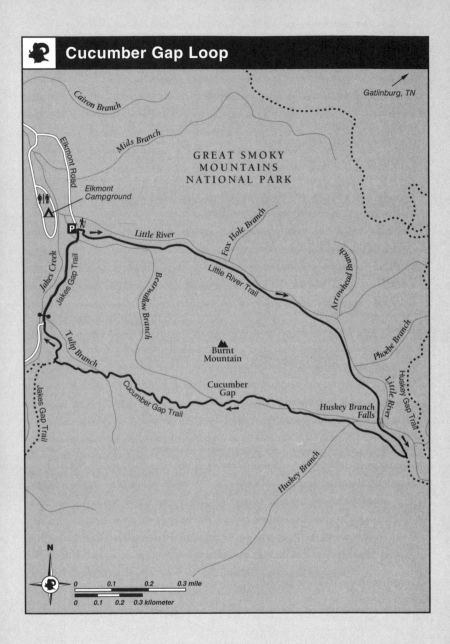

Gatlinburg, TN

GREAT SMOKY
MOUNTAINS
NATIONAL PARK

Cairon Branch

Mids Branch

Elkmont Road

Elkmont
Campground

P

Little River

Fox Hole Branch

Jakes Creek

Jakes Gap Trail

Little River Trail

Arrowhead Branch

Bearwallow Branch

Burnt
Mountain

Phoebe Branch

Tulip Branch

Cucumber
Gap

Little River

Jakes Gap Trail

Cucumber Gap Trail

Huskey Branch
Falls

Huskey Gap Trail

Huskey Branch

N

0   0.1   0.2   0.3 mile

0   0.1   0.2   0.3 kilometer

Cucumber Gap Loop.

Leave Elkmont and cruise up the ultra-attractive Little River Valley, where the watercourse tumbles over huge boulders, forming large, clear pools that invite you to take a dip in the cool mountain stream. Pass Huskey Branch Cascades. Leave the Little River on an old railroad grade that gently climbs to a gap and then descends to Jakes Creek Valley, returning to Elkmont.

TRAIL USE
Day Hiking

LENGTH
5.6 miles, 3 hours

VERTICAL FEET
±880

DIFFICULTY
– 1 **2 3** 4 5 +

TRAIL TYPE
Loop

Best Time

This is a great hike year-round. In spring, wildflowers abound along the Little River and Huskey Branch. Swimmers and sunbathers can enjoy the big waters of the Little River. Fall colors are vibrant along the streams and near Cucumber Gap. Solitude seekers will enjoy winter.

FEATURES
Ridgeline
Stream
Waterfall
Autumn Colors
Wildflowers
Swimming
Historical Interest

FACILITIES
Campground
Picnic Tables
Restrooms
Water

Finding the Trail

From the junction of US 321 and US 441/Parkway in Gatlinburg, Tennessee (signed traffic light #3), head south on US 441 into the park. In 2.7 miles, with the Sugarlands Visitor Center on your right, turn right on Fighting Creek Gap Road and follow it south and west for 4.9 miles. Turn left on Elkmont Road at the intersection and follow it 1.3 miles to Elkmont Campground. Take the first left, just before the campground check-in station, and follow this road 0.5 mile to cross the Little River. The Little River Trail starts on the left, shortly after the bridge.

Trail Description

The Little River Trail's beginning was once part of Little River Road until a mid-1990s flood washed out this upper section. The park service decided to move the trailhead ▶1 back rather than repair the road. Pass through Elkmont's former summer-home community, once known as the Appalachian Club, on a crumbling asphalt path. Vestiges of the stone entry gates and summer cottages survive. After a quarter mile, you leave the old vacation-cottage community on a wide gravel track shaded by tulip trees, sycamore, black birch, yellow birch over scads of doghobble, and rhododendron mixed with mossy boulders. The sparkling Little River to the left constantly tries to lure you to its banks with attractive shoals, crystalline pools, small islands, and big rocks ideal for sunning or feeling the cool breeze flow down the valley. A dip may be in order during the dog days of summer. At 0.4 mile, Bearwallow Branch comes in on your right.

At 1.0 mile, the path narrows after you pass the old parking area. A bluff pinches the trail to the river in places. In other spots the Little River is only audible, not visible. The Little River drains the highest point in the Smokies—Clingmans Dome—then gathers tributaries, flowing north and west through

Historical Interest 🏠

Stream ▶

Wildflowers ❀

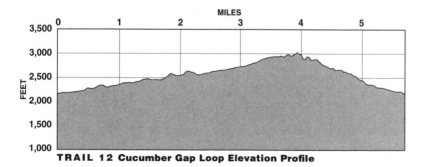

TRAIL 12 Cucumber Gap Loop Elevation Profile

The Little River *charges downstream following heavy spring rains.*

the park before emerging near the community of Townsend. The watercourse continues northwest to meet the Tennessee River near Maryville. In the park, intrepid kayakers tackle its white froth during higher flows. Foolish tubers get injured every summer floating it.

Burnt Mountain rises to your right; this hike leads completely around that wooded peak. At

Waterfall

2.0 miles, Huskey Branch flows beneath a bridge into the Little River and a large pool below. Here, Huskey Branch tumbles as a tiered cascade above and below the trail as it slices through jagged rock. ▶2 Look into the pool below Huskey Branch for swimming trout. Brook trout, technically a char, are the only native trout in the Smokies. However, brown trout and rainbow trout have been intro-

Stream

duced into the park and thrive in its waters. In the lower Little River you are most likely to see brown and rainbow trout.

Keep walking for a bit, coming to an intersection with the Cucumber Gap Trail at 2.4 miles. ▶3 Turn right onto the Cucumber Gap Trail. This path may have more vines among the trees than any other trail in the park. Ascend an old railroad grade, rock-hopping Huskey Branch at mile 2.8. ▶4 Muscadine vines are prominent elements of the trailside forest. The small native grapes ripen in early fall and are favored by all sorts of wildlife in the Smokies. The thick-skinned fruit grows throughout the Southeast; early settlers used it to make wine. Today winemak-ers cultivate the varietal. The antioxidant-laden fruit is also touted as a modern-day health food.

The path keeps rising along a small feeder stream of Huskey Branch, crossing the tributary at 3.2 miles. Occasional views open through the trees

Autumn Colors

to the right. The path passes just above Cucumber Gap at 3.5 miles; you are just below 3,000 feet of elevation. ▶5 The gap was named for the cucumber tree, which is part of the magnolia family. Its green fruit resembles a mini-cucumber and can be seen trailside in September. The tree appears throughout the mid-Appalachians, with West Virginia in the heart of its range. Outlier populations stretch to Louisiana and Missouri.

Historical Interest

The flat in Cucumber Gap was once home to a Smoky Mountain pioneer family. Look for leveled locations and piled stones in the woods, perhaps reminiscent of those people. Pass some fairly large beech trees and arrow-straight regal tulip trees before descending to cross Tulip Branch at 4.4 miles.

Meet the wide Jakes Creek Trail at 4.6 miles. ▶6 Turn right here and descend to a pole gate at 5.0 miles. Enter the former summer home community, passing the Jakes Creek Trailhead parking area. ▶7 Keep downhill on an asphalt path to the Jakes Creek Trailhead at mile 5.5. ▶8 Turn right here, follow the paved road, and soon reach the Little River Trailhead, completing your loop at 5.6 miles. ▶9

🚶	MILESTONES	
▶1	0.0	Little River Trailhead
▶2	2.0	Huskey Branch waterfall
▶3	2.4	Right on Cucumber Gap Trail
▶4	2.8	Cross Huskey Branch
▶5	3.5	Cucumber Gap
▶6	4.6	Right on Jakes Creek Trail
▶7	5.0	Jakes Creek Trailhead
▶8	5.5	Right at road split
▶9	5.6	Little River Trailhead

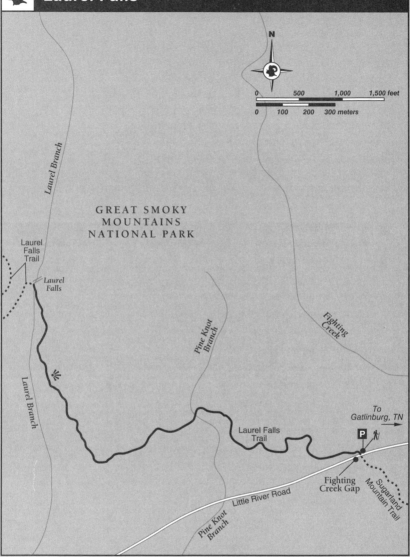

Laurel Falls

N

| 0 | 500 | 1,000 | 1,500 feet |

| 0 | 100 | 200 | 300 meters |

Laurel Branch

GREAT SMOKY
MOUNTAINS
NATIONAL PARK

Laurel
Falls
Trail

Laurel
Falls

Pine Knot
Branch

Fighting
Creek

Laurel Branch

Laurel Falls
Trail

To
Gatlinburg, TN

P

Fighting
Creek Gap

Sugarland
Mountain Trail

Little River Road

Pine Knot
Branch

Laurel Falls

This very popular hike exudes beauty that outshines its sometimes-bothersome crowds. Start at Fighting Creek Gap, then angle up the north side of Cove Mountain. Turn into Laurel Branch, where rock formations and a steep-sided valley avail views. Come to the middle of 80-foot Laurel Falls, gaining glimpses of the cataract above and below.

Best Time

Solitude seekers will want to visit the falls in the off-season, from late autumn through spring. Spring will also have the boldest falls. Winter is a good time for both solitude and views. If you're going in the summer, when the crowds are at their peak, hit the trail at dawn or dusk.

Finding the Trail

From the junction of US 321 and US 441/Parkway in Gatlinburg, Tennessee (signed traffic light #3), head south on US 441 into the park. In 2.7 miles, with the Sugarlands Visitor Center on your right, turn right on Fighting Creek Gap Road and head west for 3.8 miles to Fighting Creek Gap and the trailhead. The Laurel Falls Trail starts on the north side of the road.

Trail Description

I admit it: there was a time in my Smokies hiking career when I thought trails that were popular with tourists were uncool. In trying to establish my

TRAIL USE
Day Hiking

LENGTH
2.6 miles, 1½–2 hours

VERTICAL FEET
±680

DIFFICULTY
– 1 **2** 3 4 5 +

TRAIL TYPE
Out-and-back

FEATURES
Stream
Waterfall
Autumn Colors
Great Views
Geologic Interest

FACILITIES
None

hiking credentials, I sought out the remote, the difficult, the lesser known.

True, the hike to Laurel Falls is very popular, perhaps one of the five most popular hikes in the park. And yes, the trail is paved and used by parents pushing their babies in strollers (despite it being discouraged by the park service). But the end result of my hiking snobbery was denying myself the chance to see a very lovely waterfall that tumbles in multiple stages over a rock slab.

If hiking with the crowds turns you off, simply make the trek to Laurel Falls during off-times. This means stay away during the summer and early fall, unless you can arrive at the falls at dawn or dusk. Otherwise, save the walk here for winter or, even better, spring, when Laurel Branch will be flowing strongly off the slopes of Cove Mountain.

One thing's for sure: you won't get lost on this hike, which traces a paved path for its entirety. It leaves Fighting Creek Gap—one of the top 10 Smoky Mountain names of all time—and winds up the north slope of Cove Mountain. The track alternates among small coves and ridges, crossing Pine Knot Branch (yet another colorful Smokies name), then turns into the valley of Laurel Branch. Here, the mountain slope sharpens and the path works around boulders while you look across the Laurel

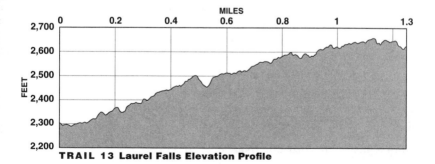

TRAIL 13 Laurel Falls Elevation Profile

Lovely Laurel Falls *is among the park's most popular destinations.*

Branch valley at Meigs Mountain. The scenery rewards the hiker who braves the crowds. The route then cuts deeper to meet Laurel Branch at 80-foot Laurel Falls.

The Laurel Falls Trail started out as a fire road built in the 1930s, constructed to provide access to a fire tower atop Cove Mountain. As the Smokies park grew in popularity, the road to the tower became known as the trail to Laurel Falls. The park service ended up paving the path in the 1960s to curb erosion. It is now the longest paved trail in the park.

The Laurel Falls Trail is marked with informative signs by which hikers from 2 to 92 gather. Join the paved path ▶1 as it heads northwesterly across the north face of Cove Mountain. High-energy kids have made numerous paths to rock formations. Mountain laurel and wild azalea rise below oaks, hickories, and maples. At 0.5 mile, ▶2 the trail bridges Pine Knot Branch on its way to meet the Little River well below.

Stream

The rise is gentle and steady. By 0.8 mile, you've turned into the Laurel Branch valley. Big boulders border the trail. The drop off the slope sharpens, giving you views across Laurel Branch and southward to Meigs Mountain. These are two of the surprises of the hike—the impressive rock cliffs and the spectacular vistas. You can hear Laurel Branch heading downslope like Pine Knot Branch to meet its mother stream, the Little River. By 1.0 mile, another fine vista ▶3 opens to the west and south, where Meigs and Blanket Mountains form a rampart.

Geologic Interest

Great Views

Continue deeper into the Laurel Branch valley. At 1.3 miles, the path suddenly leads across a bridge over Laurel Branch, and you find yourself in the middle of ▶4 Laurel Falls—and in a crowd during the summer. A wide rock slab that opens across the bridge is the primary viewing spot for the falls. The upper portion of the cataract is easily visible from

Waterfall

Geologic Interest

here. Here, Laurel Falls angles down a rock face, levels off, and then makes a second drop, widening all the while; then it flows under the trail bridge. From here, the water drops off the lower, less-viewed part of the fall, below the trail. It spills wide over a nearly vertical rock face before returning to a flow more typical of a Smoky Mountain stream, dropping for a total of 80 feet.

Photo Opportunity

The Laurel Falls Trail continues its quest for the top of Cove Mountain. The segment just beyond Laurel Falls gives you an elevated perspective of the greater waterfall scene. On your return trip, ►5 enjoy those views a second time, and be prepared to dodge baby strollers pushed by winded, dogged, less-experienced hikers. I do hope, however, that you'll still appreciate Laurel Falls for the beauty it offers both hiking novices and grizzled veterans.

	MILESTONES	
►1	0.0	Fighting Creek Gap Trailhead
►2	0.5	Pine Knot Branch
►3	1.0	View
►4	1.3	Laurel Falls
►5	2.6	Fighting Creek Gap Trailhead

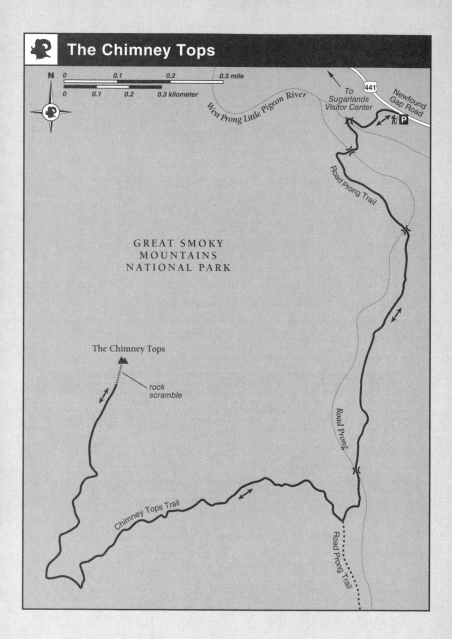

The Chimney Tops

N

0   0.1   0.2   0.3 mile
0   0.1   0.2   0.3 kilometer

West Prong Little Pigeon River

To Sugarlands Visitor Center

441

Newfound Gap Road

P

Road Prong Trail

GREAT SMOKY MOUNTAINS NATIONAL PARK

The Chimney Tops

rock scramble

Road Prong

Chimney Tops Trail

Road Prong Trail

The Chimney Tops.

Note: *This hike was affected by the Chimney Tops 2 fire of November 2016. Please check nps.gov/grsm for the latest updates.*

This busy and steep hike is nothing less than spectacular. Cross chilly mountain streams on a series of footbridges to ascend sharply amid some old trees. Emerge at the Smokies' single most recognizable rock formation: the twin spires of the Chimney Tops, which provide a dramatic view of the surrounding landscape.

Best Time

This hike is good year-round but is crowded during the warm-weather season. Try to go during off-times. In spring, fall, and winter you enjoy the best views. Avoid this hike during summer altogether unless you can hike at dawn or dusk

Finding the Trail

From the junction of US 321 and US 441/Parkway in Gatlinburg, Tennessee (signed traffic light #3), head south on US 441 for 2.7 miles into the park. With the Sugarlands Visitor Center on your right, keep south on US 441/Newfound Gap Road for 6.7 miles. The Chimney Tops parking area is on your right, just after a tunnel.

TRAIL USE
Day Hiking

LENGTH
4.0 miles, 2–3 hours

VERTICAL FEET
±1,200

DIFFICULTY
– 1 2 **3** 4 5 +

TRAIL TYPE
Out-and-back

FEATURES
Ridgeline
Stream
Autumn Colors
Wildflowers
Old-Growth
Great Views
Photo Opportunity
Swimming
Steep
Geologic Interest

FACILITIES
None

Trail Description

If you don't mind some company on the trail, this short but steep hike is nothing less than spectacular. Leave Newfound Gap Road and its cars behind on a series of footbridges over crystalline streams. Ascend sharply amid some old trees to come out on top of the Smokies' most recognizable rock formation: the twin spires of the Chimney Tops, which provide a dramatic view of the surrounding landscape.

This steep trail starts by going down. Leave the parking area ▶1 on the Chimney Tops Trail and follow the path down to Walker Camp Prong, where a footbridge awaits your crossing. The white cataract **Swimming** with a big pool attracts swimmers on a hot day, especially after a sweaty climb to the Chimney Tops. Continue on, entering Beech Flats Cove. Northern hardwoods of beech, silverbell, and yellow birch complement some preserved hemlocks to cross **Stream** Road Prong on two footbridges in short succession. Just after the fourth footbridge, you'll come to the Road Prong Trail junction, at 0.9 mile. ▶2 It leaves left for the state-line ridge, and once was a historic crossing between Tennessee and North Carolina.

Turn right, staying on the Chimney Tops Trail, **Steep** which steepens considerably. Due to the heavy traffic, the trail is rutted and has toe-grabbing roots

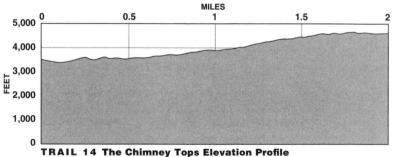

TRAIL 14 The Chimney Tops Elevation Profile

An outcrop *at the apex of the Chimney Tops yields rewarding views like this one.*

along the way. Watch your step, but don't forget to look up every now and then to admire the old-growth trees, buckeye among them, which accompany your ascent. Hikers will be standing beside the trail, hands on their knees, catching their breath. At 1.9 miles, pass a cable that helps hikers negotiate ice in winter.

Soon you top out on the rib ridge of the Chimney Tops. ▶3 It extends from Sugarland Mountain, to your left. To your right are the twin peaks that reminded some pioneer long ago of a chimney in a house. There actually is a hole in the rock, big enough to fall in. The native Cherokee, fancying the rock formation to be the branched horns of a deer, called this place Forked Antler. Be very careful as you climb the open-face rock, 4,755 feet high.

To your east, beyond the second chimney, stands Mount Le Conte. To your west is the wooded

Geologic Interest

Photo Opportunity

wall of Sugarland Mountain. Southward stands Mount Mingus. To the north lies the valley of the West Prong of the Little Pigeon River and Newfound Gap Road, your return destination. The views here can be truly incredible.

Great Views

		MILESTONES
►1	0.0	Chimney Tops Trailhead
►2	0.9	Road Prong Trail leaves left
►3	2.0	The Chimney Tops

Silers Bald via Clingmans Dome

Begin at the park's highest trailhead, near Clingmans Dome, and follow the Appalachian Trail (AT) along a knife-edge ridge. Roller-coaster along the spine of the Smokies, presenting stellar views. Reach the fast disappearing field of Silers Bald, enjoying multiple vistas.

Best Time

Clingmans Dome Road, the trail access and where this hike begins, is open from April through November. Spring and fall have the clearest skies for stupendous views. Summer is plenty cool, but can be stormy in the afternoons. If you want to camp, try to stay at Silers Bald during the week.

Finding the Trail

From the junction of US 321 and US 441/Parkway in Gatlinburg, Tennessee (signed traffic light #3), head south on US 441 for 2.7 miles into the park. With the Sugarlands Visitor Center on your right, keep south on US 441/Newfound Gap Road for 13.1 miles. Turn right on Clingmans Dome Road, passing shortly into North Carolina, and follow it about 6.9 miles to its dead end. The Forney Ridge Trail heads briefly west from the parking area, then south, away from Clingmans Dome.

Trail Description

This hike fairly exudes the aura of the high country, as you dip in and out of the spruce–fir forest

TRAIL USE
Day Hiking,
Backpacking
LENGTH
9.6 miles, 5–6 hours
VERTICAL FEET
±1,200
DIFFICULTY
– 1 2 **3** 4 5 +
TRAIL TYPE

OUT-AND-BACK FEA-
TURES
Summit
Ridgeline
Autumn Colors
Wildflowers
Spruce–Fir
Great Views
Photo Opportunity
Backcountry Camping
FACILITIES
Restrooms
Water

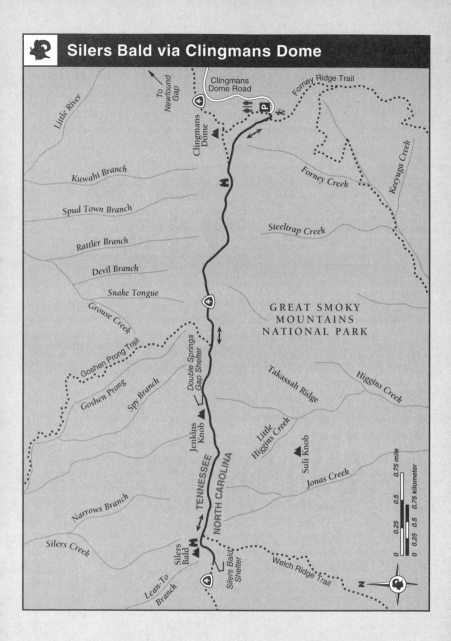

Silers Bald via Clingmans Dome

To Newfound Gap

Clingmans Dome Road

Forney Ridge Trail

Little River

Clingmans Dome

Kuwahi Branch

Forney Creek

Keeyuga Creek

Spud Town Branch

Steeltrap Creek

Rattler Branch

Devil Branch

Snake Tongue

Grouse Creek

GREAT SMOKY MOUNTAINS NATIONAL PARK

Goshen Prong Trail

Double Springs Gap Shelter

Takassah Ridge

Higgins Creek

Goshen Prong

Spy Branch

Jenkins Knob

Little Higgins Creek

Suli Knob

Jonas Creek

TENNESSEE

NORTH CAROLINA

Narrows Branch

Silers Creek

Silers Bald

Silers Bald Shelter

Welch Ridge Trail

Lean-To Branch

0.75 mile

0.75 kilometer

0.5

0.25

0.5

0.25

0

0

N

that cloaks only the highest mantles of this land.
Start your hike at the highest trailhead in the park,
6,400 feet, just below Clingmans Dome. Straddle
the very spine of the state-line ridge, joining the AT
southbound. Enjoy all-encompassing windswept
vistas into both states that are home to the Smoky
Mountains. Culminate your hike on Silers Bald,
where you can look back and see where you came
from and will return.

Start your hike at the Clingmans Dome/
Forney Ridge parking area, ▶1 leaving on the Forney Ridge Trail. Crowds mill about in summer,
taking the short quarter-mile path just past the trailhead to the right (north) up to the viewing tower
atop Clingmans Dome—instead, though, turn left
where the Clingmans Dome Trail turns right. At
0.1 mile, veer right on the Clingmans Dome Bypass
Trail. The evergreen smells of the spruce–fir forest
waft into your nostrils as you soon leave the crowds
behind. Climb moderately to intersect the AT near
Mount Buckley, elevation 6,500 feet, at 0.6 mile.

 Spruce–Fir

▲ Ridge

Continue southbound on the AT, dropping
through an old burned-over section. The lack of
tree cover opens vistas as far as the clarity of the sky
allows. Drop into a saddle to briefly ascend again,
topping out at a rock outcrop. This stone makes a
wonderful bench to look far into North Carolina.

🔲 Great Views

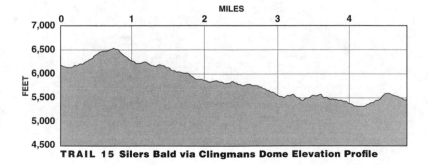

TRAIL 15 Silers Bald via Clingmans Dome Elevation Profile

Reenter spruce–fir forest, moving downward all the while. The woods are nearly always wet and cool here. The average high temperatures are warmest in July atop Clingmans Dome, and that high is only 65 degrees. It rains upward of 90 inches per year at these heights.

After a brief level section, come to the Goshen Prong Trail junction at 2.5 miles. ▶2 Continue your descent on the AT to arrive at Double Springs Gap trail shelter, elevation 5,507 feet at mile 3.1. ▶3 A small clearing stands in front of the shelter. The two springs here flow into Tennessee and North Carolina, respectively. The spring to your left, in North Carolina as you arrive at the shelter, is the easiest one from which to obtain water.

Backcountry Camping ⚠

The Silers Bald *trail shelter*

Leave the shelter behind and climb Jenkins Knob, jumbled with beech trees. Beech leaves turn brown and often stay on the tree throughout the winter, rattling in the wind. Below the knob you'll come to a declining field at mile 3.5. Welch Ridge lines the horizon as you look into North Carolina. Pass through the Narrows, where the state-line ridge becomes barely wide enough for a footpath.

Meet the Welch Ridge Trail at mile 4.4. ▶4 Now it's time to climb. Begin the final push to arrive on top of Silers Bald, 5,607 feet, at mile 4.6. ▶5 Note the USGS survey marker embedded into rock, and look back at the rugged crest of the Smokies. A small side trail to your right as you arrive at Silers allows long views into Tennessee from a rock outcrop. To your left the AT continues down the nearly disappeared bald, which the park service is allowing to reforest, to the Silers Bald trail shelter ▶6 and a spring at 4.8 miles. From here, retrace your route back to the Clingmans Dome/Forney Ridge Trailhead.

▲ Summit

📷 Photo Opportunity

🚶 **MILESTONES**

▶1	0.0	Clingmans Dome/Forney Ridge Trailhead
▶2	2.5	Goshen Prong Trail leaves right
▶3	3.1	Double Springs Gap Shelter
▶4	4.4	Welch Ridge Trail leaves left
▶5	4.6	Top of Silers Bald
▶6	4.8	Silers Bald Shelter

CHAPTER 3

Mount Le Conte, Greenbrier, and Cosby Area

Mount Le Conte, Greenbrier, and Cosby Area

The Mount Le Conte, Greenbrier, and Cosby area covers the most northeasterly part of the Tennessee Smokies. Mount Le Conte, the third highest peak in the park, stands alone, disjunct from the main mountain crest, and towers over the adjacent mountainscape from 6,593 feet. The state-line ridge extends east from Newfound Gap and presents a long continuous stretch of spruce–fir highlands, with connecting ridges also sporting the Canadian-type woodland. Other prominent peaks include Greenbrier Pinnacle and Mount Cammerer, with its historic stone tower. The area is drained by mountaintop springs gathering force to become full-fledged streams, all flowing into the Little Pigeon and Pigeon Rivers outside the park. Elevations range from nearly 6,600 feet atop Le Conte and the Tennessee shoulder of Mount Guyot to just under 1,500 feet near the Greenbrier park entrance. This vertical variation leads to natural variety as well. The flora and fauna replicate a trip up the spine of the Appalachians, from Georgia to Maine, with a decided prominence of northern plants and animals.

Newfound Gap Road forms the western boundary of the area. It has trail accesses low and high, from Sugarlands Visitor Center to Newfound Gap. US 321 runs east–west along the north park boundary, linking Le Conte, Greenbrier, and Cosby. One-way-in, one-way-out roads pierce both Cosby and Greenbrier, providing trail access. TN 32 wanders along the most northeasterly park border and ends near North Carolina's Big Creek Ranger Station and campground.

Though the land was not conducive for it, the terrain was heavily settled in pre-park days. The Sugarlands, in the northern shadow of Le Conte, was full of hardscrabble subsistence farms. Greenbrier also reflects its past in

Opposite and overleaf: Mount Le Conte *as seen from Charlies Bunion (Trail 16)*

numerous homesites, reduced to piled rock fences, crumbling chimneys, or rusting old washtubs. The subsistence lifeways of the pioneer can be found along most every streamside flat in Cosby, too. As abundant as were the valley-dwelling mountaineers, the looming high country was just as dark and wild. The evergreen mantle atop ol' Smoky was mostly trailless country then. Parts of it remain that way today.

The trail system reflects this pattern. Ridgetop paths, created after the park's inception, travel in dense woods perched atop sometimes knife-edge ridges. On the other hand, low-elevation streamside trails are rarely far from an old flat once claimed by an independent mountain man and his offspring.

Hikes in this area offer something for everyone, from high to low, from long to short, from easy strolls to rugged backpacks. The peak of Mount Le Conte is the nexus for trails that lace it from all sides. Paths here feature grand vistas, abundant waterfalls, history, and fascinating geology. Today, a primitive lodge and backpack shelter present overnight accommodations for those willing to climb to them. In Greenbrier, it is hard to hike without encountering pioneer history, yet it has superlative natural delights such as Ramsey Cascades, a cataract set amid old-growth woodlands. Likewise, Cosby has the ancient forest of Albright Grove, views from Maddron Bald and Mount Cammerer scattered amid a pioneer past.

Cosby has the area's only campground. It is large and alluring; it's puzzling why more park visitors don't use it as a base camp. Picnic areas can be found at Greenbrier, Cosby, and Sugarlands. Civilization is just a short drive away. Accommodations, restaurants, and more can be found along the nonpark roads from Gatlinburg to I-40 and the locale's eastern access.

Permits

Permits are *not* required for day hiking. Backpackers must get a backcountry permit to stay at one of the 12 designated backcountry campsites and trail shelters in this area. All campsites require a reservation, which you can make online at smokiespermits.nps.gov, then print at home.

A giant tulip tree *rises skyward at Albright Grove (Trail 23).*

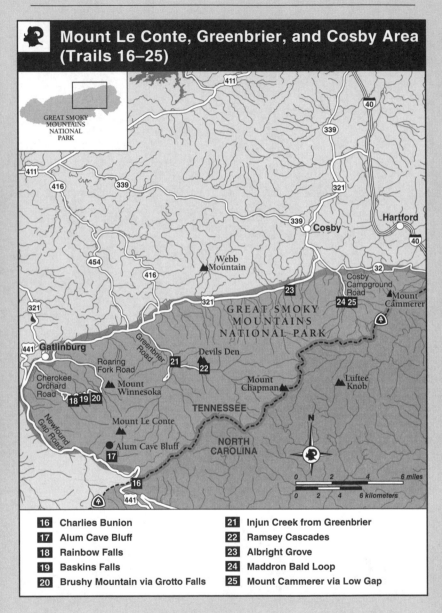

Mount Le Conte, Greenbrier, and Cosby Area (Trails 16–25)

GREAT SMOKY MOUNTAINS NATIONAL PARK

16 Charlies Bunion	**21** Injun Creek from Greenbrier
17 Alum Cave Bluff	**22** Ramsey Cascades
18 Rainbow Falls	**23** Albright Grove
19 Baskins Falls	**24** Maddron Bald Loop
20 Brushy Mountain via Grotto Falls	**25** Mount Cammerer via Low Gap

Mount Le Conte, Greenbrier, and Cosby Area

TRAIL	DIFFICULTY	LENGTH	TYPE	USES & ACCESS	TERRAIN	FLORA & FAUNA	OTHER
16	3–4	8.0	↗	🚶🥾	△ ▲	♠	Ⅿ 📷 △ ✦
17	2–3	4.6	↗	🚶	▲ 🏞	✿ 🦌 🌳	Ⅿ 🏠 ✦
18	2–3	5.4	↗	🚶	🏞 🌊	✿ ✾ 🌳	✦
19	2	3.2	↗	🚶	🏞 🌊	✿ ✾	Ⅿ 🏠 ✦
20	4	6.6	↗	🚶	△ ▲ 🏞 🌊	✿ ✾ 🌳	Ⅿ 📷 ✦
21	2–3	6.4	↗	🚶🥾	▲ 🏞	✿ ✾	△ ⬥ 🏠
22	4	8.0	↗	🚶	🏞 🌊	✿ ✾ 🌳	⇢ ✦
23	3	6.7	↻	🚶	🏞	✿ ✾ 🌳	⬥ 🏠
24	4–5	17.3	↻	🥾	▲ 🏞 🌊	✿ ✾ 🌳	Ⅿ △
25	5	11.2	↗	🚶	△ ▲ 🏞	✿ ✾	Ⅿ 📷 🏠 ✦

USES & ACCESS	TYPE	TERRAIN	FLORA & FAUNA	OTHER
🚶 Day Hiking	↻ Loop	△ Summit	✿ Autumn Colors	Ⅿ Great Views
🥾 Backpacking	↗ Out-and-back	▲ Ridge	✾ Wildflowers	📷 Photo Opportunity
🐎 Horses	↘ Point-to-point	🌊 Lake	🦌 Wildlife	△ Backcountry Camping
👥 Child Friendly		🏞 Stream	♠ Spruce–Fir	⇢ Swimming
	DIFFICULTY –1 2 3 4 5+ less more	🌊 Waterfall	🌳 Old-Growth	⬥ Secluded
				⬇ Steep
				🏠 Historical Interest
				✦ Geologic Interest

Maps

For the Mount Le Conte, Greenbrier, and Cosby area, you will need the following USGS 7.5-minute (1:24,000-scale) topographic quadrangles, listed in geographic order as you hike along your route:

Trail 16: *Clingmans Dome, Mount Le Conte*
Trail 17: *Mount Le Conte*
Trail 18: *Mount Le Conte*
Trail 19: *Mount Le Conte*
Trail 20: *Mount Le Conte*
Trail 21: *Mount Le Conte*
Trail 22: *Mount Guyot*
Trail 23: *Hartford*
Trail 24: *Hartford, Jones Cove, Mount Guyot, Luftee Knob*
Trail 25: *Hartford, Luftee Knob*

Mount Le Conte, Greenbrier, and Cosby Area

TRAIL 16

Day Hiking,
Backpacking
8.0 miles, Out-and-back
Difficulty: 1 2 **3** 4 5

Charlies Bunion................. 133

Leave busy Newfound Gap and head north on the Appalachian Trail (AT). Rise amid spruce–fir forest with occasional clearings that present warm-up views. Pass Icewater Springs trail shelter before descending a knife-edge ridge. Come to an outcrop where amazing views into the Volunteer State and beyond open wide.

TRAIL 17

Day Hiking
4.6 miles, Out-and-back
Difficulty: 1 **2 3** 4 5

Alum Cave Bluffs............... 139

Some hikes are busy for a reason. This one has several, including highlights ranging from spectacular views to old-growth forests to a natural arch—rare for the Smokies—and finally to an overhanging bluff with views of its own. A well-timed hike will let you enjoy these highlights on a less-crowded day.

TRAIL 18

Day Hiking
5.4 miles, Out-and-back
Difficulty: 1 **2 3** 4 5

Rainbow Falls 145

This deservedly popular hike reaches a waterfall on the shoulder of Mount Le Conte. Hike up attractive Le Conte Creek valley, where the creek cascades over rocks and into pools. Trek among big boulders and under old-growth trees to reach Rainbow Falls, a curtain-type cascade. *Note:* The forest along this hike was affected by the Chimney Tops 2 fire of 2016.

TRAIL 19

Day Hiking
3.2 miles, Out-and-back
Difficulty: 1 **2** 3 4 5

Baskins Falls 151

Head to a less-visited waterfall near Gatlinburg. Follow the Baskins Creek Trail over a ridge with views, then drop to aptly named Falls Branch. Make a side trip to a pioneer cemetery, then pass a home-site before reaching Baskins Falls as it tumbles over a wide bluff. *Note:* The forest along this hike was affected by the Chimney Tops 2 fire of 2016.

Brushy Mountain via Grotto Falls .. 157

This hike takes you to the appropriately named Roaring Fork to reach Grotto Falls, a popular cascade. The crowds disappear as you climb to Trillium Gap. A short ramble leads atop Brushy Mountain, where views await amid a heath-bald plant community.

TRAIL 20

Day Hiking
6.6 miles, Out-and-back
Difficulty: 1 2 **3** 4 5

Injun Creek from Greenbrier 163

This secluded hike skirts the lower reaches of Mount Le Conte. Pass a collection of former farms and homesites dotting Greenbrier. End at the Injun Creek backcountry campsite #32, just above which lies a wrecked steam-engine tractor, a high-tech contraption that crashed before the park was established.

TRAIL 21

Day Hiking,
Backpacking
6.4 miles, Out-and-back
Difficulty: 1 **2** 3 4 5

Ramsey Cascades. 169

This rewarding hike presents a waterfall and old-growth woodlands in a remote area of the park. Start out with a slight upgrade, then climb more steeply through old-growth trees in virgin woods as you near the cascades. The area remains as it has for ages.

TRAIL 22

Day Hiking
8.0 miles, Out-and-back
Difficulty: 1 2 3 **4** 5

Albright Grove 173

Hike from a less-used trailhead, passing the well-preserved Willis Baxter Cabin. Travel amid more pioneer homesites in quiet stream valleys before entering the land of giant trees—old-growth forest now preserved forever. The uppermost part of the hike makes a short loop between Dunn Creek and Indian Camp Creek, taking you past trees that helped supporters make the case for establishing Great Smoky Mountains National Park.

TRAIL 23

Day Hiking
6.7 miles, Loop
Difficulty: 1 2 **3** 4 5

Charlies Bunion

Leave busy Newfound Gap and head north on the Appalachian Trail (AT). Rise amid spruce–fir forest with occasional clearings that present warm-up views. Pass the Icewater Springs trail shelter before descending a knife-edge ridge. Come to an outcrop where amazing views into the Volunteer State and beyond open wide.

Best Time

The park tries to keep Newfound Gap Road open year-round; thus, this trek is a good way to jump into the maw of a high-country winter. Spring and fall are good choices with clear skies; summer is busy.

Finding the Trail

From the junction of US 321 and US 441/Parkway in Gatlinburg, Tennessee (signed traffic light #3), head south on US 441 for 2.7 miles into the park. With the Sugarlands Visitor Center on your right, keep south on US 441/Newfound Gap Road for 13.1 miles. The trailhead is to the left of the parking area, near the large stone podium with the plaque on it.

From the intersection of US 19 and US 441 South in Cherokee, North Carolina, drive north 3.4 miles into the park. With the Oconaluftee Visitor Center on your right, drive 16 miles farther north to Newfound Gap. The trailhead is to the right of the parking area, near the large stone podium with the plaque on it.

TRAIL USE
Day Hiking,
Backpacking

LENGTH
8.0 miles, 4–5 hours

VERTICAL FEET
±1,500

DIFFICULTY
– 1 2 **3 4** 5 +

TRAIL TYPE
Out-and-back

FEATURES
Summit
Ridgeline
Spruce–Fir
Great Views
Photo Opportunity
Backcountry Camping
Geologic Interest

FACILITIES
Restrooms
Water

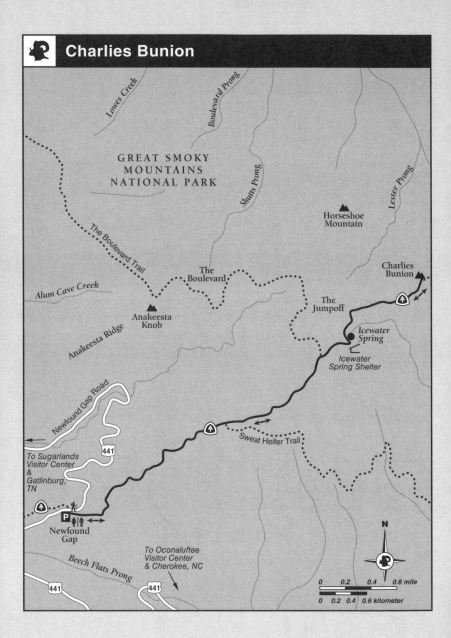

Trail Description

The view from Charlies Bunion is arguably the park's finest. Unlike a view from a fire tower or a rounded peak, Charlies Bunion boasts a vista from a cliff face with an abrupt drop of more than 1,000 feet! But you will soak in fine views on your hike to the bunion, interspersed with sections of spruce–fir high-country forest.

Unusual for the timeworn Appalachian Range, the precipitous Charlies Bunion is the result of two events in the 1920s. A devastating fire raged over the area that is the bunion in 1925, denuding the vegetation that clung to the thin mountaintop soils. Then, in 1929, heavy rains triggered a landslide of the burned-over area, leaving bare rock—and a great view—in its wake.

Head east from Newfound Gap ▶1 on possibly the most hiked quarter mile of the entire AT. As you climb away from the gap, the throngs soon disappear, turning around after getting a quick taste of America's most famous footpath. The trail is rocky and often wet, so use caution. Spruce–fir woodlands flank the track. Continue to wind up the side of Mount Kephart, named for writer and early park proponent Horace Kephart. The southern flank of Mount Le Conte stands to your left.

 Spruce–Fir

▲ **Ridge**

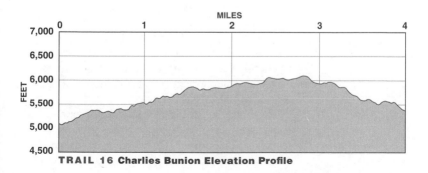

TRAIL 16 Charlies Bunion Elevation Profile

Charlies Bunion *is a rocky crag perched above the Porters Creek valley.*

The AT comes to a level area and the Sweat Heifer Trail junction at mile 1.7. ▶2 The trail is often muddy here as it passes the 6,000-foot mark only to descend to meet the Boulevard Trail at mile 2.7. ▶3 The Boulevard Trail, which links the main crest of the Appalachians to Mount Le Conte, is not nearly as easy as its name implies. Stay on the evergreen-flanked AT, opening up at the Icewater Springs trail shelter, at mile 2.9. ▶4 The shelter is surrounded by a clearing and displays impressive views. Icewater Spring, with its well-deserved name, is just beyond the shelter.

Beyond the spring, a half-mile decline on a rocky, wet slope leads to a narrow stretch of the main state-line ridge. At mile 3.6, a good vista opens and you can see the rocky point of Charlies Bunion

Backcountry Camping

Great Views

below. Arrive at a trail junction at mile 4.0, just before Charlies Bunion. The AT leaves right. Carefully follow the narrow trail 100 yards left to arrive at Charlies Bunion. ▶5

Below you lies the remote Greenbrier area of the park. To your left rises Mount Le Conte. The green heath bald of Brushy Mountain is visible. A sunny clear day allows an unparalleled view into the hills of East Tennessee. At your feet, dark-eyed juncos and Eastern chipmunks vie for some of your trail mix. This is a great place to appreciate just how high the Smoky Mountains are, and how cataclysmic events can reveal their bedrock—and great views.

Photo Opportunity

Geologic Interest

🚶	MILESTONES	
▶1	0.0	Newfound Gap Trailhead
▶2	1.7	Sweat Heifer Trail leaves right
▶3	2.7	Boulevard Trail leaves left
▶4	2.9	Icewater Springs trail shelter
▶5	4.0	Charlies Bunion

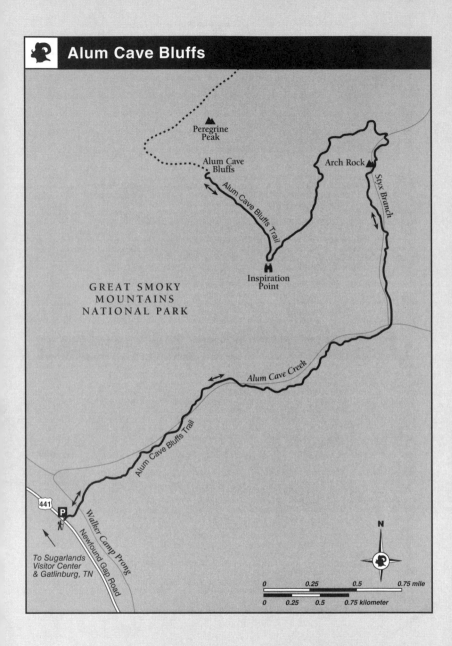

Alum Cave Bluffs

Peregrine
Peak

Alum Cave
Bluffs

Arch Rock

Styx Branch

Alum Cave Bluffs Trail

Inspiration
Point

GREAT SMOKY
MOUNTAINS
NATIONAL PARK

Alum Cave Creek

Alum Cave Bluffs Trail

441

Walker Camp Prong

Newfound Gap Road

P

To Sugarlands
Visitor Center
& Gatlinburg, TN

N

| 0 | 0.25 | 0.5 | 0.75 mile |

| 0 | 0.25 | 0.5 | 0.75 kilometer |

Alum Cave Bluffs

Some hikes are busy for a reason. This one has several, including highlights ranging from spectacular views to old-growth forests to a natural arch—rare for the Smokies—and finally to an overhanging bluff with views of its own. A well-timed hike will let you enjoy these highlights on a less-crowded day.

Best Time

Winter offers the most solitude on this busy trek. Otherwise, try to hike early in the morning or later in the evening to avoid the crowds.

Finding the Trail

From the junction of US 321 and US 441/Parkway in Gatlinburg, Tennessee (signed traffic light #3), head south on US 441 for 2.7 miles into the park. With the Sugarlands Visitor Center on your right, keep south on US 441/Newfound Gap Road for 8.9 miles. The Alum Cave Bluffs parking area will be on your left.

Trail Description

The steep slopes of Mount Le Conte contain some of the most beautiful scenery in the Smokies. This hike travels an ancient forest along Alum Cave Creek before turning up Styx Branch, where Arch Rock awaits. This geological feature is different from other classic arches you may have seen; it is more of a circular maw, with stone steps leading through it. The hike then opens onto a heath bald

TRAIL USE
Day Hiking
LENGTH
4.6 miles, 2–3 hours
VERTICAL FEET
±1,100
DIFFICULTY
– 1 **2 3** 4 5 +
TRAIL TYPE
Out-and-back

FEATURES
Ridgeline
Stream
Autumn Colors
Wildlife
Old-Growth
Great Views
Historical Interest
Geologic Interest
FACILITIES
None

Sand myrtle grows only along the Southeastern coastline and in the Southern Appalachians.

Stream

Old-Growth

where a rock promontory lives up to its name of Inspiration Point. Finally, climb a rock slope to reach Alum Cave Bluffs, a huge rock overhang with views of its own.

Try to hike during off-times to avoid the crowds. I suggest getting here at sunrise, during times when it may rain, or on winter weekdays. *Do not hike here during summer or holiday weekends,* as Smokies visitors sometimes clog this deserving highlight reel of a hike. It also gets use from folks hiking up and down on overnight trips to Mount Le Conte Lodge, which is closed during the winter.

This trail was rehabilitated in 2016, improving the situation for all. Spur trails from the two large parking areas ▶1 converge at the bridge over Walker Camp Prong, which you cross by footlog. Old-growth forest of yellow birch and spruce rise above the hiker-only trail as it slices through a rhododendron sea. Bridge Alum Cave Creek on a footlog. Notice that some of the hemlocks close to the trailhead are being preserved, but you will also see red spruce, another evergreen. Watch for a massive red spruce left of the trail at 0.4 mile. This is a good spot to look around and take inventory of the ancient grove.

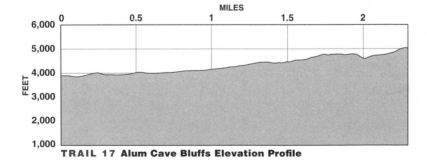

TRAIL 17 Alum Cave Bluffs Elevation Profile

Alum Cave Bluffs *overlooks the verdant forests of yon Smoky Mountains.*

Authentic old-growth woodland is not an agglomeration of even-aged primeval trees. To the contrary, even aged trees are a result of disturbance. An old-growth forest has many big trees, along with younger trees that grow when they get the chance. When a big tree falls, it creates a light gap. Young trees sprout in this light gap, and other partially mature trees thrive in the additional sun. Other times, in the dim of the dark forest, trees gain foothold on nurse logs.

Nurse logs—fallen and decaying trees—allow a seedling to gain root and then feed the young trees with the energy they contain. Later, the new trees grow and spread roots around the fallen log. Over time, a nurse log returns to the soil, and the newly grown tree looks as if it grew up with legs.

This heavily traveled trail has many exposed roots, so watch your footing as well as the stately

The great forests *for which the Smokies are known cloak the lower slopes of Mount Le Conte.*

giants above and the crystalline stream beside you, with its beige, gray, and tan rocks. Cross Alum Cave Creek on another footlog at mile 1.0. ►2 The trail swerves left and begins to follow Styx Branch, which it bridges at 1.3 miles. Watch for a gigantic buckeye tree just after this crossing that brings you over to the left-hand bank. Next, come to one of nature's more time-consuming projects, Arch Rock, at 1.4 miles, ►3 just after another footlog crossing of Styx Branch.

Geologic Interest

At first, it seems that the path dead-ends. However, a set of stone stairs leads the way through the tunnel-like arch. Continue ascending, stepping over Styx Branch a final time at 1.5 miles. Open onto an area, known as a heath bald, covered with small, low bushes. Rock outcrops are mixed among the low-slung Catawba rhododendron, sand myrtle, and mountain laurel, along with a few wind-sculpted trees.

Great views open from Inspiration Point at 2.0 miles. ►4 See the Chimneys and Sugarland Mountain across the gulf, the rock slides of Anakeesta Ridge, and slides nearer to the west. Unstable soils have simply sloughed off the mountainside, usually following heavy rain. Give yourself ample time to relax at this superlative setting.

Great Views

Leave the bald, cruising the rock face of Peregrine Peak, a stony knob of Mount Le Conte. (Peregrine falcons were successfully reintroduced on Mount Le Conte.) The mostly open rock trail can get quite icy in winter. The park service has strung wire handrails along the declivitous slope. Arrive at Alum Cave Bluffs, residing at 5,000 feet of elevation, at 2.3 miles. ►5 The rock overhang with a dusty floor really isn't a cave. During the Civil War, soldiers led by Chief Thomas Walker and his band of Confederate Cherokees mined the bluff for saltpeter to make gunpowder for the South. You can usually smell sulfur at the bluff. In the winter, large icicles

Wildlife

Historical Interest

form atop the overhang and crash down when the air warms. Nature is constantly at work on the Alum Cave Bluffs Trail.

🚶	**MILESTONES**		
►1	0.0	Alum Cave Trailhead
►2	1.0	Cross Styx Branch
►3	1.4	Arch Rock
►4	2.0	Inspiration Point
►5	2.3	Alum Cave Bluffs

Rainbow Falls

This deservedly popular hike reaches a waterfall on the shoulder of Mount Le Conte. Hike up attractive Le Conte Creek valley, where the creek cascades over rocks and into pools. Trek among big boulders and under old-growth trees to reach Rainbow Falls, a curtain-type cascade. *Note:* The forest along this hike was affected by the Chimney Tops 2 fire of 2016.

Best Time

The falls is at its boldest in winter and spring. Wildflowers are abundant in spring also. Summer can be too crowded.

Finding the Trail

From the junction of US 321 and US 441/Parkway in Gatlinburg, Tennessee (signed traffic light #3), head south and west 0.6 mile on US 441, and turn left on Historic Nature Trail at signed traffic light #8 (look for the Shoot 'Em Up Cinema on your right). Follow Historic Nature Trail 0.6 mile, and keep straight at the intersection on Cherokee Orchard Road to enter the park. In 1.9 miles, bear right at the fork, continue another 0.6 mile, and turn right into the parking area for the Rainbow Falls Trailhead, just past the Bullhead Trail.

Trail Description

There's no doubt about it: waterfalls attract hikers. They are a scenic destination, an endpoint that changes with the seasons. At Rainbow Falls, you

TRAIL USE
Day Hiking
LENGTH
5.4 miles, 3–4 hours
VERTICAL FEET
±1,650
DIFFICULTY
– 1 **2 3** 4 5 +
TRAIL TYPE
Out-and-back

FEATURES
Stream
Waterfall
Autumn Colors
Wildflowers
Old-Growth
Geologic Interest
FACILITIES
Restrooms

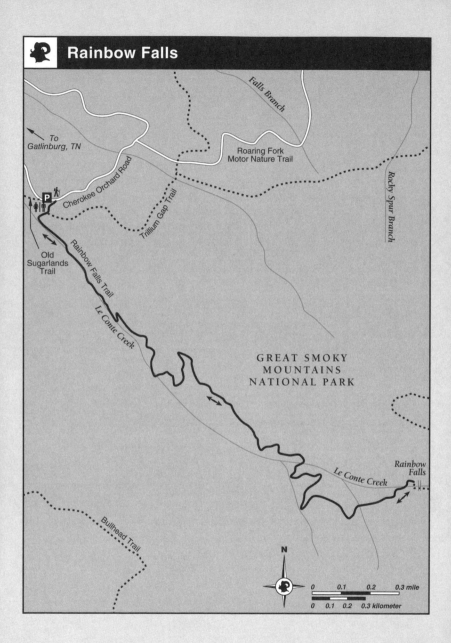

Rainbow Falls

To Gatlinburg, TN

Falls Branch

Roaring Fork Motor Nature Trail

Rocky Spur Branch

Cherokee Orchard Road

Trillium Gap Trail

Old Sugarlands Trail

Rainbow Falls Trail

Le Conte Creek

GREAT SMOKY MOUNTAINS NATIONAL PARK

Le Conte Creek

Rainbow Falls

Bullhead Trail

N

0   0.1   0.2   0.3 mile
0   0.1   0.2   0.3 kilometer

may get a frozen curtain falling off the sheer rock face. In spring, the heavy flow may have a pile of melting ice under it. In summer, throngs trek through deep woods to the rock cathedral on the cool north side of Mount Le Conte. In fall, colorful trees flank hikers as they find a thin veil of water gently spilling over stone.

When the sun spills just right over the mist from the fall, a rainbow forms, giving the cataract its name. Leaving the main parking area, ▶1 cruising a wooded slope. Several user-created trails make this area potentially confusing. You will shortly end up at the intersection with the Trillium Gap Trail. ▶2 Stay with the Rainbow Falls Trail, soon coming alongside Le Conte Creek. This rocky, fast-moving brook became known as Mill Creek because there were so many small-scale corn-grinding water-powered tub mills along its banks. It seems more rock than water as it bounds toward the town of Gatlinburg from the highlands of Mount Le Conte. Overhead, red maples, oaks, black birches, and a scattering of preserved hemlocks shade the trail. The well-beaten, root-covered track is scattered with gravel. Spur paths lead to the boisterous creek.

Keep uphill and upstream in the wildflower- and rhododendron-filled valley. At 0.5 mile, the

 Stream

 Autumn Colors

 Wildflowers

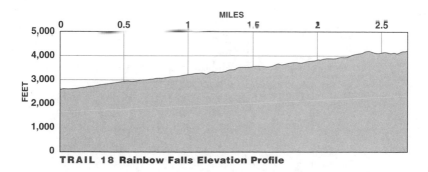

MILES

TRAIL 18 Rainbow Falls Elevation Profile

Rainbow Falls *splashes into a snowbank.*

trail switchbacks then turns back up the valley. Come alongside Le Conte Creek at 0.9 mile, only to turn away again, joining a drier slope with galax, mountain laurel, and chestnut oaks. At 1.1 miles, on another switchback, an obscured view extends toward Gatlinburg. The path then passes some big boulders upon which hikers scramble. A small overhang could provide shelter from a thunderstorm.

 Geologic Interest

The Rainbow Falls Trail works into the valley again, coming alongside Le Conte Creek at 1.6 miles. Cooler-climate trees, such as yellow birch and cherry, show a presence. Look also for big preserved hemlocks. At 1.8 miles, cross Le Conte Creek on a footbridge. ▶3 Take in creek views here at nearly 3,700 feet. Enter a world of big trees, passing a

massive hemlock on trail right at 1.9 miles. ►4 Start
switchbacking up a rich, mossy slope between Le
Conte Creek and a tributary, avoiding the shortcuts
used by thoughtless hikers.

At 2.3 miles, the trail reaches a tributary just
below a small waterfall, a preview of your destination. Rock-hop the tributary. ►5 Come back
alongside Le Conte Creek at 2.5 miles, then bridge
it at 2.6 miles. ►6 The trail leads farther up and
to another bridge. You are here! Uphill, beyond a
boulder field, spills Rainbow Falls. ►7 The stream
tumbles 80 feet over a wide stone face into a rocky
cathedral. You must do a little boulder scrambling
to get close to the falls. Be careful, as the rocks are
often slick. A good view can be had from the trail.

On your way back—if the trail is busy—count
how many hikers ask you, "How much farther?"
This path seems to attract hikers with more desire
than stamina to make the 1,600-foot climb.

Old-Growth

Waterfall

⋏	**MILESTONES**	
►1	0.0	Rainbow Falls Trailhead
►2	0.1	Stay straight as Trillium Gap Trail leaves left
►3	1.8	Bridge Le Conte Creek
►4	1.9	Huge hemlock
►5	2.3	Rock-hop tributary below fall
►6	2.6	Bridge Le Conte Creek
►7	2.7	Rainbow Falls

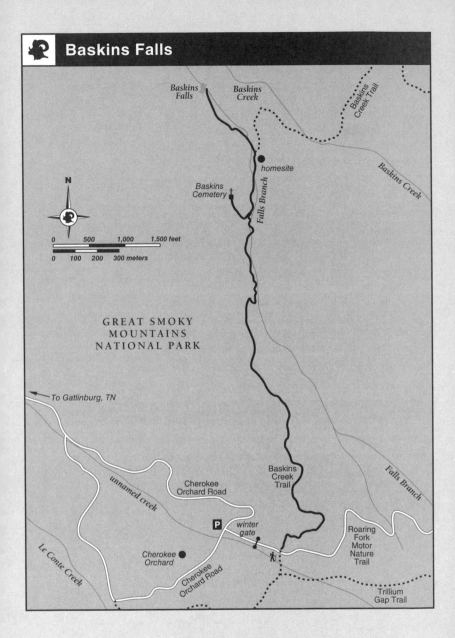

Baskins Falls

Baskins Falls

Baskins Creek

Baskins Creek Trail

Baskins Creek

homesite

Falls Branch

Baskins Cemetery

N

0   500   1,000   1,500 feet
0   100   200   300 meters

GREAT SMOKY
MOUNTAINS
NATIONAL PARK

To Gatlinburg, TN

unnamed creek

Cherokee
Orchard Road

Baskins
Creek
Trail

Falls Branch

P   winter
gate

Cherokee
Orchard

Roaring
Fork
Motor
Nature
Trail

Le Conte Creek

Cherokee
Orchard Road

Trillium
Gap Trail

Baskins Falls

Head to a less-visited waterfall near Gatlinburg. Follow the Baskins Creek Trail over a ridge with views, then drop to aptly named Falls Branch. Make a side trip to a pioneer cemetery, then pass a homesite before reaching Baskins Falls as it tumbles over a wide bluff. *Note:* The forest along this hike was affected by the Chimney Tops 2 fire of 2016.

Best Time

This waterfall walk is best in spring, when Falls Branch is at its boldest. It can also be good in winter, when Baskins Falls freezes.

Finding the Trail

From the junction of US 321 and US 441/Parkway in Gatlinburg, Tennessee (signed traffic light #3), head south and west 0.6 mile on US 441, and turn left on Historic Nature Trail at signed traffic light #8 (look for the Shoot 'Em Up Cinema on your right). Follow Historic Nature Trail 0.6 mile, and keep straight at the intersection on Cherokee Orchard Road to enter the park. In 1.9 miles, bear right at the fork, and in another 0.9 mile, reach another fork— here, Cherokee Orchard Road keeps straight, while Roaring Fork Motor Nature Trail heads right. Park at this intersection. Walk up Roaring Fork Motor Nature Trail for 0.2 mile to reach the Baskins Creek Trail, on your left. (There is room for one or two cars at the trailhead.) In winter, Roaring Fork Motor Nature Trail will be gated, but you can simply walk around the gate to access the trail.

TRAIL USE
Day Hiking

LENGTH
3.2 miles, 1½–2 hours

VERTICAL FEET
±1,180

DIFFICULTY
– 1 **2** 3 4 5 +

TRAIL TYPE
Out-and-back

FEATURES
Stream
Waterfall
Autumn Colors
Wildflowers
Great Views
Historical Interest
Geologic Interest

FACILITIES
None

Trail Description

It is amazing how much less visited is Baskins Falls versus its two nearby counterparts, Grotto Falls and Rainbow Falls. All three of the cataracts flow off the north slope of Mount Le Conte within a few miles of one another, but that is where the resemblance ends—save for the areas of Rainbow Falls and Baskins Falls that were affected by the Chimney Tops 2 fire of 2016.

Rainbow Falls and Grotto Falls can be swarming with hikers, while Baskins Falls basks in relative solitude. It may be the parking and trailhead: the Baskins Creek Trail's western trailhead has room for just one or two cars—if you don't know to park on Cherokee Orchard Road and then walk 0.2 mile to the trailhead. The hike is plenty rewarding as it cruises over a piney ridge with partial views, then drops into aptly named Falls Branch, where Baskins Falls is found. Along the way, you will pass through formerly settled country where the Baskins clan and others lived. The Baskins Cemetery and old homesites provide evidence of this settled past in a now-forested, very hilly terrain. Baskins Falls—tumbling 35 or so feet in stages over a stone bluff—was used as a natural shower by locals before indoor plumbing came to the region.

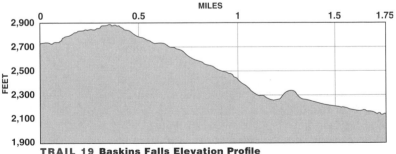

TRAIL 19 Baskins Falls Elevation Profile

Baskins Falls *was used as a natural shower by local residents during pre-park days.*

Join the Baskins Creek Trail northbound, ►1 leaving Roaring Fork Motor Nature Trail—if you go southbound, you quickly intersect the Trillium Gap Trail. Leave the watershed of Le Conte Creek, then rise unswervingly to a shoulder ridge of Mount Le Conte. Westerly views of Cove Mountain open among pine, sourwood, black gum, and oak. Keep along the unnamed ridge dividing Le Conte Creek from Falls Branch. By 0.8 mile, the path starts to drop into Falls Branch valley. At 0.9 mile, ►2 step over Falls Branch, a small waterway at this point. Cruise along the slender watercourse as it flows under a sea of rhododendron. Quickly pass a rock overhang that has sheltered more than a few people during a summer Smokies thunderstorm, and then come near a second overhang.

Reach a trail intersection at 1.2 miles. ►3 Head left toward Baskins Cemetery, passing through a

Great Views

Autumn Colors

Stream

Baskins Falls *at higher flows*

former cleared flat before angling steeply up the hillside to reach the graveyard at 1.4 miles. All but one grave are simple unmarked fieldstones. The site is less than level, but it faces east—the primary requirement of Christian pioneer cemeteries in order for those interred to see Jesus' resurrection coming. Backtrack and then resume the Baskins Creek Trail, passing through a flat where it's easy to spot a homesite to the right of the trail; the level locale still has a vestigial rock foundation and crumbled chimney. You can bet the inhabitants bathed under Baskins Falls after a long day of hoeing corn on the adjacent hills.

Historical Interest

At 1.6 miles, come to another trail junction. ▶4 Here, head left on the spur leading to Baskins Falls. The path and creek squeeze through narrows. Falls Branch tumbles over a ledge out of sight, while the path works around the right side of the ledge and then curves to its base. Trek along the base of the ledge, and reach ▶5 Baskins Falls at 1.8 miles. The 35-foot tumbler drops in two stages over a break in the very wide ledge, then splashes off rocks at the bottom, with no real pool. Take a gander at it from all angles. In late summer and autumn, it can slow to a trickle. The north-facing waterfall can be a real stunner in winter, however, after a prolonged freeze. After you've had your fill of the falls, retrace your steps to the trailhead. ▶6

Geologic Interest

Waterfall

Photo Opportunity

🚶	MILESTONES		
▶1	0.0	Roaring Fork Motor Nature Trail Trailhead	
▶2	0.9	Step over Falls Branch	
▶3	1.2	Spur to Baskins Cemetery	
▶4	1.6	Spur to Baskins Falls	
▶5	1.8	Baskins Falls	
▶6	3.2	Roaring Fork Motor Nature Trail Trailhead	

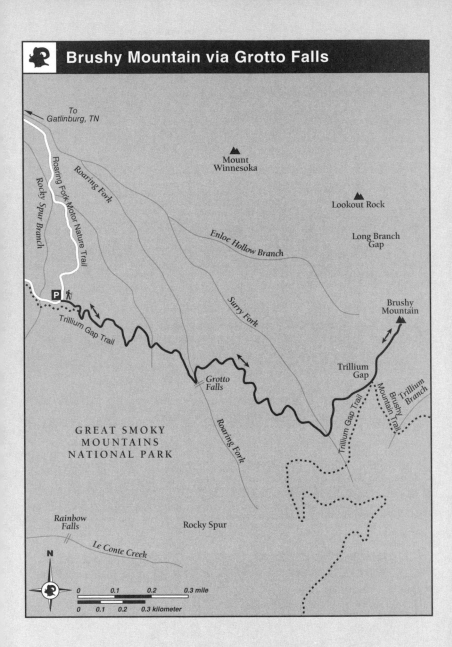

Brushy Mountain via Grotto Falls

To
Gatlinburg, TN

Rocky Spur Branch

Roaring Fork Motor Nature Trail

Roaring Fork

Mount
Winnesoka

Lookout Rock

Enloe Hollow Branch

Long Branch
Gap

Surry Fork

Brushy
Mountain

P

Trillium Gap Trail

Grotto
Falls

Trillium Gap

Trillium Gap Trail

Brushy Mountain Trail

Trillium Branch

Roaring Fork

GREAT SMOKY
MOUNTAINS
NATIONAL PARK

Rainbow
Falls

Rocky Spur

Le Conte Creek

N

| 0 | 0.1 | 0.2 | 0.3 mile |

| 0 | 0.1 | 0.2 | 0.3 kilometer |

Brushy Mountain via Grotto Falls

This hike takes you to appropriately named Roaring Fork to reach Grotto Falls, a popular cascade. The crowds disappear as you climb to Trillium Gap. A short ramble leads atop Brushy Mountain, where views await amid a heath bald plant community.

Best Time

Roaring Fork Motor Nature Trail is generally closed from late November until mid-March, cutting off trailhead access, though you can walk from Cherokee Orchard Road, adding 1.8 miles each way. In spring Grotto Falls are bold, and the views from Brushy Mountain are extensive. During warmer times, the trail to Grotto Falls can be crowded. Fall is a good choice, with clear skies presenting far-reaching panoramas.

Finding the Trail

From the junction of US 321 and US 441/Parkway in Gatlinburg, Tennessee (signed traffic light #3), head south and west 0.6 mile on US 441, and turn left on Historic Nature Trail at signed traffic light #8 (look for the Shoot 'Em Up Cinema on your right). Follow Historic Nature Trail 0.6 mile, and keep straight at the intersection on Cherokee Orchard Road to enter the park. In 1.9 miles, bear right at the fork, and in another 0.9 mile, reach another fork. Here, Cherokee Orchard Road keeps straight—head right on Roaring Fork Motor Nature Trail. Follow the one-way road 1.7 miles to the Trillium Gap

TRAIL USE
Day Hiking

LENGTH
6.6 miles, 3–4 hours

VERTICAL FEET
±1,680

DIFFICULTY
− 1 2 **3 4** 5 +

TRAIL TYPE
Out-and-back

FEATURES
Summit
Ridgeline
Stream
Waterfall
Autumn Colors
Wildflowers
Old-Growth
Great Views
Photo Opportunity
Geologic Interest

FACILITIES
None

Heath Balds

Heath balds form an interesting plant community in the Southern Appalachians. Generally treeless, they are concentrations of plants found on high ridges. The plants, including azaleas, blueberries, and sand myrtle, along with rhododendron and mountain laurel, grow in tight, wind-sculpted thickets that native mountaineers dubbed "hells," since they were "hell to get into, and hell to get out of." Their origin is about as unclear as grassy balds, though exposure, soils, and fire are thought to play a role in their evolution.

connector access on your right, just as the motor trail makes a hard left.

Stop to absorb the ambiance of this place with its perpetual cool breeze under whispering beech trees.

Trail Description

This trek is a tale of two hikes. Down low you have water and crowds, while up high you enjoy solitude and vistas—all on the same hike. The first part travels to Grotto Falls, which tumbles over a deep rock overhang. You actually walk behind and under the falls on the way to Trillium Gap Trail. This part of the trail can be very crowded, but beyond Grotto Falls the pathway is likely to be deserted.

You then climb into northern hardwoods mixed with spruce to reach Trillium Gap. From here the

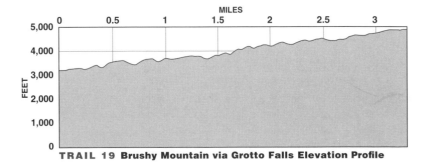

TRAIL 19 Brushy Mountain via Grotto Falls Elevation Profile

Hikers walk *through the overhang at Grotto Falls.*

path cuts into an evergreen heath bald atop, which
has extensive panoramas of the Smokies and the
nearby lands that border it. For an easy family hike,
just walk to Grotto Falls and back.

Take the well-used connector path ►1 leading
to the Trillium Gap Trail, upward among preserved
hemlocks, many of them old-growth. Carolina **Old-Growth**
silverbell, black birch, and yellow birch also line the
rocky, root-covered track. Continue along a stream,
then reach a trail junction at 0.2 mile. ►2 Turn left
here to join the Trillium Gap Trail.

Stream

Step over a tributary, and keep working your way between ridges and little hollows on the side of Mount Le Conte. The cool, north-facing slope harbors ferns, doghobble, and buckeye. Cross another small branch at 0.6 mile. You may notice more hemlocks aren't being preserved than are. Skeletal trunks rise in the forest. Step over another branch at 0.9 mile, and another at 1.0 mile.

Curve into the Roaring Fork valley at 1.1 miles. Saddle up to the mountain cataract. Watch for a **Waterfall** preliminary 15-foot two-tiered waterfall. It splits between two big boulders and forms a big pool below. The open rock face atop this fall beckons trailside relaxers.

You reach Grotto Falls at 1.4 miles. ▶3 Roar-**Photo** ing Fork dives into a plunge pool around which **Opportunity** hikers gather. Then you see people walking behind the falls. The overhang behind the falls is how the cascade gets its name. It's fun to walk behind the spilling water, the official track.

Cruise behind the falls and continue up the Trillium Gap Trail. The crowds drop to your average backcountry trail, rather than those you find on an easy waterfall hike. Step over a trickling branch at 2.0 miles. You have broken the 4,000-foot elevation barrier. A few spruce trees appear among the northern hardwoods. Big boulders and rock fields border **Geologic** the path. Mosses and ferns find purchase on these **Interest** trailside boulders. Pass a craggy rock bluff at 2.4 miles. ▶4 At 2.5 miles, rock-hop Surry Fork, your last water source.

The woodland understory becomes grassier as you approach Trillium Gap. Reach the gap at 3.0 miles. ▶5

To reach the top of Brushy Mountain, veer left from the gap and follow the path tunneling bushy evergreens. At 3.3 miles, you come to trail's end. **Great Views** ▶6 Viewpoints diverge from the main trail. Brushy Mountain offers panoramas both above and below your 4,900-foot elevation. Above and to your south stands the imposing bulk of Mount Le Conte. To your east lies the Porters Creek valley. Below, to the north, stretch Gatlinburg and East Tennessee.

 Photo Opportunity

🚶	**MILESTONES**	
►1	0.0	Trillium Gap Trail Connector
►2	0.2	Left on Trillium Gap Trail
►3	1.4	Grotto Falls
►4	2.4	Craggy bluff
►5	3.0	Trillium Gap
►6	3.3	Brushy Mountain

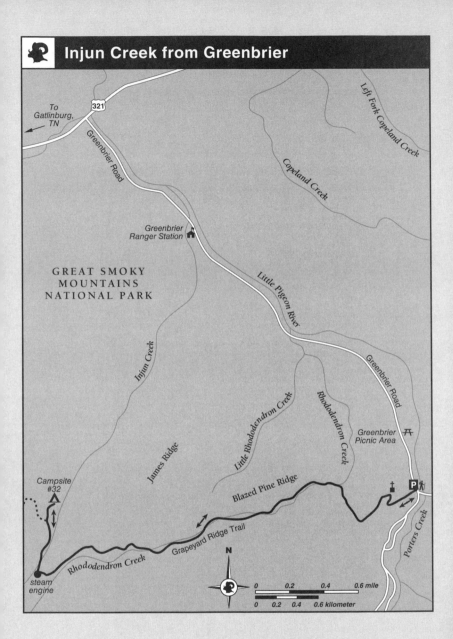

Injun Creek from Greenbrier

To Gatlinburg, TN

321

Greenbrier Road

Greenbrier Ranger Station

GREAT SMOKY MOUNTAINS NATIONAL PARK

Little Pigeon River

Left Fork Copeland Creek

Copeland Creek

Greenbrier Road

Greenbrier Picnic Area

Injun Creek

James Ridge

Little Rhododendron Creek

Rhododendron Creek

Blazed Pine Ridge

Campsite #32

Grapeyard Ridge Trail

Rhododendron Creek

steam engine

Porters Creek

N

0   0.2   0.4   0.6 mile
0   0.2   0.4   0.6 kilometer

Injun Creek from Greenbrier

This secluded hike skirts the lower reaches of Mount Le Conte. Pass a collection of former farms and homesites dotting Greenbrier. End at the Injun Creek backcountry campsite #32, just above which lies a wrecked steam-engine tractor, a high-tech contraption that crashed before the park was established.

Best Time

Hikers heading here in fall will have the easiest stream crossings and the driest trail. Wildflowers are abundant in spring. Winter is a good time to see the plentiful trailside homesites. Summer could be warm.

Finding the Trail

From the junction of US 321 and US 441/Parkway in Gatlinburg, Tennessee (signed traffic light #3), go east on US 321/East Parkway for 6.1 miles to the Greenbrier section of the park. Turn right and drive up Greenbrier Road for 3.1 miles to the intersection with Ramsey Prong Road, which crosses a bridge to your left. Park just before the intersection. The Grapeyard Ridge Trail starts on the right side of Greenbrier Road.

Trail Description

Greenbrier was one of the most heavily settled areas of what was to become Great Smoky Mountains National Park. In the shadow of Mount Le Conte,

TRAIL USE
Day Hiking,
Backpacking

LENGTH
6.4 miles, 3–4 hours

VERTICAL FEET
±850

DIFFICULTY
− 1 2 **3** 4 5 +

TRAIL TYPE
Out-and-back

FEATURES
Ridgeline
Stream
Autumn Colors
Wildflowers
Backcountry Camping
Secluded
Historical Interest

FACILITIES
None

the rocky, mountainous area drains slopes that flow north toward Gatlinburg and Pittman Center. The land is hardly arable, but mountain pioneers scraped out a living along the creek bottoms and sloped tributaries. This hike travels past several homesites located along Rhododendron Creek, a pleasant stream. You will become very familiar with the creek during several creek crossings as Grapeyard Ridge Trail seeks James Gap. From there, you descend into the Injun Creek watershed.

The old farm–turned–backcountry campsite where you end the trek makes a great picnic or camping spot. Pull up a rock under the shade of a tree or simply sprawl out on the grass and contemplate what it might have been like to live here without the electrical accoutrements that accompany us through modern life.

Start the Grapeyard Ridge Trail on a Civilian Conservation Corps–built path ▶1 that cobbles together old roads used by area settlers, passing rock walls and other wagon tracks splintering off the one you're following. At 0.3 mile, on a left-turning switchback, a spur path leads right to a pioneer cemetery. A mixed woodland of sweet gum, holly, maple, and pine forms the forest.

Historical Interest 🏠

Autumn Colors 🍁

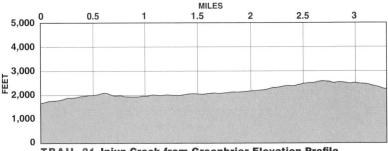

TRAIL 21 Injun Creek from Greenbrier Elevation Profile

This machine *gave a Smokies creek a name.*

Ascend to a gap and the remnants of a homesite chimney at 0.6 mile. ►2 The dull roar of Middle Prong Little Pigeon River fades. The trail follows a small rill to Rhododendron Creek in a young, spindly forest that was open land fourscore past. At 0.8 mile, step over the small rill and enter a persistent field. Make the first of several crossings of Rhododendron Creek and its tributaries, none of which are deep, though you may wet your shoes a bit in winter or after heavy rains.

Stream

Wind up the creek valley, noting the homesites on both sides of the path. Watch for exposed trailside white quartz. A 1931 topographic map of the Smokies, commissioned by the Department of the Interior, shows 11 homes in the Rhododendron Creek watershed. Watch for more closing fields in stream bottoms, which contrast greatly with the numerous rhododendron tunnels you pass through.

Historical Interest

Wildflowers

At 1.8 miles, a rock marks a spur trail leading left to a confusing network of old roads leading to forgotten homesites and graves of settlers who left the Smokies after it became a park. Down-trail, see where stones line the creek, marking a pioneer's attempt to tame Rhododendron Creek. Farmers in this rocky land couldn't afford to lose precious topsoil to sporadic flash floods that flushed the valley.

At 2.1 miles, leave Rhododendron Creek ►3 and begin the steady ascent to James Gap. A green cornucopia of rhododendron, mountain laurel, moss, and galax flanks the path. Oaks and hickories stand overhead and drop their mast on the trail in fall. Another homesite, marked with a mere pile of rock rubble, sits in the saddle of James Gap at 2.8 miles. ►4 Enter the Injun Creek watershed. As you descend, the inspiration for the creek's name appears in a rivulet on your right. The body and wheels of a tractorlike steam engine stand upturned, with water running beneath them. Somewhere in the naming of this creek an errant mapmaker thought the name

Autumn Colors

Ridge

referred to the Cherokee that roamed this land long ago and not a steam engine that made its final turn in the Great Smoky Mountains.

Historical Interest

The old road–turned–trail descends to reach the spur path to Injun Creek backcountry campsite #32. ▶5 Turn right on the side trail to reach the camp at 3.2 miles. Enter yet another homesite. Walk around and look at the lasting changes the settlers made on the land, such as leveling the ground with rock walls. The campsite makes for a good break spot. On your return journey, visualize this area in the future as the forest continues reestablishing its dominion over the Smokies.

Backcountry Camping

🚶	MILESTONES	
▶1	0.0	Grapeyard Ridge Trailhead
▶2	0.6	Gap and homesite
▶3	2.1	Leave Rhododendron Creek
▶4	2.8	James Gap
▶5	3.2	Injun Creek campsite #32

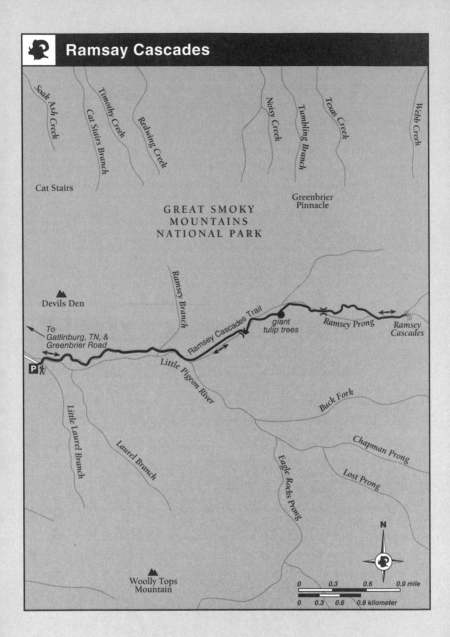

Ramsay Cascades

Soak Ash Creek

Timothy Creek

Cat Stairs Branch

Redwing Creek

Noisy Creek

Tumbling Branch

Texas Creek

Webb Creek

Cat Stairs

GREAT SMOKY
MOUNTAINS
NATIONAL PARK

Greenbrier
Pinnacle

Devils Den

Ramsey Branch

Ramsey Cascades Trail

giant
tulip trees

Ramsey Prong

Ramsey
Cascades

To
Gatlinburg, TN, &
Greenbrier Road

Little Pigeon River

P

Little Laurel Branch

Laurel Branch

Buck Fork

Chapman Prong

Lost Prong

Eagle Rocks Prong

N

Woolly Tops
Mountain

0   0.3   0.6   0.9 mile
0   0.3   0.6   0.9 kilometer

Ramsey Cascades

This rewarding hike presents a waterfall and old-growth woodlands in a remote area of the park. Start out with a slight upgrade, then climb more steeply through old-growth trees in virgin woods as you near the cascades. The area remains as it has been for ages.

Best Time

This hike is good year-round, but spring affords a plethora of wildflowers. Hikers can swim in summer. Fall has brilliant old-growth forests. In winter, Ramsey Cascades may be frozen, which attracts hikers, too.

Finding the Trail

From the junction of US 321 and US 441/Parkway in Gatlinburg, Tennessee (signed traffic light #3), go east on US 321/East Parkway for 6.1 miles to the Greenbrier section of the park. Turn right and drive up Greenbrier Road for 3.1 miles to the intersection with Ramsey Prong Road, which crosses a bridge to your left. Turn left onto Ramsey Prong Road, crossing the bridge, and then follow the road 1.5 miles to its dead end at the trailhead.

Trail Description

The hike leaves the trailhead, ►1 passing around boulders. The Middle Prong Little Pigeon River crashes through the valley amid huge gray boulders and thousands of smaller rocks, sometimes slowing

TRAIL USE
Day Hiking

LENGTH
8.0 miles, 4½–5½ hours

VERTICAL FEET
±2,250

DIFFICULTY
– 1 2 3 **4** 5 +

TRAIL TYPE
Out-and-back

FEATURES
Stream
Waterfall
Old-Growth
Autumn Colors
Wildflowers
Swimming
Geologic Interest

FACILITIES
None

Stream

Geologic Interest 🔖

This is the valley of the big trees: tulip trees, Carolina silverbells, buckeyes, and more.

Old-Growth 🌳

into ultraclear pools, sometimes sliding around tree-covered islands, but always moving downstream. Soon cross the prong on a very long footbridge. The river is wide here. Stop for a moment and look upstream and downstream at this watercourse shaded in sycamores, birch, and rhododendron.

The wide track continues up the west side of Middle Prong. Huge boulders litter the mountainside. At 0.3 mile, a gigantic boulder forms a rock shelter. Climb away from the stream. Level off at 0.8 mile. Keep east in rocky terrain. Bridge Ramsey Branch at 1.3 miles, flowing down from Greenbrier Pinnacle, shading the trail to your left. At 1.5 miles, the trail comes to an old auto turnaround. ►2 The Ramsey Cascade Trail continues straight and climbs more steeply as it enters smaller and narrower Ramsey Prong valley.

The trail morphs into a primitive footpath as it tunnels under rhododendron, climbing more steeply. Cross Ramsey Prong on a footlog at 2.1 miles. ►3 Note the shaded pool below a rock overhang just below the bridge—that swimming hole stays chilly year-round!

At 2.5 miles, pass between two massive tulip trees that act as trailside gates, leading to a third tulip tree—the biggest of them all. ►4 Impressive!

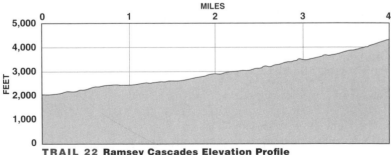

TRAIL 22 Ramsey Cascades Elevation Profile

Ramsey Prong *flows through snow-covered rocks.*

At 2.8 miles, stone steps lead past a small rock shelter on trail right.

Span Ramsey Prong yet again on a footlog at 3.0 miles. ►5 Exposed roots over the people-worn path can make the trail tricky, especially while you're looking around at all the big trees. Now the path works left, crisscrossing a trickling tributary as it wanders through a cove full of big buckeyes and cherry trees. Return to Ramsey Prong at 3.6 miles. Keep ascending amid a mosaic of moss, boulders, birches, and rhododendron.

 Wildflowers

Rock-hop a tributary just before reaching the falls. Plunging down the green valley, nestled at 4,300 feet in elevation, between the high ridges

Waterfall of Guyot Spur and Pinnacle Lead, falls Ramsey Cascades at mile 4.0. ▶6 Here, Ramsey Prong tumbles in a series of stairstep drops, framed by evergreens. Though it falls fewer than 100 feet, the cascade sends out quite a spray, which freezes in winter. Note the spruce trees, indicating your elevation. Picnickers and trail-weary hikers flock to the ample big boulders to watch this natural water show.

🚶	MILESTONES	
▶1	0.0	Ramsey Cascades Trailhead
▶2	1.5	Old auto turnaround
▶3	2.1	Bridge Ramsey Prong
▶4	2.5	Giant tulip trees
▶5	3.0	Bridge Ramsey Prong
▶6	4.0	Ramsey Cascades

Albright Grove

Hike from a lesser-used trailhead, passing the well-preserved Willis Baxter Cabin. Travel amid more pioneer homesites in quiet stream valleys before entering the land of giant trees—old-growth forest now preserved forever. The uppermost part of the hike makes a short loop between Dunn Creek and Indian Camp Creek, taking you by trees that helped supporters make the case for establishing the Smoky Mountains National Park.

Best Time

During fall you will see not merely big trees but big trees cloaked in autumn finery. After the leaves have fallen, the many pioneer homesites of the area are more evident, as are big trees beyond the edge of the trail. This area is also a fine spring-wildflower destination. Winter offers maximum seclusion.

Finding the Trail

From the junction of US 321 and US 441/Parkway in Gatlinburg, Tennessee (signed traffic light #3), go east on US 321/East Parkway 15.6 miles to Baxter Road, which is just beyond Jellystone Park Campground. Turn right onto Baxter Road and follow it for 0.3 mile to Laurel Springs Road. Veer sharply right onto gravel Laurel Springs Road, and follow it for 100 yards to a pole gate and trail sign on the left. The Maddron Bald Trail starts here.

TRAIL USE
Day Hiking
LENGTH
6.7 miles, 3–3½ hours
VERTICAL FEET
±1,500
DIFFICULTY
– 1 2 **3** 4 5 +
TRAIL TYPE
Loop

FEATURES
Stream
Autumn Colors
Wildflowers
Old-Growth
Secluded
Historical Interest
FACILITIES
None

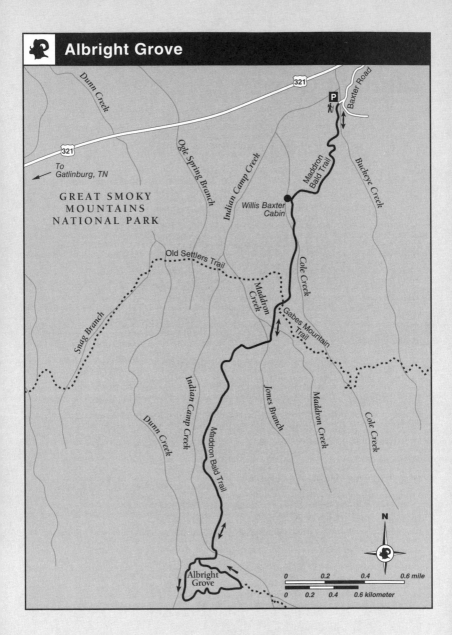

Albright Grove

321

P

Baxter Road

Dunn Creek

321

To
Gatlinburg, TN

GREAT SMOKY
MOUNTAINS
NATIONAL PARK

Ogle Spring Branch

Indian Camp Creek

Maddron Bald Trail

Willis Baxter
Cabin

Cole Creek

Buckeye Creek

Old Settlers Trail

Maddron Creek

Gabes Mountain Trail

Snug Branch

Dunn Creek

Indian Camp Creek

Maddron Bald Trail

Jones Branch

Maddron Creek

Cole Creek

N

Albright
Grove

0   0.2   0.4   0.6 mile
0   0.2   0.4   0.6 kilometer

Trail Description

A hard-to-find trailhead keeps many hikers off this trail. However, with good directions, it's a cinch. After finding the starting point, head up a wide bed on the Maddron Bald Trail. Pass the Willis Baxter Cabin, still intact after more than a century. Pass through a trail junction and start to climb a bit, then reach the side trail into Albright Grove. This nature trail loops through a giant forest of hemlock and tulip trees located between Dunn and Indian Camp Creeks. The immensity of this woodland, named after a former director of the park service, Horace Albright, makes this a trek that you will want to share with your friends.

> Some of these trees, such as Carolina silverbell and Fraser magnolia, are giants for their species.

The Maddron Bald Trail starts by passing a pole gate. ▶1 Buckeye Creek rushes downstream left of the trail. Head up an open roadbed beneath a second-growth deciduous forest, once farmland. Remember the size of these trees so that you can compare them to the big trees to come. The trail curves right toward Cole Creek and levels off, reaching the Willis Baxter Cabin at 0.6 mile. ▶2 This one-room cabin was built in 1889. Note the notched logs at the cabin corners. A small rocked-in spring and rock walls lie nearby. (Developed springs are almost always found near old pioneer cabins and homesites.)

Historical Interest

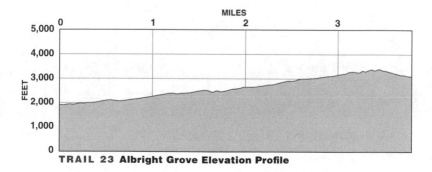

TRAIL 23 Albright Grove Elevation Profile

The Willis Baxter Cabin *stands against a pale winter sky.*

Keep up Maddron Bald Trail, bridging Cole Creek, then reach a trail junction at 1.2 miles. ▶3 Gabes Mountain Trail leaves left to Cosby, and Old Settlers Trail leaves right to Greenbrier. History buffs can make a little side trip down Old Settlers Trail to see more homesites. Maddron Bald Trail slices between boulders and narrows, slipping over Maddron Creek and Jones Branch, which flow beneath the Civilian Conservation Corps–built trail. The path then passes through a small gap and drifts into the Indian Camp Creek streamshed. Indian Camp Creek dutifully roars in the lowlands below. The valley floor reveals rock walls and other trailside pioneer signs.

Stream

Reach an old auto turnaround at 2.3 miles. The path narrows yet again as it leaves the turnaround and the former civilized world. Big trees, primarily preserved hemlocks, immediately tower overhead. Come to Indian Camp Creek at 2.8 miles. ▶4 A long footbridge avails a dry-footed crossing. Ascend steeply away from the creek, passing a seeping rock face that flows over the trail. The trail heads toward Dunn Creek before reaching a trail junction at 2.9 miles. ▶5

Old-Growth

Stay forward with the Albright Grove Loop Trail, entering a sheltered valley with Indian Camp Creek to the east and Dunn Creek to the west. The north-facing slope ranges between 3,100 and 3,400 feet, ideal conditions for a Southern Appalachian cove hardwood forest. Deep, rich, and moist soils harbor not just massive trees but one of the temperate climate's most diverse plant communities overall. The dominant trees are hemlock, buckeye, Carolina silverbell, tulip trees, beech trees, yellow birch, and more. The list of smaller plants and herbs of the cove hardwood forest is long enough to numb a biologist.

Dunn Creek is audible through the rhododendron near the trail. Yellow birch trees shade mossy

Horace Albright successfully fought a mountain road that would have traversed the Smokies crest, similar to Skyline Drive at Shenandoah National Park.

rocks and ferns. Turn away from Dunn Creek and climb along a hillside. A short path leads left to a tulip tree that has been towering since before the United States was established. Curve into a cove where buckeye trees dominate. From this cove, the Albright Grove Nature Trail climbs to a ridgetop flat where hikers repose in the forest.

The tree grove was named for Horace Albright, the second director of the National Park Service. He was a big proponent of a national park for the Smokies, thinking that national parks should be well distributed throughout the country.

The Albright Grove Loop Trail then heads up the ridge nose. Cruise along a hillside with downward views toward Indian Camp Creek. The loop ends at 3.6 miles, ▶6 meeting the Maddron Bald Trail once again. From here, it is 0.3 mile back down to the lower end of the Albright Grove Loop Trail ▶7 and a 2.9-mile backtrack to the Maddron Bald Trailhead. ▶8

🚶	**MILESTONES**		
▶1	0.0	Maddron Bald Trailhead
▶2	0.6	Willis Baxter Cabin
▶3	1.2	Old Settlers Trail and Gabes Mountain Trail
▶4	2.8	Bridge Indian Camp Creek
▶5	2.9	Right on Albright Grove Nature Trail
▶6	3.6	Left on Maddron Bald Trail
▶7	3.9	Meet lower end of Albright Grove Loop Trail and backtrack
▶8	6.7	Maddron Bald Trailhead

Maddron Bald Loop

This is one of the best backpacking loops in the entire park! First, hike along the lower reaches of Gabes Mountain, passing Hen Wallow Falls and entering virgin woodland to camp at Sugar Cove. Next, head up Maddron Bald Trail to Albright Grove, which contains some of the park's largest trees. Camp along resonant high-country Otter Creek. Surmount Maddron Bald, which sports awe-inspiring views. Return via the rugged Snake Den Trail, where more vistas open on heath balds.

Best Time

This destination is good year-round, though winter can be cold and harsh up high. The multiple creek crossings may be high in spring. High-elevation streamside camps are cool, even in summer. Fall offers low water and clear skies.

Finding the Trail

From the junction of US 321 and US 441/Parkway in Gatlinburg, Tennessee (signed traffic light #3), head east 18.1 miles on US 321 until it comes to a T-intersection with TN 32. Follow TN 32 a little more than a mile, turning right (south) into the signed Cosby section of the park. After 1.9 miles up Cosby Entrance Road, watch for a road splitting left to the picnic area. Turn left here and immediately park. The Gabes Mountain Trail starts a short distance downhill, back toward the entrance to Cosby, on the west side of Cosby Entrance Road.

TRAIL USE
Backpacking
LENGTH
17.3 miles, 6 hours
VERTICAL FEET
±4,000
DIFFICULTY
– 1 2 3 **4 5** +
TRAIL TYPE
Loop

FEATURES
Ridgeline
Stream
Waterfall
Autumn Colors
Wildflowers
Old-Growth
Great Views
Backcountry Camping
FACILITIES
(SEASONAL)
Campground
Picnic Area
Restrooms
Water

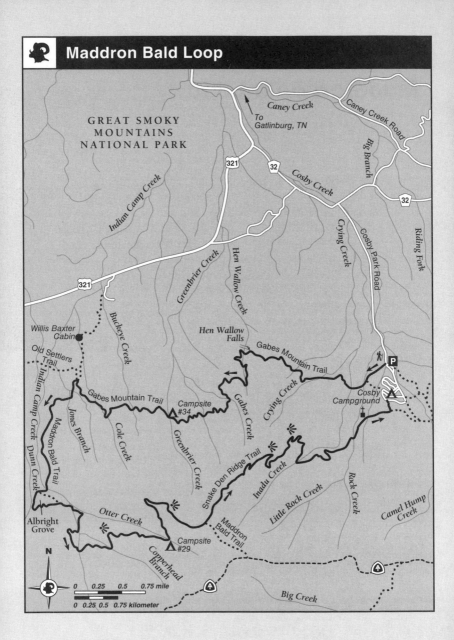

Maddron Bald Loop

**GREAT SMOKY
MOUNTAINS
NATIONAL PARK**

Caney Creek

Caney Creek Road

To
Gatlinburg, TN

Big Branch

321

32

Cosby Creek

32

Crying Creek

Riding Fork

Indian Camp Creek

Cosby Park Road

321

Greenbrier Creek

Hen Wallow Creek

Bucheye Creek

Willis Baxter
Cabin

Hen Wallow
Falls

Gabes Mountain Trail

Cosby
Campground

Old Settlers
Trail

Indian Camp Creek

Gabes Mountain Trail

Campsite
#34

Gabes Creek

Crying Creek

Jones Branch

Cole Creek

Greenbrier Creek

Snake Den Ridge Trail

Inadu Creek

Little Rock Creek

Rock Creek

Camel Hump
Creek

Maddron Bald Trail

Dunn Creek

Otter Creek

Albright
Grove

N

Copperhead
Branch

Campsite
#29

Maddron
Bald
Trail

Big Creek

0   0.25   0.5   0.75 mile

0   0.25 0.5   0.75 kilometer

East Tennessee *opens from the view down the Indian Camp Creek valley.*

Trail Description

Join the Gabes Mountain Trail ►1 just downhill from the Cosby picnic area. Day hikers can make the trip to Hen Wallow Falls for a rewarding 4.4-mile round-trip trek. Pine, oak, and hickory forest, bordered by rhododendron and mountain laurel, shades the track. Reach a trail junction at 0.3 mile. A spur trail leads left to Cosby Campground. Stay right here to bridge Rock Creek. Step over streamlets flowing from Snake Den Mountain. More substantial tributaries have small bridges. Bridge Crying Creek before coming to an old auto turnaround at 1.1 miles. Climb past an old homestead—look for rocks piled in a vain attempt to make this hardscrabble, sloped land more arable.

Continue upstream along Crying Creek before turning away at 1.3 miles to shortly pass through an unnamed gap. A little trail leads right from the gap

The Civilian Conservation Corps operated a camp at Otter Creek in the 1930s while workers labored on area trails.

 Historical Interest

to the lonesome grave of Sally Sutton. Dip to a small stream before rising to reach Bear Neck Gap at 1.7 miles. ▶2 The mountain slope sharpens considerably. Vines drape among the trees of a cove hardwood forest. Winter views of Three Top Mountain and Round Mountain open to the north.

At 2.2 miles, a spur leaves right toward Hen Wallow Falls. ▶3 A profusion of rocks lies at the base of the 60-foot falls, which slides in a thin veil over a stone face, before splattering into the boulder jumble. Cross Lower Falling Branch by a culvert above the falls. The trail switchbacks, curves around a dry hollow, and ascends the valley of Lower Falling Branch. Reach an upper crossing of Lower Falling Branch just below a wide set of cascades. Cross it a third and last time. Notice the abundance of white quartz rocks in the streambed here.

Waterfall

Old-Growth

Split a gap in Gabes Mountain at 3.3 miles. Work into the Greenbrier Creek valley, where the big trees form a forest primeval. Old-growth silverbells, buckeyes, and tulip trees shade the path. Step over small Gabes Creek. Begin winding in and out of small coves where the giants have taken their place, growing undisturbed through the American centuries.

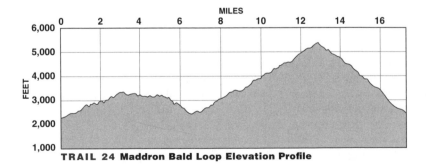

TRAIL 24 Maddron Bald Loop Elevation Profile

Drift into Sugar Cove backcountry campsite #34 at 4.9 miles, your first night's destination. ▶4 Multiple sites are strung along the creek. Beyond the camp, Gabes Mountain Trail climbs around Buckeye Lead, passing through a gap in a quarter mile. Big trees stand sentinel along the track. From here, the path mostly descends toward Cole Creek, which you cross twice in succession at 5.9 miles.

 Backcountry Camping

 Stream

Drift back into settled, more level country to reach a trail intersection at 6.6 miles. ▶5 Turn left on the Maddron Bald Trail. The path slices between boulders and narrows, slipping over Maddron Creek and Jones Branch, which flow beneath the Civilian Conservation Corps–built trail. The path then passes through a small gap and shifts to the Indian Camp Creek streamshed. Drop to the valley floor, passing rock walls and other pioneer evidence beside the trail.

Historical Interest

Reach an old auto turnaround at mile 7.6. The path narrows yet again as it leaves the turnaround and the former civilized world. Big trees immediately tower overhead. Come to Indian Camp Creek and a long footbridge at 8.0 miles. Ascend steeply away from the creek, passing a seeping rock face that flows over the trail. The path heads toward Dunn Creek before reaching a trail junction at 8.3 miles. ▶6 Stay right with the Albright Grove Loop Trail as it circles through old-growth woods and returns to Maddron Bald Trail.

Old-Growth

Old-Growth

Meet the Maddron Bald Trail at 9.0 miles. ▶7 Turn right to meet Indian Camp Creek at a potentially tough crossing just above its confluence with Otter Creek. Keep climbing, now along Otter Creek. Soon cross Copperhead Branch, then shortly cross Indian Camp Creek again. These crossings can be troublesome in high water.

The path curves around a relatively level cove, rife with buckeye trees, after crossing a small, unnamed feeder branch. The path curves back,

Spruce trees rise *from the heath on Maddron Bald.*

looking for another creek to cross. And it soon
meets Indian Camp Creek for the last time at 9.9

 Waterfall

miles. A scenic, tiered cascade descends above the
trail passage. Next, the graded trail crosses Copperhead Branch for the final time.

After leaving Copperhead Branch, the path rises
to the point of a ridge and a heath bald at 10.5
miles. ▶8 Look for a side trail leading left to an overlook at a rocky point. You are 4,215 feet high. Look

Great Views

far into East Tennessee below. To your right, Maddron Bald forms a rampart. Behind you, Old Black
and the crest of the Smokies make their impressive
heights known. Otter Creek, rippling down the valley below, forms the background music for the vista.

The Maddron Bald Trail leaves the vista and angles toward Otter Creek on a steep slope, working around rock outcrops. Reach Otter Creek backcountry campsite #29 at 11.3 miles. ►9 This rationed campsite, your second night's destination, has a few flats stretched along the stream.

 Backcountry Camping

The path rises to meet Maddron Bald, then becomes canopied in laurel. Make a hard right turn and continue climbing. Wind-flagged spruce trees rise from the brushy bald at 11.9 miles. ►10 Sand myrtle grows low, and spur trails head off to rock lookouts. Briefly descend, then make the last push for Snake Den Ridge Trail. Spruce trees lord over the forest.

 Great Views

Meet Snake Den Ridge Trail at 12.8 miles. ►11 You are at the high point of the loop, over 5,300 feet. Continue in spruce and yellow birch amid open brush with limited vistas. Ahead, Snake Den Trail rewards hikers with views of Cosby Knob, Low Gap, and Mount Cammerer as you curve through the low-growing heath balds. Reach a notable view at 14.2 miles. ►12

 Great Views

The path doesn't stay on the ridgecrest for long, angling back into deep green woods and then switchbacking again and again, too many times to count, eventually reaching another heath bald and repeating the pattern. Pass another great view at 14.9 miles. Turn into the Inadu Creek watershed, crossing the stream at 15.6 miles. ►13 Continue down the wildflower-rich vale.

Come to an old auto turnaround. Left of the turnaround, a short path leads to a cement square, laid for forgotten reasons, and a view of Rock Creek. Cross Rock Creek by bridge at 16.5 miles. Enter the formerly settled lands of Cosby. Pass a cemetery at 16.8 miles.

Historical Interest

Reach a trail junction at 17.1 miles. ►14 Here, a horse path leaves right to meet the Low Gap Trail. Stay left on an old road, reaching Cosby

Campground near campsite #B51 at 17.3 miles. ►15
From here, work your way through the campground
downhill to the hiker parking area. The campground
walk is not included in the final trail mileage because
there are numerous routes.

	MILESTONES	
►1	0.0	Gabes Mountain Trailhead
►2	1.7	Bear Neck Gap
►3	2.2	Spur trail to Hen Wallow Falls
►4	4.9	Campsite #34
►5	6.6	Left on Maddron Bald Trail
►6	8.3	Right on Albright Grove Loop Trail
►7	9.0	Rejoin Maddron Bald Trail
►8	10.5	View from Heath Bald
►9	11.3	Campsite #29
►10	11.9	Maddron Bald
►11	12.8	Left on Snake Den Ridge Trail
►12	14.2	View from heath bald
►13	15.6	Cross Inadu Creek
►14	17.1	Stay left toward Cosby Campground
►15	17.3	Cosby Campground

Mount Cammerer via Low Gap

Revel in great views from a historic restored lookout tower. Leave Cosby Campground, and head up Cosby Creek valley through gorgeous woodland to the state line. Meet the Appalachian Trail (AT) at Low Gap. Cruise the state line to emerge at an outcrop and tower where the world falls away.

Best Time

Hikers find their way to Mount Cammerer year-round. Fall through spring offer the most far-reaching views. Summer afternoons can be stormy.

Finding the Trail

From the junction of US 321 and US 441/Parkway in Gatlinburg, Tennessee (signed traffic light #3), head east 18.1 miles on US 321 until it comes to a T-intersection with TN 32. Follow TN 32 a little more than a mile, turning right (south) into the signed Cosby section of the park. After 1.9 miles up Cosby Entrance Road, watch for a road splitting left to the picnic area, then the hiker parking area. Turn left here and immediately park. The Low Gap Trail starts at the upper end of the parking area.

Trail Description

Called "White Rock" by Tennesseans and "Sharp Top" by Carolinians before the park's inception, this mountaintop rock outcrop was named in perpetuity for Arno B. Cammerer, former director of the National Park Service. No matter the name,

TRAIL USE
Day Hiking
LENGTH
11.2 miles, 5–7 hours
VERTICAL FEET
±2,780
DIFFICULTY
– 1 2 3 4 **5** +
TRAIL TYPE
Out-and-back

FEATURES
Summit
Ridgeline
Stream
Autumn Colors
Wildflowers
Great Views
Photo Opportunity
Geologic Interest
Historical Interest
FACILITIES
(SEASONAL)
Campground
Picnic Tables
Restrooms
Water

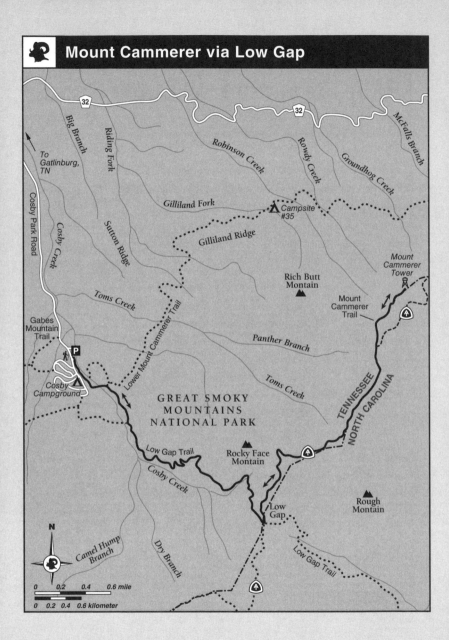

Mount Cammerer via Low Gap

To Gatlinburg, TN

Cosby Park Road

Big Branch

Riding Fork

Robinson Creek

Rowdy Creek

Groundhog Creek

McFalls Branch

Gilliland Fork

Campsite #35

Gilliland Ridge

Mount Cammerer Tower

Cosby Creek

Sutton Ridge

Rich Butt Montain

Mount Cammerer Trail

Toms Creek

Lower Mount Cammerer Trail

Panther Branch

Gabes Mountain Trail

P

Cosby Campground

Toms Creek

GREAT SMOKY
MOUNTAINS
NATIONAL PARK

TENNESSEE

NORTH CAROLINA

Low Gap Trail

Rocky Face Montain

Cosby Creek

Low Gap

Rough Montain

N

Camel Hump Branch

Dry Branch

Low Gap Trail

0   0.2   0.4   0.6 mile

0   0.2   0.4   0.6 kilometer

this sentinel delivers incredible panoramas from its place on the Smokies crest. A historic wood and stone fire tower, long in disuse, was restored by a group known as Friends of the Smokies. This restoration makes Mount Cammerer an even more desirable destination.

Friends of the Smokies, a private support group working in concert with the park, restored the lookout tower.

The trail's beginning, within the greater realm of Cosby Campground, can be a bit confusing, with numerous trail junctions in the first half mile. But exercise a little persistence and soon you are ascending the gorgeous valley of Cosby Creek, where tall trees shade mossy boulders and Cosby Creek forms a watery attraction alongside which wildflowers grow in spring. It is a steady climb to Low Gap, but the trail is in good shape. From there, the AT has its ups, but the hardest part to Cammerer is over.

Leave the hiker parking area ▶1 and drop to an old path of crumbling asphalt. Cosby Creek is downhill to your left. Soon pass the campground amphitheater. A cold piped spring is on trail left just before the amphitheater. The now-lovely woodland around you was once farmland. The path soon splits as the Cosby Nature Trail meanders through the woods to the left—stay with the signs indicating Low Gap, passing over two creeks via footbridges. The second creek is Cosby Creek. Reach the upper part of the Cosby Nature Trail, but this time stay right.

Stream

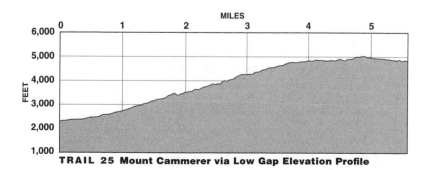

TRAIL 25 Mount Cammerer via Low Gap Elevation Profile

Mount Cammerer Tower *rises above wind-flagged spruce trees.*

The Low Gap Trail soon reaches an open area and the Lower Mount Cammerer Trail at 0.4 mile. ▶2

Leave the trail junction and continue climbing toward Low Gap. This area, also once farmland, is now rich in wildflowers. Pass a water-monitoring station on Cosby Creek just before reaching a trail junction at 0.8 mile. Here, a connector trail leads 0.4 mile back to Cosby Campground and 0.6 mile to Snake Den Ridge Trail. This connector allows hikers and equestrians to avoid the campground if they are going to Snake Den Ridge.

Wildflowers ✹

Stay with the Low Gap Trail, continuing the steady-but-not-too-steep uptick toward the Smokies crest, now in tall woodland. You are walking the old maintenance road to the Mount Cammerer fire tower. The wide track allows you to look around more rather than watch your every step. Tulip trees, maple, preserved hemlock, and black birch form a green cathedral overhead. Moss and ferns grow on the boulder-strewn ground, which becomes a wildflower garden in spring. Come back alongside Cosby Creek, where pretty cascades form white ribbons dropping between mossy boulders.

At mile 1.3, the trail makes the first of several switchbacks, leaving the dark creekside world behind. The ascent steepens as the trail works the slopes of Rocky Face Mountain to your left. Cross a tributary at 1.8 miles. ▶3 Keep rising. Step over now-tiny Cosby Creek again at mile 2.4. ▶4

The Low Gap Trail works around rock outcrops. The last stretch is a straight shot to make brushy Low Gap and the AT at mile 2.9. ►5 The elevation here is 4,242 feet. At Low Gap, turn left, northbound on the AT, and resume your ascent. A mile of steady climbing leads through northern hardwoods of cherry and yellow birch, along with scattered spruce. The AT levels out below Sunup Knob at mile 4.0. ►6 Winter views of the heath balds along lower Mount Cammerer open. Then trail is as level as they come in the Smokies, rising slightly near the junction with the Mount Cammerer Trail at mile 5.0. ►7

Follow the Mount Cammerer Trail along the state-line ridge into mountain laurel. The AT drops toward Davenport Gap. After a slight dip, reach the outcrop and tower at mile 5.6. ►8 You don't need to get in the tower to enjoy the vistas from the jutting rocks—you can see in every direction. However, the inside of the octagonal structure provides refuge from winds.

The rock cut of I-40 is visible to your east, and the road follows the Pigeon River. Mount Sterling and its metal fire tower rise to your south. In the foreground to your north is the appropriately named Stone Mountain. Beyond Stone Mountain, Tennessee stretches until the horizon's end. Maybe a place this spectacular deserves three names.

Geologic Interest

▲ **Ridge**

▲ **Summit**

Great Views

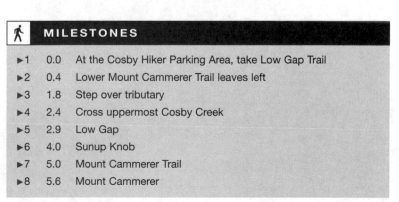

🚶	**MILESTONES**	
►1	0.0	At the Cosby Hiker Parking Area, take Low Gap Trail
►2	0.4	Lower Mount Cammerer Trail leaves left
►3	1.8	Step over tributary
►4	2.4	Cross uppermost Cosby Creek
►5	2.9	Low Gap
►6	4.0	Sunup Knob
►7	5.0	Mount Cammerer Trail
►8	5.6	Mount Cammerer

Twentymile and Fontana Lake Area

Twentymile and Fontana Lake Area

The Twentymile and Fontana Lake area is the least accessible and least visited area of the Smokies. Boater-only accesses, a dearth of nearby towns, and long, winding drives combine to keep crowds down.

Located in the most northwesterly section of the North Carolina Smokies, this area includes three major drainages that flow south from the state-line ridge: Twentymile, Hazel, and Eagle Creeks. Fontana Lake forms the south boundary. The Appalachian Trail (AT) traverses most of the state-line crest. Elevations range from higher than 5,000 feet along the state line down to 1,300 feet at Twentymile Ranger Station. Fontana Lake stands 1,710 feet at full pool. Eagle Creek and Hazel Creek flow into Fontana Lake, while Twentymile Creek feeds Cheoah Lake. Hazel Creek is laden with history. A little more than a century ago, a timber town, Proctor, harbored more than 1,000 residents who worked lumbering operations. Today, the forest has recovered, and Hazel Creek is now known as the Smokies' most storied trout fishery. Rough, remote Eagle Creek requires many fords to hike its watershed. Both of these creeks are accessed primarily by boat on Fontana Lake, including a fee shuttle operating out of Fontana Marina. Landlocked hikers can access this area from the north side of Fontana Dam, Twentymile Ranger Station, and over the mountain crest from Tennessee.

All the watersheds are noteworthy not just for fishing but also for national park–level magnificence. Twentymile Creek and its major tributary, Moore Spring Branch, exhibit deep, above-average-size pools divided by seemingly ceaseless cascades. Eagle Creek exudes a back-of-beyond wild aura and a slender hiker-only path that epitomizes the Smokies backcountry. Hazel Creek is one of the largest streams in the park. Its tributary network gives water lovers more opportunities to explore aquatic scenery and the verdant woodlands that surround them, combined with human history.

Opposite and overleaf: Fontana Lake *as seen from Shuckstack fire tower (Trail 28)*

Too low for spruce–fir, the high country is instead cloaked in northern hardwoods in most places. An exception is the most famous Southern Appalachian mountain meadow of them all: Gregory Bald. This grassy clearing, punctuated with blueberry bushes and wild azaleas, reveals pronounced views, berries in season, and the most colorful display of flame azaleas on the planet. This is one of two balds being preserved by the park, the other being Andrews Bald, near Clingmans Dome. Yet even better views can be had atop Shuckstack Mountain, where one of two historic park fire towers is preserved. This destination on the AT presents a 360-degree panorama of the Smokies crest, Fontana Lake, and the Nantahala National Forest to the south.

All park camping in this area is backcountry only. Car campers can overnight at Cable Cove or Tsali Campground in the Nantahala National Forest on Fontana Lake's south shore. Paddlers and boaters can camp at boat-only backcountry campsites on the lake and also lakeside hiker-accessible sites. Area trails are generally lightly used, except for the AT.

When boating to a trailhead, plan ahead, whether you're using your own boat or a shuttle. Fontana Marina and Cable Cove (in the Nantahala National Forest) are the two best boat-launching options for exploring the Fontana Smokies. Also, be apprised that Fontana Lake generally is at full pool from late May through early September. Lower lake levels make accessing the lake trailheads a little tougher and may require you to scramble over open, potentially muddy lakebed.

Permits

Permits are *not* required for day hiking. Backpackers must get a backcountry permit to stay at one of the 23 designated backcountry campsites and trail shelters in this area. All campsites require a reservation, which you can make online at smokiespermits.nps.gov, then print at home.

Twentymile and Fontana Lake Area (Trails 26–31)

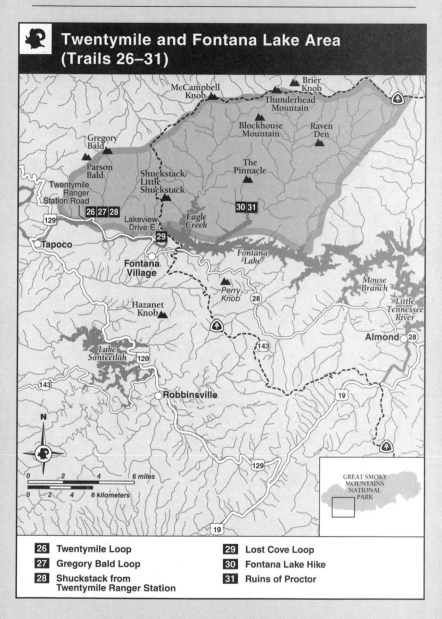

26 Twentymile Loop	**29** Lost Cove Loop
27 Gregory Bald Loop	**30** Fontana Lake Hike
28 Shuckstack from Twentymile Ranger Station	**31** Ruins of Proctor

Twentymile and Fontana Lake Area

TRAIL	DIFFICULTY	LENGTH	TYPE	USES & ACCESS	TERRAIN	FLORA & FAUNA	OTHER
26	2	7.6	Loop	Day Hiking, Backpacking, Horses	Stream, Waterfall	Autumn Colors, Wildflowers	Backcountry Camping, Swimming, Secluded
27	4	15.5	Loop	Backpacking, Horses	Summit, Ridge, Stream, Waterfall	Autumn Colors, Wildflowers	Great Views, Photo Opportunity, Backcountry Camping, Swimming, Steep
28	3	11.0	Out-and-back	Day Hiking, Backpacking	Summit, Ridge, Stream, Waterfall	Autumn Colors, Wildflowers	Great Views, Photo Opportunity, Backcountry Camping, Swimming, Steep
29	3–4	11.5	Loop	Day Hiking, Backpacking	Summit, Ridge, Lake, Stream	Autumn Colors, Wildflowers	Great Views, Photo Opportunity, Backcountry Camping, Swimming, Secluded, Steep, Historical Interest
30	3	13.3	Point-to-point	Day Hiking, Backpacking, Horses	Ridge, Lake, Stream	Autumn Colors, Wildflowers	Great Views, Backcountry Camping, Swimming, Historical Interest
31	1	2.0	Out-and-back	Day Hiking, Backpacking, Child Friendly	Lake, Stream	Autumn Colors, Wildflowers	Photo Opportunity, Backcountry Camping, Swimming, Historical Interest

USES & ACCESS	TYPE	TERRAIN	FLORA & FAUNA	OTHER
Day Hiking	Loop	Summit	Autumn Colors	Great Views
Backpacking	Out-and-back	Ridge	Wildflowers	Photo Opportunity
Horses	Point-to-point	Lake	Wildlife	Backcountry Camping
Child Friendly		Stream	Spruce–Fir	Swimming
	DIFFICULTY −12345+ less more	Waterfall	Old-Growth	Secluded
				Steep
				Historical Interest
				Geologic Interest

Maps

For the Twentymile and Fontana Lake area, you will need the following USGS 7.5-minute (1:24,000-scale) topographic quadrangles, listed in geographic order as you hike along your route:

Trail 26: *Tapoco, Fontana Dam*
Trail 27: *Tapoco, Fontana Dam, Cades Cove, Calderwood*
Trail 28: *Tapoco, Fontana Dam*
Trail 29: *Fontana Dam*
Trail 30: *Tuckasegee, Fontana Dam*
Trail 31: *Tuckasegee*

Twentymile and Fontana Lake Area

Leave a quiet trailhead to circle past Twentymile
Cascades. Bisect dry ridges to reach Moore Spring
Branch watershed. Numerous footlog bridge stream
crossings present panoramas of deep pools and
frothier cascades.

TRAIL 26

Day Hiking,
Backpacking, Horses
7.6 miles, Loop
Difficulty: 1 **2** 3 4 5

Ascend Twentymile Creek, passing Twentymile
Cascades and along dark pools before leaving the
stream. Reach Gregory Bald, with its views and
world-renowned wild azalea displays. Camp below
the bald at Sheep Pen Gap. Pass over what remains
of Parson Bald, and return via Moore Spring Branch,
with its plentiful cascades.

TRAIL 27

Backpacking, Horses
15.5 miles, Loop
Difficulty: 1 2 3 **4** 5

This is one of the better "climb it because it's there"
hikes. Leave Twentymile Ranger Station, travel
along pool-and-drop Twentymile Creek, and pass
Twentymile Cascades. Climb from the valley onto a
dry ridgeline, meeting the Appalachian Trail (AT). A
final ascent leads to a restored metal fire tower with
a stupendous 360-degree view.

TRAIL 28

Day Hiking,
Backpacking
11.0 miles,
Out-and-back
Difficulty: 1 2 **3** 4 5

This loop makes for a rewarding but long day hike
or good backpack. Travel the history-sprinkled
Lakeshore Trail with many pre-park relics. Enjoy
views of Fontana Lake. Climb along secluded Lost
Cove Creek to the AT. Reach astonishing vistas from
atop Shuckstack fire tower. Trace the AT down to
the trailhead and Fontana Lake.

TRAIL 29

Day Hiking,
Backpacking
11.5 miles, Loop
Difficulty: 1 2 **3** **4** 5

TRAIL 30

Day Hiking,
Backpacking, Horses
13.3 miles,
Point-to-Point
Difficulty: 1 2 **3** 4 5

Fontana Lake Hike 227

Regularly done as a day hike, this trip can be an excellent backpack for water lovers and backpack beginners. Take a boat shuttle to Hazel Creek and a piney creekside camp. Follow Lakeshore Trail past old homesites to Eagle Creek and a lakeside camp. Pass more pioneer history as the Lakeshore Trail delivers you to Fontana Dam.

TRAIL 31

Day Hiking,
Backpacking,
Child Friendly
2.0 miles,
Out-and-back
Difficulty: **1** 2 3 4 5

Ruins of Proctor 235

Take a boat shuttle on scenic Fontana Lake to Hazel Creek. Make an easy stroll to a backcountry camp, once the lumber town of Proctor. Explore the former townsite, heading up Hazel Creek to reach the relics of a mill, now covered in forest. Discover other area sites, including the Calhoun House.

Twentymile Loop

Leave a quiet trailhead to circle past Twentymile Cascades. Bisect dry ridges to reach Moore Spring Branch watershed. Numerous footlog bridge stream crossings present panoramas of deep pools and frothier cascades.

Best Time

Late winter and spring offer the most water to enjoy Twentymile Cascades and all the other unnamed falls on Twentymile Creek and Moore Spring Branch. The watersheds are also rich wildflower areas.

Finding the Trail

From the junction of US 321/TN 73 and East Lamar Alexander Parkway in Townsend, Tennessee, take US 321 west and then north 7.5 miles, and exit left (west) onto Foothills Parkway. Follow Foothills Parkway 16.9 miles south to its end at US 129 in Chilhowee. Turn left (south) onto US 129 and follow it 15 winding miles into North Carolina to reach NC 28. Turn left (east) onto NC 28 and follow it 2.6 miles to Twentymile Ranger Station, on your left.

From the intersection of US 19 and Veterans Boulevard in Bryson City, North Carolina, take US 19/US 74 south for 8.8 miles. Then veer right (west) and follow NC 28 for 11.4 miles to the intersection with NC 143. Zero your trip odometer here, and continue 17.7 miles west on NC 28 south to the Twentymile Ranger Station, which will be on your right about 5 miles past the turnoff to Fontana Dam Marina and Visitor Center.

TRAIL USE
Day Hiking,
Backpacking, Horses
LENGTH
7.6 miles, 3½–4½ hours
VERTICAL FEET
±1,300
DIFFICULTY
– 1 **2** 3 4 5 +
TRAIL TYPE
Loop

FEATURES
Stream
Waterfalls
Autumn Colors
Wildflowers
Backcountry Camping
Swimming
Secluded
FACILITIES
Picnic table

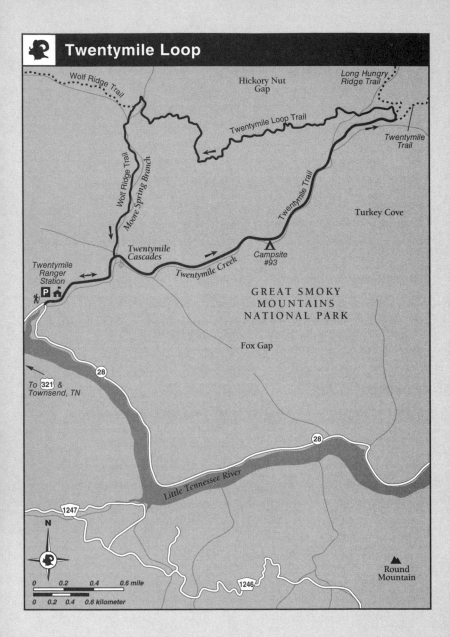

Twentymile Loop

Wolf Ridge Trail

Hickory Nut
Gap

Long Hungry
Ridge Trail

Twentymile Loop Trail

Twentymile
Trail

Wolf Ridge Trail

Moore Spring Branch

Twentymile Trail

Turkey Cove

Twentymile
Cascades

Twentymile Creek

Campsite
#93

Twentymile
Ranger
Station

GREAT SMOKY
MOUNTAINS
NATIONAL PARK

Fox Gap

28

To 321 &
Townsend, TN

28

Little Tennessee River

1247

N

1246

Round
Mountain

0   0.2   0.4   0.6 mile

0   0.2   0.4   0.6 kilometer

Trail Description

This streamside loop hike never gets too far from the sound of falling water—a key ingredient that makes the Smokies what they are. First, walk along Twentymile Creek, with its big pools that far outsize the amount of water it carries to Cheoah Lake. Stay with the Twentymile Trail, shortly reaching tiered Twentymile Cascades, an accessible waterfall that is fun to play around. Continue up the stream, bridging Twentymile Creek numerous times, getting looks into the fast-dropping stream as it dashes white through a green cathedral. Make a trail junction at now-grown Proctor Field Gap. Veer left on the hiker-only Twentymile Loop Trail, bridging Twentymile Creek one last time. Rise into silent wooded Long Hungry Ridge. Moore Spring Branch, a fine trout stream, serenades your downgrade. A short backtrack leads you to the trailhead.

Start your loop on the Twentymile Trail on a wide, roadlike path. ▶1 Twentymile Creek stairsteps south for Cheoah Lake. A forest of beech, black birch, and rhododendron rises from the ferny forest floor. Your hillside vantage allows views into the deep pools of Twentymile Creek, bordered by mossy rocks. The stream carries a higher amount of sediment relative to other Smoky Mountain streams and thus has a brownish tint. The sediment also causes the stream to cloud up after thunderstorms. It doesn't affect the fishery, though. Feisty rainbow trout can be found in every pool. A skilled angler will have a ball battling these colorful fish. At 0.5 mile, bridge Moore Spring Branch just before it meets Twentymile Creek. Reach a trail junction. ▶2

Turn right, staying with Twentymile Trail as the Wolf Ridge Trail, your return route, leaves left. Make a short, quick climb, then reach the spur trail to Twentymile Cascades. ▶3 From the main path, you can already gain a wide perspective of the cascades as they drop 40 or so feet over a distance of

🡒 Stream

🡒 Waterfall

30 yards, making multiple falls and rock slides into multiple pools divided by multiple ledges. The largest descent is the last one, as the creek pours over a sloped rock slab. Ample dunking pools beckon. Smooth gray sunning rocks give you a spot to dry.

Resume your ascent along Twentymile Creek, which continues splashing over big boulders into shadowy pools, backed against a rising wall of rhododendron. Scan for big boulders scattered in the forest. Bridge the stream at 1.5 miles and then again at 1.7 miles to reach Twentymile Creek backcountry campsite 93, ▶4 located in a flat on the curve of the stream. The main trail bridges Twentymile Creek again at the upper end of the campsite at 1.8 miles.

Backcountry Camping ⚠️

Cross a stream flowing out of Turkey Cove at 2.2 miles. Rise deeper into the mountains. Span Twentymile Creek at 2.5 miles, just below a boulder-strewn cascade. Watch for a big gravel bar and pool before bisecting the stream again at 2.6 miles. Here, the path turns away from the creek into piney woods to reach Proctor Field Gap and a trail junction at 3.2 miles. ▶5 The forest has overtaken the field from which it drew a name. Here, the hiker-only Twentymile Loop Trail leaves left, while the Long Hungry Ridge Trail keeps straight for

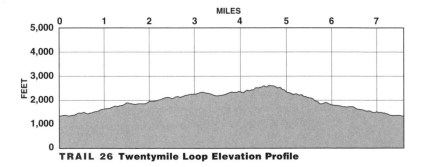

TRAIL 26 Twentymile Loop Elevation Profile

Ferns and rhododendrons *line Twentymile Trail.*

Campsite #92. The Twentymile Trail leaves right for the Appalachian Trail.

Take the narrow Twentymile Loop Trail as it drifts downhill to bridge an unnamed streamlet. Next, cross Twentymile Creek on a footlog. Here, the force of the stream pounds into a mossy stone bluff, then slows as a pool before pushing over boulders. The path weaves up Long Hungry Ridge in a dry forest of white pine, oak, and hickory. The secluded woodland is an ideal place for contemplative solitude, to absorb the essence of the Southern

Secluded

Appalachians. Split a gap on Long Hungry Ridge at 4.5 miles. Continue in upland forest, and bisect a second gap at 4.9 miles. ▶6 Views open across the valley of Wolf Ridge.

Descend to reach Moore Spring Branch at 5.8 miles in a rocky glen, where a 5-foot aquatic curtain drops into a deep pool. Turn down Moore Spring Branch and join the Wolf Ridge Trail at 5.9 miles. ▶7 Keep downstream, bridging Moore Spring **Stream** 🔁 Branch on footlogs at 6.0, 6.3, 6.6, 6.7, and 6.8 miles. They are fun to cross because they also give you enhanced vistas into the water. Deep pools, rock slides, and white frothy cascades cloaked in greenery characterize this superlatively scenic Smoky Mountain stream. Pass by a rare-for-the-Smokies dry rock overhang just before your loop ends at 7.1 miles. ▶8 It's just a half-mile backtrack to the trailhead. ▶9

🚶	**MILESTONES**	
▶1	0.0	Twentymile Trailhead
▶2	0.5	Right with Twentymile Trail
▶3	0.6	Twentymile Cascades
▶4	1.8	Campsite #93
▶5	3.2	Twentymile Loop Trail
▶6	4.9	Gap in Long Hungry Ridge
▶7	5.9	Join Wolf Ridge Trail
▶8	7.1	Right on Twentymile Trail
▶9	7.6	Twentymile Trailhead

Gregory Bald Loop

Ascend Twentymile Creek, passing Twentymile Cascades and along dark pools before leaving the stream. Reach Gregory Bald, with its views and world-renowned wild azalea displays. Camp below the bald at Sheep Pen Gap. Pass over what remains of Parson Bald, and return via Moore Spring Branch, with its plentiful cascades.

Best Time

June is the time to be on Gregory Bald to see the flame azaleas. Early August is better for picking blueberries. Views are best in fall after the first cool fronts sweep through. Winter and spring bring good views also, but the weather up top can be iffy.

Finding the Trail

From the junction of US 321/TN 73 and East Lamar Alexander Parkway in Townsend, Tennessee, take US 321 west and then north 7.5 miles, and exit left (west) onto Foothills Parkway. Follow Foothills Parkway 16.9 miles south to its end at US 129 in Chilhowee. Turn left (south) onto US 129 and follow it 15 winding miles into North Carolina to reach NC 28. Turn left (east) onto NC 28 and follow it 2.6 miles to Twentymile Ranger Station, on your left.

From the intersection of US 19 and Veterans Boulevard in Bryson City, North Carolina, take US 19/US 74 south for 8.8 miles. Then veer right (west) and follow NC 28 for 11.4 miles to the intersection with NC 143. Zero your trip odometer here, and continue 17.7 miles west on NC 28 south to the

TRAIL USE
Backpacking, Horses

LENGTH
15.5 miles, 9–11 hours

VERTICAL FEET
±3,570

DIFFICULTY
– 1 2 3 **4** 5 +

TRAIL TYPE
Loop

FEATURES
Summit
Ridgeline
Stream
Waterfall
Autumn Colors
Wildflowers
Great Views
Photo Opportunity
Backcountry Camping
Swimming
Steep

FACILITIES
Picnic table

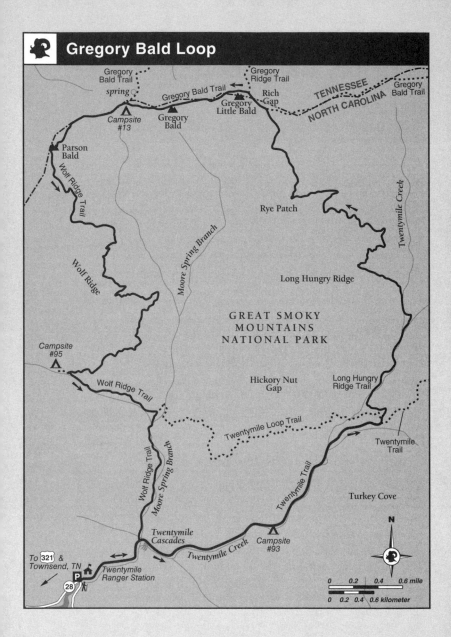

Gregory Bald Loop

Gregory
Bald Trail

Gregory
Ridge Trail

spring

Gregory Bald Trail

Rich
Gap

TENNESSEE

NORTH CAROLINA

Gregory
Bald Trail

Campsite
#13

Gregory
Bald

Gregory
Little Bald

Parson
Bald

Wolf Ridge Trail

Twentymile Creek

Wolf Ridge

Moore Spring Branch

Rye Patch

Long Hungry Ridge

GREAT SMOKY
MOUNTAINS
NATIONAL PARK

Campsite
#95

Wolf Ridge Trail

Hickory Nut
Gap

Long Hungry
Ridge Trail

Long Hungry
Ridge Trail

Twentymile Loop Trail

Twentymile
Trail

Wolf Ridge Trail

Moore Spring Branch

Twentymile Trail

Turkey Cove

N

Twentymile
Cascades

To 321 &
Townsend, TN

P

28

Twentymile
Ranger Station

Twentymile Creek

Campsite
#93

0   0.2   0.4   0.6 mile

0   0.2   0.4   0.6 kilometer

Parson Bald, *once a grassy meadow, is all but grown over.*

Twentymile Ranger Station, which will be on your right about 5 miles past the turnoff to Fontana Dam Marina and Visitor Center.

Trail Description

This hike combines the best the high and low country have to offer. Four backcountry campsites allow backpackers to vary the mileage and length of their trips. Those in top-notch mountain hiking shape can do it as a strenuous day hike. The Twentymile Trail leads through a magnificent stream valley past Twentymile Cascades, then Twentymile Creek campsite and on to Upper Flats campsite, both available for overnight stays. A little more creekside hiking leads to an arduous climb, topping out on Long Hungry Ridge at Rye Patch. From there, ramble high ridges to make Gregory Bald, the Southern Appalachians' most famed highland meadow, with

The park service maintains grassy, brushy Gregory Bald, dotted with wind-sculpted trees at its present 15-acre size.

its staggering views and flower displays. High-country camping is an option at Sheep Pen Gap, a grassy glade shaded with yellow spruce, below Gregory Bald.

Your return route passes nearly overgrown Parson Bald. Leave the state line via the steep Wolf Ridge Trail, negotiating never-ending switchbacks. Pass isolated Dalton Branch campsite, another overnight alternative, before crisscrossing Moore Spring Branch, with its deep pools and stairstep falls.

Stream ⚡ Twentymile Trail ▶1 rises above Twentymile Creek, flowing below in alternating pools and rapids. Rich woods pocked with big boulders shade the track. At 0.5 mile, Moore Spring Branch flows in from your left. ▶2 Bridge the creek just before beginning the loop portion of the hike. Stay right with the Twentymile Trail, as the Wolf Ridge Trail, your return route, leaves left. Shortly come to **Waterfall** ◖▮ Twentymile Cascades. ▶3 A series of ledges divides pools, culminating in a rock slide located at the base of the cascade.

Continue hiking up Twentymile Creek, admiring more cascades and trout-filled pools, half-hidden **Wildflowers** ❋ behind rhododendron and black birch. Bridge the stream at 1.5, 1.7, and 1.8 miles. Twentymile **Backcountry Camping** ◣ Creek backcountry campsite #93 is located in a flat just before the bridge at 1.8 miles. ▶4 Bridge

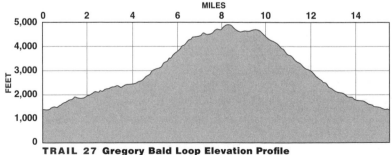

TRAIL 27 Gregory Bald Loop Elevation Profile

Twentymile Creek twice more at 2.5 miles and 2.6 miles. The path temporarily leaves Twentymile Creek, ascending through pines to make Proctor Field Gap and a trail junction at 3.2 miles. ▶5

Stay straight and pick up the Long Hungry Ridge Trail, dipping to step over Proctor Branch. Swing around the point of a ridge, then dip alongside Twentymile Creek again. At 4.3 miles, reach Upper Flats backcountry campsite #92, elevation 2,520 feet. ▶6 Upper Flats has several good tent sites from which to choose at its perch between Twentymile Creek and Greer Branch. Large rocks emerge from the ground, forming natural seats at the camps.

Beyond Upper Flats, immediately rock-hop Twentymile Creek, then step over Rye Patch Branch. The once-moderate grade steepens as the trail crosses Rye Patch Branch a final time at 4.9 miles, your last easy water. Ascend a dry ridge slope amid oaks. Partial views open to the southeast. Make sharp switchbacks at 5.5, 6.2, and 6.4 miles. At 6.7 miles, level off at Rye Patch, 4,400 feet. This once-open area is now mostly overgrown, but it remains an ideal resting spot after you've climbed to the crest of Long Hungry Ridge.

The balance of the Long Hungry Ridge Trail is easy, ending in Rich Gap and the Tennessee state line at 7.6 miles. ▶7 Turn left on the Gregory Bald Trail, walking the state line on what was the Appalachian Trail (AT) before Fontana Dam was built. Northern hardwoods such as buckeye, cherry, and beech rise over a grassy floor.

Reach another trail junction at 7.7 miles. ▶8 If you're thirsty, take the unmarked left route 0.3 mile and refresh yourself at Moore Spring, the site of an old AT shelter. Continue straight on the Gregory Bald Trail and climb 0.6 mile to the grassy meadow of Gregory Bald at 8.3 miles. ▶9 A nearly 360-degree view opens. Cades Cove lies below to

⚠ Backcountry Camping

🧍 Steep

▲ Ridge

Gregory Bald *presents a feast of mountains from its grassy crest.*

Great Views

Backcountry Camping

Wildflowers

the north. Flame azaleas bloom in June. Blueberries follow after that. The bald is large and has many elements, so allow time to explore it all.

Reenter woods on the western end of the bald, descending to the Wolf Ridge Trail junction and Sheep Pen Gap backcountry campsite #13, elevation 4,560, at 8.8 miles. ►10 The grassy glade of open, level woodland is one of the Smokies' finer backcountry locales; it is very heavily used, however. You can get water by walking 200 yards down the Gregory Bald Trail to a spring. Sunset from atop Gregory Bald is a Smoky Mountains sight to see.

Continue the loop, heading southwest on the Wolf Ridge Trail through level woodland, making a slight uptick before making Parson Bald at 9.6 miles. ►11 The park service does not maintain this bald, unlike Gregory Bald. It has grown up with trees and blueberry and azalea bushes, limiting views but proffering colorful beauty. All too soon you have passed through the bald's remnants.

Head from the state line into North Carolina, beginning an irregular but steep descent down Wolf Ridge, punctuated with frequent switchbacks amid oaks. Watch for white quartz pebbles on the trail. Come within earshot of Moore Spring Branch at 11.8 miles, only to turn away from the stream on a sharp switchback.

Steep

Dip toward Dalton Branch, meeting the quarter-mile side trail leading to Dalton Branch backcountry campsite #95 at 13.1 miles. ►12 Veer left and pick up an old road leading to the Twentymile Loop trail junction at 13.9 miles. Bridge Moore Spring Branch five times on fun footlogs, admiring the pools and falls of the watercourse, to arrive at the Twenty-mile Trail junction at 15.0 miles. ►13 Retrace the Twentymile Trail 0.5 mile to the trailhead, ►14 completing your loop.

Backcountry Camping

		MILESTONES
►1	0.0	Twentymile Trailhead
►2	0.5	Right with Twentymile Trail
►3	0.6	Twentymile Cascades
►4	1.8	Campsite #93
►5	3.2	Straight on Long Hungry Ridge Trail
►6	4.3	Campsite #92
►7	7.6	Left on Gregory Bald Trail
►8	7.7	Pass the spur to Moore Spring
►9	8.3	Gregory Bald
►10	8.8	Campsite #13, left on Wolf Ridge Trail
►11	9.6	Parson Bald
►12	13.1	Spur to campsite #95
►13	15.0	Twentymile Trail
►14	15.5	Twentymile Trailhead

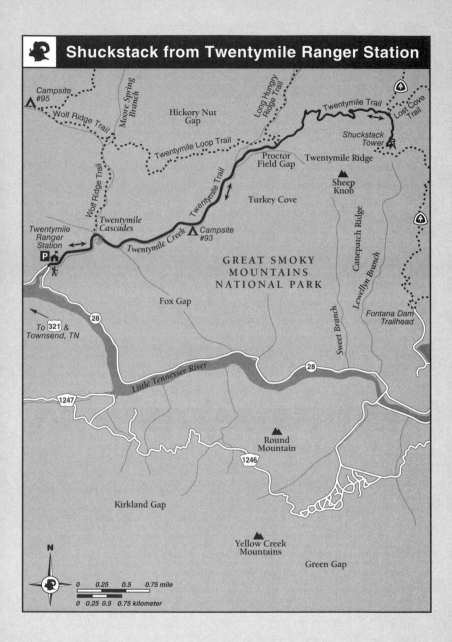

Campsite #95

Wolf Ridge Trail

Moore Spring Branch

Hickory Nut Gap

Long Hungry Ridge Trail

Twentymile Trail

Lost Cove Trail

Twentymile Loop Trail

Shuckstack Tower

Wolf Ridge Trail

Proctor Field Gap

Twentymile Ridge

Twentymile Cascades

Twentymile Trail

Turkey Cove

Sheep Knob

Twentymile Ranger Station

Twentymile Creek

Campsite #93

Canepatch Ridge

Llewellyn Branch

GREAT SMOKY MOUNTAINS NATIONAL PARK

Fox Gap

Sweet Branch

Fontana Dam Trailhead

To 321 & Townsend, TN

28

Little Tennessee River

28

1247

Round Mountain

1246

Kirkland Gap

Yellow Creek Mountains

Green Gap

N

0   0.25   0.5   0.75 mile

0   0.25   0.5   0.75 kilometer

Shuckstack from Twentymile Ranger Station

This is one of the better "climb it because it's there" hikes. Leave Twentymile Ranger Station, travel along pool-and-drop Twentymile Creek, and pass Twentymile Cascades. Climb from the valley onto a dry ridgeline, meeting the Appalachian Trail (AT). A final ascent leads to a restored metal fire tower with a stupendous 360-degree view.

Best Time

The clear skies of fall and winter avail the farthest-reaching views from Shuckstack Tower. In winter the cascades of Twentymile Creek may be frozen, adding a wintry treat to the trek. Views in summer can be hazy.

Finding the Trail

From the junction of US 321/TN 73 and East Lamar Alexander Parkway in Townsend, Tennessee, take US 321 west and then north 7.5 miles, and exit left (west) onto Foothills Parkway. Follow Foothills Parkway 16.9 miles south to its end at US 129 in Chilhowee. Turn left (south) onto US 129 and follow it 15 winding miles into North Carolina to reach NC 28. Turn left (east) onto NC 28 and follow it 2.6 miles to the Twentymile Ranger Station, on your left.

From the intersection of US 19 and Veterans Boulevard in Bryson City, North Carolina, take US 19/US 74 south for 8.8 miles. Then veer right (west) and follow NC 28 for 11.4 miles to the intersection with NC 143. Zero your trip odometer here, and

TRAIL USE
Day Hiking,
Backpacking
LENGTH
11.0 miles, 6–8 hours
VERTICAL FEET
±2,660
DIFFICULTY
– 1 2 **3** 4 5 +
TRAIL TYPE
Out-and-back

FEATURES
Summit
Ridgeline
Stream
Waterfall
Autumn Colors
Wildflowers
Great Views
Photo Opportunity
Backcountry Camping
Swimming
Steep
FACILITIES
Picnic table

Shuckstack resembles the piles of discarded cornstalks, or "shuck stacks," gathered by farmers for winter cattle feed.

continue 17.7 miles west on NC 28 south to the Twentymile Ranger Station, which will be on your right about 5 miles past the turnoff to Fontana Dam Marina and Visitor Center.

Trail Description

A sure, steady, but not-too-steep path leads from the lowlands of Twentymile Ranger Station to the metal fire tower atop Shuckstack Mountain, where an above-the-treetops vista awaits from one of two preserved metal fire towers within the park boundaries. The flora changes with the elevation, adding vegetational variety to the trek. The hike isn't as daunting as the mileage may indicate. Anybody in decent shape can—with ample rest breaks—make this hike. It's uphill the whole way but downhill all the way back!

The wide Twentymile Trail ▶1 ascends astride Twentymile Creek, which falls in a pool–drop–pool fashion. The deep pools of Twentymile Creek harbor lively rainbow trout. At 0.5 mile, bridge Moore Spring Branch above its confluence with Twentymile Creek. ▶2 Beyond the bridge, stay right with the Twentymile Trail, as the Wolf Ridge Trail heads left. A brief uptick leads to the spur trail to Twentymile Cascades. ▶3 Look down as the cataract descends

Stream

Waterfall

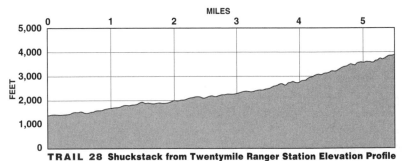

TRAIL 28 Shuckstack from Twentymile Ranger Station Elevation Profile

Looking toward the main crest *of the Smokies from Shuckstack fire tower*

40 feet in stairstep fashion over wide stone ledges. In summer you could get wet in a pool, then dry off on a sunny rock. The water will feel especially good after a sweaty climb in the Southern humidity.

The trail continues mimicking the curves and gradient of Twentymile Creek. Big boulders stand among the hardwoods, while the northeast-facing side of the valley is cloaked in thickets of rhododendron. Doghobble finds its trailside place. This low, arching shrub grows only in the Southern Appalachians. In late spring, doghobble produces clusters of small, bell-shaped flowers that droop from its arms. The waist-high thickets prove quite an impediment for most creatures, including people and dogs. In pioneer days, hunted bears would crash through such thickets using their powerful bodies, losing the dogs that were in pursuit of them, giving the plant its name.

✽ **Wildflowers**

Bridge the stream at 1.5 miles, then again at 1.8 miles to reach Twentymile Creek backcountry campsite #93. ▶4 The overnighting locale lies in a flat bordered by the stream on one side and a rising hill on the other. The Twentymile Trail bridges Twentymile Creek again at the upper end of the campsite, then rises well above the stream. Bridge

▲ **Backcountry Camping**

a creeklet flowing out of Turkey Cove at 2.2 miles, and continue penetrating farther into the park. Bridge Twentymile Creek at 2.5 miles, just below a boulder-strewn cascade. Watch for a big gravel bar and pool before bridging the stream again at 2.6 miles. Here, the path turns away from the creek, rising in piney woods to reach Proctor Field Gap and a trail junction at 3.2 miles. ▶5 Resting logs are scattered at the intersection.

Take a right turn at the trail junction, staying on the Twentymile Trail. The path now parallels Proctor Branch, flowing off to your left, while small rills flow under the now-narrower trail. The woods still reflect a streamside habitat. Cross your last trickle at 3.9 miles. The going gets higher and drier as you make your way into xeric woods composed of oak, mountain laurel, pine, sourwood, sassafras, and blueberry bushes.

Stream ⮒

Sassafras trees are easy to identify. Their leaves have three basic shapes: oval, three-lobed, and mitten-shaped. Mature sassafras trees have a reddish-brown, deeply furrowed bark. They are known for their aromatic scent. Scratch the bark from a twig, and the sweet smell is unmistakable. American natives used sassafras for medicinal purposes. Pioneers made tea by boiling the roots, and some people still do today. Birds eat the berries. The wood of sassafras shrinks when dried and is used for fence posts and hand tools. Sassafras roots were one of the first exports from the American colonies to Europe.

Though you're climbing, this is about as good as climbing gets, with the steady grade and good footing. Dark galax leaves line the path. Twentymile Ridge rises to your right. Keep looking upward along that ridge for the slender tower of Shuckstack. In winter the views are clear, but even when the leaves are on, you can spot it. The final ascent to the AT is completed in a series of switchbacks to arrive at Sassafras Gap at 5.1 miles. ▶6 This four-way trail junction is another spot where tower seekers take a break.

Turn right, southbound, on the more heavily trodden AT. Meander a minute before climbing from Sassafras Gap and skirting the north slope of Shuckstack. Emergent rocks rise from the steep mountainside. Reach the spur to Shuckstack at 5.4 miles. ►7 The acute left turn rises up the craggy knob 0.1 mile to the top of Shuckstack and a fire tower, elevation 4,020 feet. ►8 The chimney from the tower watcher's cabin stands quiet. The concrete cistern reflects a time when, during the spring and fall fire seasons, these towers would be manned by park rangers.

 Summit

Atop the tower, views extend in every direction. The main crest of the Smokies and the state line lie northeast. Fontana Lake covers the flooded valley of the Little Tennessee River to the southeast. The rampart of Gregory Bald stands to the northwest. Your route up the Twentymile Creek valley lies to the southwest. Waves of mountains extend southward into the Nantahala National Forest. From this vantage point, the surrounding Southern Appalachians look especially rugged. Soak up the views before backtracking to the trailhead.

Great Views

Photo Opportunity

🚶	**MILESTONES**	
►1	0.0	Twentymile Trailhead
►2	0.5	Right with Twentymile Trail
►3	0.6	Twentymile Cascades
►4	1.8	Campsite #93
►5	3.2	Proctor Field Gap
►6	5.1	At Sassafras Gap, turn right (south) on the Appalachian Trail
►7	5.4	Left on spur to Shuckstack
►8	5.5	Fire tower with 360-degree view

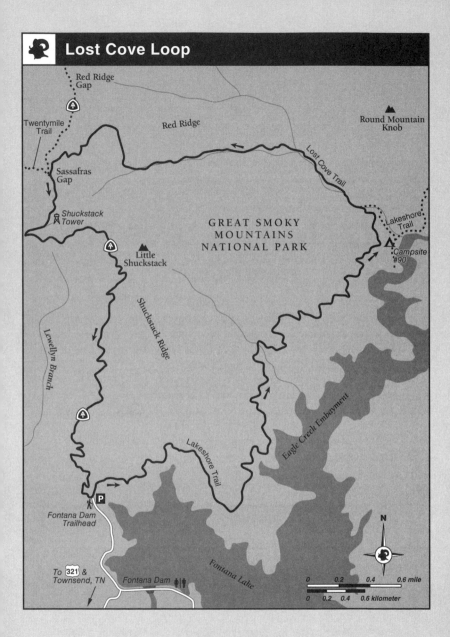

Lost Cove Loop

Red Ridge Gap

Twentymile Trail

Red Ridge

Round Mountain Knob

Sassafras Gap

Lost Cove Trail

Lakeshore Trail

Shuckstack Tower

GREAT SMOKY MOUNTAINS NATIONAL PARK

Campsite #90

Little Shuckstack

Shuckstack Ridge

Lewellyn Branch

Eagle Creek Embayment

Lakeshore Trail

Fontana Dam Trailhead

P

To 321 & Townsend, TN

Fontana Dam

Fontana Lake

N

| 0 | 0.2 | 0.4 | 0.6 mile |
| 0 | 0.2 | 0.4 | 0.6 kilometer |

Lost Cove Loop

This loop makes for a rewarding but long day hike or good backpack. Travel the history-sprinkled Lakeshore Trail with many pre-park relics. Enjoy views of Fontana Lake. Climb along secluded Lost Cove Creek to the Appalachian Trail (AT). Reach astonishing vistas from atop Shuckstack fire tower. Trace the AT down to the trailhead and Fontana Lake.

Best Time

Winter offers clear skies for gaining views atop Shuckstack fire tower and also allows more looks into pioneer relics along the Lakeshore Trail. In spring, the part of the loop along the AT can be busy with thru-hikers. Fall has clear skies and solitude.

Finding the Trail

From the junction of US 321/TN 73 and East Lamar Alexander Parkway in Townsend, Tennessee, take US 321 west and then north 7.5 miles, and exit left (west) onto Foothills Parkway. Follow Foothills Parkway 16.9 miles south to its end at US 129 in Chilhowee. Turn left (south) onto US 129 and follow it 15 winding miles into North Carolina to reach NC 28. Turn left (east) onto NC 28, passing Fontana Village Resort on your right at 9 miles. In another 1.5 miles, turn left onto Fontana Dam Road, with the sign for Fontana Dam on your right. Follow the signs, cross the dam, and then stay right just beyond the dam to dead-end at the trailhead, 2.2 miles from NC 28.

TRAIL USE
Day Hiking,
Backpacking
LENGTH
11.5 miles,
6½–8½ hours
VERTICAL FEET
±3,100
DIFFICULTY
– 1 2 **3 4** 5 +
TRAIL TYPE
Loop

FEATURES
Ridgeline
Summit
Lake
Stream
Autumn Colors
Wildflowers
Great Views
Photo Opportunity
Backcountry Camping
Swimming
Secluded
Steep
Historical Interest
FACILITIES
Picnic Tables
Restrooms near
Fontana Dam
Water

From the intersection of US 19 and Veterans Boulevard in Bryson City, North Carolina, take US 19/US 74 south for 8.8 miles. Then veer right (west) and follow NC 28 for 11.4 miles to the intersection with NC 143. Zero your trip odometer here and continue 9.9 miles west on NC 28. Turn right onto Fontana Dam Road, with the sign for Fontana Dam on your left; follow the signs, cross the dam, and then stay right just beyond the dam to dead-end at the trailhead, 2.2 miles from NC 28.

Trail Description

This loop can be a full day's hike or easily stretched into an overnight backpack. It's also a great Smokies sampler hike. It presents pre-park history, lake

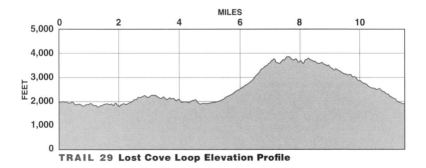

TRAIL 29 Lost Cove Loop Elevation Profile

views, mountain streams, old homesites, and ridge running and is capped off with a great view from a fire tower accessed via the AT. You start at the Fontana Dam Trailhead, following a former highway reverted to wilderness because of the dam's construction. Roller-coaster over rib ridges divided by streams flowing into Fontana Lake.

Reach Lost Cove Creek, with backcountry camping. You have the option of walking downstream to meet the Eagle Creek arm of Fontana Lake before traveling up secluded Lost Cove. A steep final ascent brings you to Sassafras Gap and the AT. One last uptick reaches Shuckstack fire tower and a panorama that rewards every uphill step you took. Views stretch as far as the clarity of the sky allows. From the top of the tower it's all downhill. Pass a natural vista from a rock face. The AT switchbacks down a dry ridge, leveling off at occasional gaps, before returning to the lowlands near Fontana Dam.

Pick up the Lakeshore Trail from the Fontana Dam Trailhead ▶1 as it follows the wide bed of old North Carolina Highway 288. This area wasn't originally slated to be part of the Smoky Mountains National Park—it was added only after Fontana Lake was to be built to furnish power for the Alcoa aluminum plant in Maryville, Tennessee, for the World War II effort. The land around the dam and Fontana Lake was condemned and purchased by the federal government. The land on the north side of the impoundment was then deeded over to the park, making the boundary at Fontana Lake's edge. This was all hastily done before World War II. That is why this area has more "modern" relics and evidence such as this wide highway grade and even roadside jalopies.

Oaks dominate the forest, along with plentiful tulip trees regenerating even atop the roadbed. Creek bottoms are clothed in rhododendron and

The rangers who staffed these fire towers lived in them full-time during the spring and fall fire seasons.

birch. Step over Payne Branch at 0.8 mile, ▶2 then ascend to surmount a gap. Descend along a trickling tributary. Watch for some big holly trees here. Pass the ruins of an old car beside a nearly disappeared farm clearing; walnut trees are reclaiming the former field.

Historical Interest 🏠

Rejoin the old auto highway at 1.5 miles. ▶3 Ahead more rusty hulks of vehicles lie abandoned along the old road. Views of the Eagle Creek embayment open to your right through the pines. Leave the road for the final time at 2.4 miles. ▶4 Stay left here, traveling straight up a rhododendron-shaded branch, crossing the stream, then climbing to a gap. This pattern will soon repeat itself many times over.

Great Views 🔭

Bisect streams at 3.0, 3.1, and 3.5 miles, the last being Birchfield Branch. ▶5 More stream and ridge undulations occur. The lake seems but an illusion at this point. Eventually Lost Cove Creek rushes audibly below. A few switchbacks deliver you to Lost Cove Creek Trail at 5.1 miles. ▶6

This loop turns left up the Lost Cove Trail. The dark hollow is tight here, and Lost Cove Creek plummets over mossy boulders into pools. Rock-hop the creek three times in the next 0.2 mile. The valley widens and you enter Lost Cove, where several homes once stood. Watch for a partial stone chimney to the right of the trail at 5.6 miles. More crossings lie ahead—if the water is high, your feet will get wet. Under normal flows, the stream can be easily rock-hopped. You probably won't realize it, but you rock-hop Cold Springs Branch, the major tributary of Lost Cove Creek, before reaching Upper Lost Cove backcountry campsite #91 at 5.8 miles. ▶7 The site is sloped but offers seclusion in a vale of spring-wildflower profusion.

Stream

Historical Interest 🏠

Backcountry Camping ⚠️

The slender footpath steepens beyond the campsite. Stream crossings ease up, until you are stepping over more rock than water. The path turns away from what is left of Lost Cove Creek at 6.9 miles and

Panoramic views *from the fire tower*

ascends steeply. A few switchbacks ease the climb. Huff and puff your way into Sassafras Gap at 7.8 miles. ▶8 The small gap beckons a rest.

 Steep

Turn left, southbound, on the AT. It shows much more use than Lost Cove Trail. A brief level stretch is followed by an assault on the boulder-strewn north flank of Shuckstack. Reach the spur trail to the fire tower at 8.2 miles. Stay left and switchback up the rocky summit to reach the fire tower and old lookout cabin site at 8.3 miles. ▶9 The chimney and water cistern mark the site of what was a job offering a lot of solitude. Climb the metal tower. Undulating panoramas open in all directions. You can see Fontana Lake, the Lost Cove Creek valley, the main chain of the Smokies, Twentymile Creek valley, and the wall of Gregory Bald in the background. Looks like that firewatcher job came with a few perks!

Great Views

Return to the narrow hiker-only AT, and continue southbound. Make a sharp switchback, then pass an open stone face offering natural southern vistas. Drop to a gap betwixt Shuckstack and Little Shuckstack at 9.2 miles. ►10 Continue the downgrade, briefly entering a hollow to step over a trickling stream at 10.0 miles. ►11 Occasional westerly views of Fontana Lake open. The switchbacks continue under the hickories and oaks. Emerge at the Fontana Dam Trailhead at 11.5 miles, ►12 completing the loop.

🚶 MILESTONES

►1	0.0	Fontana Dam Trailhead
►2	0.8	Payne Branch
►3	1.5	Old highway
►4	2.4	Leave old highway
►5	3.5	Birchfield Branch
►6	5.1	Left on Lost Cove Trail
►7	5.8	Campsite #91
►8	7.8	Left on Appalachian Trail
►9	8.3	Shuckstack fire tower
►10	9.2	Gap between Shuckstack and Little Shuckstack
►11	10.0	Trickling stream
►12	11.5	Fontana Dam Trailhead

Fontana Lake Hike

Regularly done as a day hike, this trip can be an excellent backpack for water lovers and backpack beginners. Take a boat shuttle to Hazel Creek and piney creekside camp. Follow Lakeshore Trail past old homesites to Eagle Creek and a lakeside camp. Pass more pioneer history as the Lakeshore Trail delivers you to Fontana Dam.

Best Time

Fontana Lake is at its most scenic when in full pool during summer. Swimming also is good then. Spring offers cooler temperatures and wildflowers. Winter is a poor choice because of annual lake drawdowns.

Finding the Trail

From the junction of US 321/TN 73 and East Lamar Alexander Parkway in Townsend, Tennessee, take US 321 west and then north 7.5 miles, and exit left (west) onto Foothills Parkway. Follow Foothills Parkway 16.9 miles south to its end at US 129 in Chilhowee. Turn left (south) onto US 129 and follow it 15 winding miles into North Carolina to reach NC 28. Turn left (east) onto NC 28, passing Fontana Village Resort on your right at 9 miles. In another 1.5 miles, turn left on Fontana Dam Road, with the sign for Fontana Dam on your right. Just after the turnoff, take the first right at the sign for Fontana Marina.

From the intersection of US 19 and Veterans Boulevard in Bryson City, North Carolina, take US

TRAIL USE
Day Hiking,
Backpacking, Horses
LENGTH
13.3 miles, 7–9 hours
VERTICAL FEET
+1,860/−1,840
DIFFICULTY
− 1 2 **3** 4 5 +
TRAIL TYPE
Point-to-Point

FEATURES
Ridgeline
Lake
Stream
Autumn Colors
Wildflowers
Great Views
Backcountry Camping
Swimming
Historical Interest
FACILITIES
Camping
Picnic Tables
Restrooms near
Fontana Dam
Water

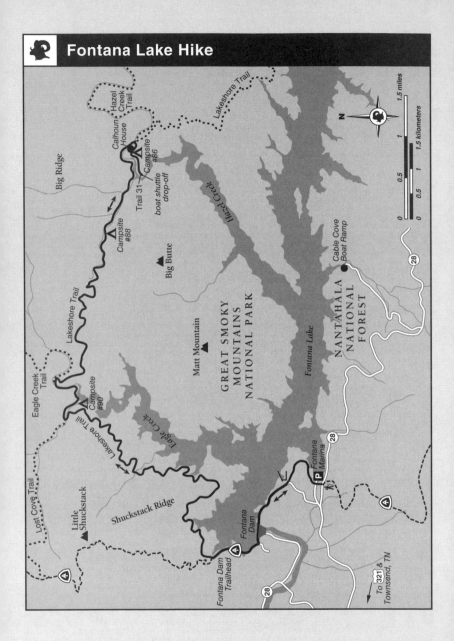

Fontana Lake Hike

Hazel Creek Trail

Lakeshore Trail

Lakeshore Trail

Calhoun House

Campsite #86

Trail 31

boat shuttle drop-off

Big Ridge

Campsite #88

Big Butte

Hazel Creek

N

1.5 miles

1

1.5 kilometers

0.5

1

0.5

0

0

Cable Cove Boat Ramp

28

Lakeshore Trail

Matt Mountain

GREAT SMOKY MOUNTAINS NATIONAL PARK

NANTAHALA NATIONAL FOREST

Fontana Lake

Eagle Creek Trail

Campsite #90

Eagle Creek

Lakeshore Trail

Lost Cove Trail

Little Shuckstack

Shuckstack Ridge

Fontana Marina

P

28

Fontana Dam

Fontana Dam Trailhead

28

321

To 321 & Townsend, TN

19/US 74 south for 8.8 miles. Then veer right (west) and follow NC 28 for 11.4 miles to the intersection with NC 143. Zero your trip odometer here and continue 9.9 miles west on NC 28. Turn right onto Fontana Dam Road, with the sign for Fontana Dam on your left; then make another quick right at the sign for Fontana Marina.

Trail Description

If you like a combination of mountains, streams, and lakes, this hike is for you and any younger or inexperienced backpackers you may wish to bring along. It's doable as a day hike, but you'd best get started early.

Be apprised that this trip takes planning—you must arrange a boat shuttle to the trailhead. Contact Fontana Marina at 828-498-2129 to arrange for a one-way pay shuttle; you will hike back to the marina.

Fontana Dam is the highest dam east of the Mississippi River.

The boat shuttle takes you on a pleasure ride from Fontana Marina to Hazel Creek, where you see wave upon wave of mountains from a watery grandstand. Your drop-off point is where Hazel Creek flows into Fontana Lake. Backpackers can walk a mere half mile to a pine-shaded campsite on the banks of Hazel Creek. Talk about an easy first day! Use your free time to explore the old townsite of Proctor, fish Hazel Creek, swim in the lake, or relax at camp.

From there, the hike leads west up historic Possum Hollow where settler evidence abounds. Surmount Pinnacle Ridge to reach Eagle Creek, a tumultuous mountain rill. Ahead, another campsite lies at the confluence of Eagle Creek, Lost Cove Creek, and Fontana Lake. Simultaneously enjoy tumbling streams and a mountain-rimmed lake.

The final part of the hike bisects rib ridges extending from Shuckstack Mountain, divided by tumbling watersheds, all mixed in with still more homesites and even a few old jalopies left from pre-park days. Intersect the Appalachian Trail (AT) and walk over Fontana Dam to Fontana Marina, completing a water-and-woods loop.

The boat shuttle ▶1 drops you off at the mouth of Hazel Creek. Soak in mountain vistas on the ride—the lake trip is part of this overall experience. The Hazel Creek Trail, shaded by black birch, sycamore, and ferns aplenty, takes you to Proctor backcountry campsite #86, at 0.5 mile. ▶2 White pines carpet the camp with needles as cool Hazel Creek rushes by. Soon reach a wide bridge and trail junction.

Backcountry Camping

Cross the bridge and stay left, taking the Lakeshore Trail toward the Calhoun House, owned and used by the park. Pass the house, climbing a bluff only to descend back to Hazel Creek. Turn into Possum Hollow at 1.2 miles. ▶3 Remnants of the old community of Proctor, including relic fields, train axles, chimneys, and foundations, are very evident along this valley of Sheehan Branch.

Historical Interest

Continue up an old wagon road, passing spurs to pioneer cemeteries. The gently ascending trail narrows. Pass the spur trail to campsite #88 at 2.0 miles. ▶4 This small, less-than-ideal camp sits on a slope. An intact brick chimney stands just ahead.

Wildflowers

Backcountry Camping

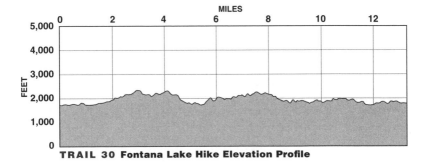

TRAIL 30 Fontana Lake Hike Elevation Profile

Waves of mountains *rise from Fontana Lake.*

Continue along an ever-diminishing watercourse to reach a gap in Pinnacle Ridge at 3.1 miles.

From here, the Lakeshore Trail follows a graded park-created path rather than a historic pioneer track. Descend through hickory, oak, pine, and mountain laurel woods, occasionally coasting into lonely hardwood coves. Watch for quartz-encrusted boulders beside the trail at 3.9 miles. Enjoy sporadic lake views. The cry of Eagle Creek accompanies a few final switchbacks, and you reach the Eagle Creek Trail at 5.1 miles. ▶5

 Stream

Turn left to descend along boulder-sprinkled Eagle Creek, still on the Lakeshore Trail. Cross an iron trestle bridge and soon Fontana Lake comes into view. Cross Lost Cove Creek on a footlog to arrive at the strategically located and busy Lost Cove backcountry campsite #90 at 5.5 miles. ▶6 This oak- and hickory-shaded camp offers fishing and swimming in both Fontana Lake and the mountain streams nearby. A network of user-created trails makes finding the continuance of the Lakeshore Trail a

Backcountry Camping

Fontana Lake *snakes into the mountains near campsite #90.*

challenge. As you look out on the lake from the campsite, the Lakeshore Trail is uphill and to your right, entering the Lost Cove Creek valley.

Travel up the cool, rhododendron-dominated valley. Turbulent Lost Cove Creek crashes below. Reach the Lost Cove Trail junction at 6.0 miles. ►7 Stay left with the Lakeshore Trail, climbing to the first of innumerable gaps dividing drainages into Fontana Lake. This portion of the Lakeshore Trail has many old roads and trails leading off it, so make sure you stay on the right path. Fontana Lake is on your left the whole way.

Autumn Colors

The trail follows a familiar pattern: up and around a point of a ridge, down into a creek-filled hollow, up the side of a ridge and over the point, and down again into a hollow. Step over Birchfield Branch at 7.6 miles. ►8 Intersect a former road, Old NC 28, at 8.7 miles. ►9 It still has some junker cars from the 1930s nearby. Homesites and other evidence of human habitation are all around this

Historical Interest

section of trail. Enjoy views of Fontana Lake from piney points. Leave the old road at 9.6 miles, ▶10 heading right to pass through a fast disappearing farm clearing. Bisect a gap, then return to the old roadbed. Emerge at the Fontana Dam Trailhead at 11.1 miles. ▶11

Road-walk to reach the north side of Fontana Dam at 11.7 miles. ▶12 Cross Fontana Dam, appreciating the immensity of the project and the views of Fontana Lake. Follow the AT to the left, away from Fontana Dam Road and reenter woodland. Pass a trail shelter nicknamed the Fontana Hilton, so dubbed because it was considered fancy when first erected. After running a low ridgeline through thick woods, the AT crosses a road leading to the marina. The marina is a short distance downhill to your left. Turn left on the road to complete your loop, at 13.4 miles. ▶13

Great Views

🚶	**MILESTONES**	
▶1	0.0	Fontana Marina (boat-shuttle departure point)
▶2	0.5	Campsite #86
▶3	1.2	Possum Hollow
▶4	2.0	Campsite #88
▶5	5.1	Eagle Creek Trail
▶6	5.5	Campsite #90
▶7	6.0	Lost Cove Trail
▶8	7.6	Birchfield Branch
▶9	8.7	Meet old NC 28
▶10	9.6	Leave old NC 28
▶11	11.1	Pass Fontana Dam Trailhead
▶12	11.7	Fontana Dam
▶13	13.4	Fontana Marina

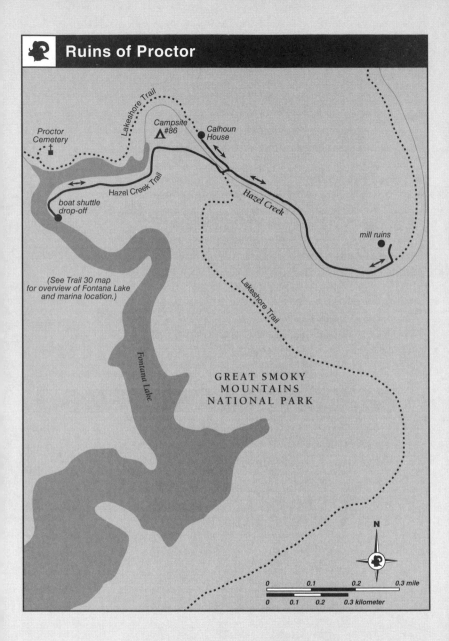

Ruins of Proctor

Proctor Cemetery

Lakeshore Trail

Campsite #86

Calhoun House

boat shuttle drop-off

Hazel Creek Trail

Hazel Creek

mill ruins

(See Trail 30 map for overview of Fontana Lake and marina location.)

Lakeshore Trail

Fontana Lake

GREAT SMOKY MOUNTAINS NATIONAL PARK

N

| 0 | 0.1 | 0.2 | 0.3 mile |
| 0 | 0.1 | 0.2 | 0.3 kilometer |

Ruins of Proctor

Take a boat shuttle on scenic Fontana Lake to Hazel Creek. Make an easy stroll to a backcountry camp, once the lumber town of Proctor. Explore the former townsite, heading up Hazel Creek to reach the relics of a mill, now covered in forest. Discover other area sites, including the Calhoun House.

Best Time

Late spring and summer are the best times to enjoy the boat ride on Fontana Lake. Warm weather also favors exploring the waters of Hazel Creek. The easy trail is enjoyable any time of year.

Finding the Trail

From the junction of US 321/TN 73 and East Lamar Alexander Parkway in Townsend, Tennessee, take US 321 west and then north 7.5 miles, and exit left (west) onto Foothills Parkway. Follow Foothills Parkway 16.9 miles south to its end at US 129 in Chilhowee. Turn left (south) onto US 129 and follow it 15 winding miles into North Carolina to reach NC 28. Turn left (east) onto NC 28, passing Fontana Village Resort on your right at 9 miles. In another 1.5 miles, turn left on Fontana Dam Road, with the sign for Fontana Dam on your right. Just after the turnoff, take the first right at the sign for Fontana Marina.

From the intersection of US 19 and Veterans Boulevard in Bryson City, North Carolina, take US 19/US 74 south for 8.8 miles. Then veer right (west) and follow NC 28 for 11.4 miles to the intersection

TRAIL USE
Day Hiking,
Backpacking,
Child Friendly

LENGTH
2.0 miles, 4–6 hours,
including boat shuttle

VERTICAL FEET
±70

DIFFICULTY
– **1** 2 3 4 5 +

TRAIL TYPE
Out-and-back

FEATURES
Lake
Stream
Autumn Colors
Wildflowers
Photo Opportunity
Backcountry Camping
Swimming
Historical Interest

FACILITIES
Restrooms near
Fontana Dam
Water

235

OPTIONS

Proctor Cemetery

Hike a half mile beyond the Calhoun House on the Lakeshore Trail to reach the spur to Proctor Cemetery. Many homesites and settler evidence lie up Possum Hollow beyond the cemetery.

with NC 143. Zero your trip odometer here and continue 9.9 miles west on NC 28. Turn right, with the sign for Fontana Dam on your left; then make another quick right at the sign for Fontana Marina.

Trail Description

Great Smoky Mountains National Park has a few tourist towns in its shadow. The towns have T-shirt shops, restaurants, museums, games, and rides . . . many swirling, climbing, splashing, round-and-round rides. If you want to lure your offspring to the park to feast upon the natural beauty contained within its boundaries, take them on this walk. It starts with a boat ride!

Take a boat shuttle from Fontana Marina, located far from the tourist towns, and cruise Fontana Lake. The crest of the Smokies rises on one

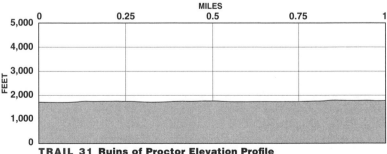

TRAIL 31 Ruins of Proctor Elevation Profile

side, while the peaks of the Nantahala National Forest flank the other. Narrow coves slice high green
ridges. You will travel easterly along the impoundment, which dammed the waters of the Little Tennessee River.

The sinuous lake stretches as far as the eye can
see, but you turn northeasterly up the Hazel Creek
embayment. Welch Ridge and Matt Mountain peer
down from above. If you can turn your head away
from the mountains and look into the water, you'll
notice the lake's unbelievable clarity—rocks, sub-
merged logs, and fish are visible 20 or more feet
deep. The Hazel Creek embayment narrows, twists,
and turns its last mile or so, following the course of
the streambed underneath. Thickly wooded ridges
crowd the now-slender waterway. Soon the sounds
of Hazel Creek rushing to meet the waters of Fontana Lake reach your ears.

It's time to jump off the boat and explore the
ruins of Proctor. This boat ride and stroll through
the Smoky Mountain past leave visitors with smiles
on their faces and the contrived attractions of the
tourist towns forgotten.

This adventure requires planning. Contact Fontana Marina at 828-498-2129 to arrange for a drop-
off and pickup shuttle. I recommend starting early
to get the most for your money—the shuttle isn't
cheap, but it's a unique way to enjoy the Smoky
Mountains National Park. It takes around an hour
to hike to the mill ruins and back to the boat drop-
off. If you start early, you'll have plenty of time to
explore the place at your leisure, have a picnic, fish,
and swim in Fontana Lake or in the chilly waters
of the Baptism Pool, a deep section of Hazel Creek.

By the way: because a backcountry campsite
is located a half mile from the boat drop-off, those
interested in camping can simply carry their stuff
from the lake to the campsite without needing a
backpack or any specialized gear. In fact, campers

Great Views

Lake

Sunlight filters *onto a lonely chimney from a time forgotten.*

here bring so-called luxury items such as camp chairs and coolers. Consider bringing less physically able campers to the site to experience the Smokies backcountry. You can simply arrange your pickup for the next day—or the day after.

In the 1830s, Moses Proctor settled near the town that was to bear his name. Others filtered in, farmers mostly. Small-scale mining and lumber operations took place. But in 1907, the Southern Railway ran through the nearby Little Tennessee River Valley, allowing easier access to Proctor. Ritter Lumber Company bought large tracts of land in the Hazel Creek Valley, then ran a spur rail line up Hazel Creek. They established a lumber boomtown at once-sleepy Proctor. The population grew to more than a thousand people, with all the services needed to feed, house, and entertain the lumbermen and their families.

By 1928, the town had peaked. An estimated 200 million board feet of lumber had been cut, processed, and shipped out on the railroad. The townspeople followed the lumber. At this time there was already talk of a national park being established here. By the mid-1940s, the entire valley was left to the beasts of the Smokies. The forest has recovered nicely, though signs of the logging days are visible.

Your exact drop-off spot may vary, depending on the lake level. ▶1 Immediately join the Hazel Creek Trail, traveling a wide gravel path. A canopy of black birch, red maple, and rhododendron borders the track. The stream drains the North Carolina high country west of Clingmans Dome. Hazel Creek, a storied fishing venue, is one of the bigger watercourses in the park.

At 0.5 mile, you reach the signpost for Campsite #86, Proctor. ▶2 To your left, trails lead under the big white pines that drop their fragrant needles on the large camping flat. This was once the playground for Proctor School, where the children of the

 Stream

 Backcountry Camping

Historical Interest

lumbermen were educated. The school stood on the hill to your right as you stand at the campsite sign-post. Sometimes it's hard to imagine that civilization once held fast in these now-wooded hills. But if you walk around, you will find artifacts large and small. Leave them for others to discover and enjoy.

Reach a trail junction and bridge at 0.6 mile. ▶3 Ahead, the Lakeshore Trail briefly follows what was Struttin' Street in the Proctor days, before leaving east for Forney Creek. Cross the bridge, then turn left on the Lakeshore Trail, heading downstream along Hazel Creek to reach the Calhoun House, built in 1923. I have seen the home locked and closed and at other times open for exploration. The park service formerly used it in their operations, but now it is kept as a purely historic building. The huge white oaks in front of the house saw Proctor in its heyday.

Stream

Historical Interest

Now backtrack to the bridge, this time heading up the Hazel Creek Trail. Note the old field to your left, growing up in walnut trees. Look for squared-off flat spots, old roadbeds, metal washtubs, and other imprints of Proctor. You are now circling around the huge flat upon which the lumber mill, trains, logs, boards, and attendant facilities stood. What once was a loud and noisy place has reverted to nature but still holds its past underneath the brush and trees.

At 1.0 mile, look left for a clear trail leading into the woods away from Hazel Creek. The path travels a berm between former log ponds. Shortly reach the brick and concrete mill ruins, ▶4 along with assorted junk, even a bathtub. *As is the case with any abandoned structure, look around, but be careful.* Notice how nature is reclaiming the area, with trees growing in, around, and over the ruins.

🚶	**MILESTONES**		
▶1	0.0	Boat drop-off at the mouth of Hazel Creek
▶2	0.5	Campsite #86
▶3	0.6	Bridge over Hazel Creek
▶4	1.0	Mill ruins

CHAPTER 5

Deep, Forney, and Noland Creeks Area

Deep, Forney, and Noland Creeks Area

The Deep, Forney, and Noland Creeks area consists of three major drainages that flow from the highest point in the park—Clingmans Dome—into North Carolina near Bryson City. A variance in flora and fauna characterizes the extreme elevation changes. Altitudes range from higher than 6,600 feet along the state-line ridge dividing North Carolina and Tennessee down to 1,700 feet near the park entrance at Deep Creek and the full pool level of Fontana Lake.

Both Forney Creek and Noland Creek flow into Fontana Lake. Deep Creek flows into the Tuckasegee River, which flows into Fontana Lake. Up high, you will encounter one of the larger swaths of Canadian-type spruce–fir forest, an ice age relic cloaking only the highest reaches of the park. The spruce–fir zone includes not only the main crest but also the upper ridges that divide the streamsheds: Forney Ridge, Noland Divide, and Thomas Divide.

Descending in elevation, the forest types blend into northern hardwoods, cove hardwoods, and pine–oak on drier sites. Along the streams, dense temperate jungles of black birch, yellow birch, sycamore, and tulip trees rise above massive thickets of rhododendron and doghobble. Crystalline streams crash over rocks, occasionally slowing to form pools where trout furtively ply a rich subaquatic food chain.

The lower portions of these now deeply wooded valleys were once settled by pre-park pioneers, who gave their names to many of the tributaries: Bumgardner Branch, Huggins Creek, and more. In addition to being settled, parts of the area were logged, from a small-scale selective cutting operation on Deep Creek to a near-complete forest takedown using railroads on Forney Creek. The woodland has recovered well from both pioneer settlement and timber operations. Coincidentally, hikers use many of the old timber-harvesting railroad grades as trails. Later, the Civilian Conservation Corps

Opposite and overleaf: Verdant forests *rise in the hills and hollows of the Great Smoky Mountains.*

enhanced or otherwise created more trails, some of which unfortunately have been abandoned.

The streams and ridges attract hikers, backpackers, equestrians, anglers, tubers, and campers who overnight at Deep Creek Campground. Visitors also stay in Bryson City, adjacent to the park. The hikes described are primarily loops, including both day hikes and overnight treks. The area's primary features—the vista at Andrews Bald, the spruce–fir forests, several waterfalls on gorgeous streams, a slice of Fontana Lake, and pioneer home-steads—can be seen here. Hikers enter the high country from Clingmans Dome Road. Hikers enter the "lowlands" near Bryson City, from the Deep Creek Campground and day-use area, as well as Lakeview Drive, also known as the Road to Nowhere.

Permits

Permits are *not* required for day hiking. Backpackers must get a backcountry permit to stay at one of the 23 designated backcountry campsites and trail shelters in this area. All campsites require a reservation, which you can make online at smokiespermits.nps.gov, then print at home.

Maps

For the Deep, Forney, and Noland Creeks area, you will need the following USGS 7.5-minute (1:24,000-scale) topographic quadrangles, listed in geographic order as you hike along your route:

Trail 32: *Noland Creek*
Trail 33: *Bryson City, Clingmans Dome*
Trail 34: *Bryson City*
Trail 35: *Bryson City, Clingmans Dome, Smokemont*
Trail 36: *Clingmans Dome*
Trail 37: *Clingmans Dome, Silers Bald, Noland Creek*
Trail 38: *Clingmans Dome*

Deep, Forney, and Noland Creeks Area (Trails 32–38)

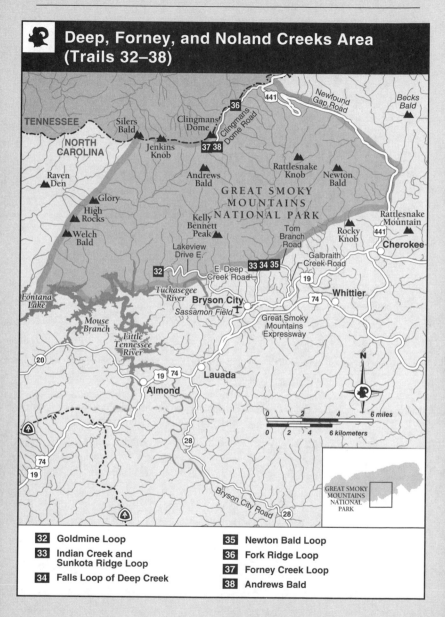

32	Goldmine Loop	
33	Indian Creek and Sunkota Ridge Loop	
34	Falls Loop of Deep Creek	
35	Newton Bald Loop	
36	Fork Ridge Loop	
37	Forney Creek Loop	
38	Andrews Bald	

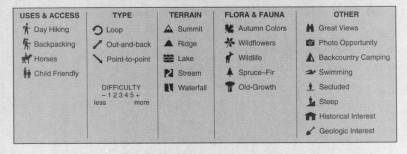

Deep, Forney, and Noland Creeks Area

TRAIL	DIFFICULTY	LENGTH	TYPE	USES & ACCESS	TERRAIN	FLORA & FAUNA	OTHER
32	2	3.2	Loop	Day Hiking, Backpacking, Horses	Lake, Stream	Autumn Colors, Wildflowers	Backcountry Camping, Swimming, Secluded, Historical Interest
33	3	12.0	Loop	Day Hiking, Backpacking, Horses	Ridge, Stream, Waterfall	Autumn Colors, Wildflowers	Backcountry Camping, Secluded, Historical Interest
34	1–2	2.4	Loop	Day Hiking, Child Friendly	Stream, Waterfall	Autumn Colors, Wildflowers	Photo Opportunity, Swimming, Historical Interest
35	5	22.5	Loop	Backpacking, Horses	Ridge, Stream, Waterfall	Autumn Colors, Wildflowers, Wildlife	Backcountry Camping, Swimming, Secluded, Historical Interest
36	5	20.1	Loop	Backpacking, Horses	Ridge, Stream	Autumn Colors, Wildflowers, Spruce–Fir	Great Views, Backcountry Camping, Swimming, Secluded, Steep
37	5	19.4	Loop	Backpacking, Horses	Ridge, Stream, Waterfall	Autumn Colors, Wildflowers, Spruce–Fir	Great Views, Photo Opportunity, Backcountry Camping, Swimming, Steep, Historical Interest
38	2	3.6	Out-and-back	Day Hiking, Child Friendly	Summit, Ridge	Autumn Colors, Wildflowers, Spruce–Fir	Great Views, Photo Opportunity

USES & ACCESS	TYPE	TERRAIN	FLORA & FAUNA	OTHER
🏃 Day Hiking	↻ Loop	△ Summit	✻ Autumn Colors	Ⓜ Great Views
🎒 Backpacking	↗ Out-and-back	▲ Ridge	✺ Wildflowers	📷 Photo Opportunity
🐎 Horses	↘ Point-to-point	≋ Lake	🦌 Wildlife	⛺ Backcountry Camping
👫 Child Friendly		⚑ Stream	🌲 Spruce–Fir	➷ Swimming
	DIFFICULTY	⚑ Waterfall	🌳 Old-Growth	⚊ Secluded
	– 1 2 3 4 5 +			⚊ Steep
	less more			🏠 Historical Interest
				✎ Geologic Interest

Deep, Forney, and Noland Creeks Area

Travel a seldom-trod area of the Smokies, finding forgotten chimneys of old homesites. Gain views of Fontana Lake and small streams that feed it. Several old roads and trails spur off the loop, luring budding historians.

On this rewarding but long day hike, pass two waterfalls and then walk along old homesteads amid riverine habitat of Indian Creek. Climb to Martins Gap and return via the quiet Sunkota Ridge Trail, with its drier forest.

This great family day hike has numerous rewards. Visit Juney Whank Falls, then cruise hills above Deep Creek before returning to visit cataracts on Indian Creek. Enjoy a streamside cruise on lower Deep Creek, passing Tom Branch Falls.

Head up the famed fishing waters of Deep Creek to a streamside camp beneath white pines. Next, climb to a backcountry campsite 5,000 feet high on Thomas Divide. Follow the quiet Thomas Divide Trail back to Deep Creek.

TRAIL 36

Backpacking, Horses
20.1 miles, Loop
Difficulty: 1 2 3 4 **5**

Fork Ridge Loop 277

This challenging backpack loop has major elevation changes. Explore spruce–fir ridges and camp near high-elevation streams. Descend beneath big spruce and yellow birch trees on Fork Ridge to junglelike Deep Creek. Climb to the Appalachian Trail with views from Mount Collins.

TRAIL 37

Backpacking, Horses
19.4 miles, Loop
Difficulty: 1 2 3 4 **5**

Forney Creek Loop 285

This tough but rewarding backpacking trek involves numerous creek fords and an elevation change of more than 4,000 feet one-way! Travel Forney Ridge, passing Andrews Bald, to make Forney Creek. Ascend Forney Creek and visit Forney Creek Cascades on your return trip.

TRAIL 38

Day Hiking,
Child Friendly
3.6 miles,
Out-and-back
Difficulty: 1 **2** 3 4 5

Andrews Bald 293

From the park's highest trailhead, explore the extraordinary spruce–fir forest community on the way to the meadow of Andrews Bald, resplendent with stunning views.

Goldmine Loop

Travel a seldom-trod area of the Smokies, finding forgotten chimneys of old homesites. Gain views of Fontana Lake and small streams that feed it. Several old roads and trails spur off the loop, luring budding historians.

Best Time

Summer is when Fontana Lake is at full pool and best for swimming. During fall the trails are their driest. Open winter woods reveal old homesites most clearly and offer maximum solitude.

Finding the Trail

From the intersection of US 19 and US 441 South in Cherokee, North Carolina, head east on US 19 to Bryson City, North Carolina. After 10 miles, turn right just after the Swain County Courthouse onto Everett Street, which becomes Fontana Road and then Lakeview Drive. The parking area is 8.8 miles from the courthouse in Bryson City, at the end of Lakeview Drive.

Trail Description

The Goldmine Loop is an undiscovered gem of a day hike in the Smoky Mountains. Along the way you will see pioneer homesites and a slice of Fontana Lake and journey through the tunnel on the Road to Nowhere. Several old roads and trails branch off the Goldmine Loop, so watch your direction.

TRAIL USE
Day Hiking,
Backpacking, Horses

LENGTH
3.2 miles, 1½–2½ hours

VERTICAL FEET
±650

DIFFICULTY
– 1 **2** 3 4 5 +

TRAIL TYPE
Loop

FEATURES
Lake
Stream
Autumn Colors
Wildflowers
Backcountry Camping
Swimming
Secluded
Historical Interest

FACILITIES
None

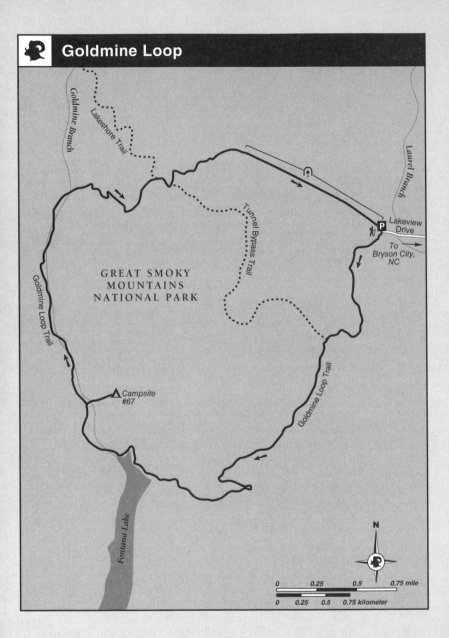

Goldmine Loop

Goldmine Branch

Lakeshore Trail

Laurel Branch

Tunnel Bypass Trail

GREAT SMOKY
MOUNTAINS
NATIONAL PARK

Lakeview
Drive

P

To
Bryson City,
NC

Goldmine Loop Trail

△ Campsite
#67

Goldmine Loop Trail

Fontana Lake

N

| 0 | 0.25 | 0.5 | 0.75 mile |

| 0 | 0.25 | 0.5 | 0.75 kilometer |

With your back to the Lakeview Drive parking area, ►1 pick up the Tunnel Bypass Trail across Lakeview Drive. The tunnel is to your right and will be your return route. Once on the singletrack Tunnel Bypass Trail, briefly traipse through a mountain laurel and rhododendron thicket, and then climb to a small gap at 0.3 mile. Several faint abandoned trails converge here. Proceed straight through the gap under pine, oak, and hickory woodland dotted with flowering dogwood. Skirt a knob to arrive at another gap and a trail junction at 0.4 mile. ►2 Here, the Tunnel Bypass Trail leaves right 1.2 miles for the Lakeshore Trail, avoiding a trip through the tunnel bisecting Tunnel Ridge. This loop heads left with the Goldmine Loop Trail on a modest ridge.

Turn left on the Goldmine Loop Trail, and descend the slim crest well above Fontana Lake. At 0.9 mile, curve left to find Tunnel Branch and an old roadbed. A homesite was likely just upstream but is now under a tangle of briers. The moisture-loving forest of beech, black birch, and tulip trees is denser than on the ridgetop. Tunnel Branch flows downhill under a sea of rhododendron to meet its mother waters of Fontana Lake, formerly the free-flowing Tuckasegee River.

The old road turns away from Tunnel Branch and comes to Fontana Lake and the embayment of Goldmine Branch at 1.3 miles. ►3 Rich woodland reflects

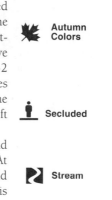

Autumn Colors

Secluded

Stream

The sites of homes, schools, and churches now lie under Fontana Lake.

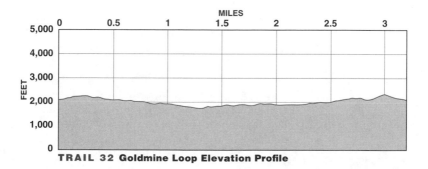

TRAIL 32 Goldmine Loop Elevation Profile

Paddlers can access *Smokies trails from Fontana Lake.*

off the still blue-green waters of the impoundment. When drawn down, the lake's exposed mud bottom impairs the scenery.

Intersect another old road. Funny thing about these pre-park, pre-dam roads—they'll take you **Lake** right to the lake, where you can see that the road continues but is now under water. A short trip left will take you to the lake, but the official Goldmine Loop Trail veers right away from the lake to cross a tiny creek and then Hyatt Branch. Span Goldmine Branch at 1.5 miles. Look for a small falls below the Goldmine Branch crossing. Judging by what the poor pioneers left behind, there was never any gold in these parts. Intersect the spur trail to Goldmine **Backcountry** Branch campsite #67 at 1.6 miles. ▶4 This campsite, **Camping** located at an open homesite a few hundred yards up the side trail, makes for a great one-night trip. Odds are you'll have the campsite to yourself.

Resume a northbound, sometimes-muddy track astride small and shallow Goldmine Branch. Ahead, the trail briefly leaves the road and skirts to the right of a homesite to rejoin the old road. The diminutive valley harbors a rhododendron tunnel under which you pass. Homesite clearings persist despite decades of park reforestation. A chimney stands mute near the path at 2.2 miles. ►5 Consider the events that took place before that hearth.

🌼 **Wildflowers**

🏠 **Historical Interest**

Swing past the homesite in another rhododendron tunnel to emerge atop the hollow. The old road continues straight, but the Goldmine Loop makes a sharp right, heads uphill to a saddle, and then veers left for a short but steep climb to meet the Lakeshore Trail at 2.5 miles. ►6

Turn right on the Lakeshore Trail. Cruise easterly through oak woods, passing the other end of the Tunnel Bypass Trail. Keep forward to reach the Lakeview Drive tunnel. Let your eyes adjust, and you can walk through it sans flashlight. Traverse the 0.2-mile long tunnel to emerge near Lakeview Drive and reach the trailhead. ►7

🚶	**MILESTONES**	
►1	0.0	Lakeview Drive Trailhead
►2	0.4	Left on Goldmine Loop Trail
►3	1.3	Fontana Lake
►4	1.6	Spur trail to Goldmine Branch campsite #67
►5	2.2	Trailside chimney
►6	2.5	Right on Lakeshore Trail
►7	3.2	Lakeview Drive Trailhead

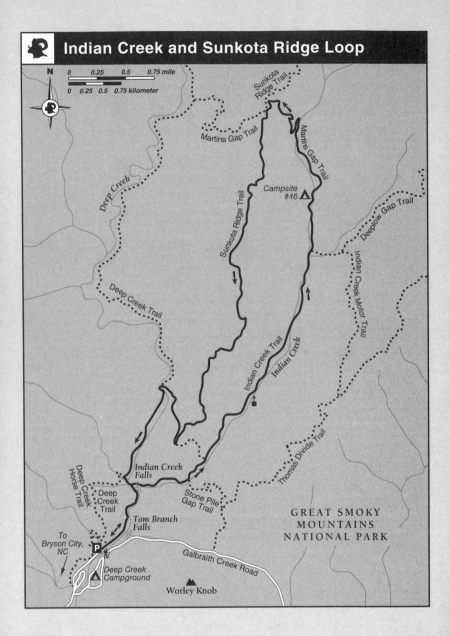

Indian Creek and Sunkota Ridge Loop

N

| 0 | 0.25 | 0.5 | 0.75 mile |
| 0 | 0.25 | 0.5 | 0.75 kilometer |

Sunkota Ridge Trail

Martins Gap Trail

Martins Gap Trail

Deep Creek

Campsite #46 △

Deeplow Gap Trail

Sunkota Ridge Trail

Deep Creek Trail

Indian Creek Motor Trail

Indian Creek Trail

Indian Creek

Thomas Divide Trail

Deep Creek Horse Trail

Indian Creek Falls

Deep Creek Trail

Stone Pile Gap Trail

GREAT SMOKY MOUNTAINS NATIONAL PARK

Tom Branch Falls

To Bryson City, NC

P

Deep Creek Campground

Galbraith Creek Road

Worley Knob

Indian Creek and Sunkota Ridge Loop

On this long but rewarding day hike, pass two waterfalls and then walk along old homesteads amid the riverine habitat of Indian Creek. Climb to Martins Gap and return via the quiet Sunkota Ridge Trail, with its drier forest.

Best Time

Winter offers maximum solitude and leafless woods, where you can see the homesites of Indian Creek more clearly. Spring presents wildflowers and the waterfalls at their boldest. Fall colors on Sunkota Ridge can be stunning. The trailhead and first 0.7 mile of the hike may be a madhouse in summer. The secluded part of the hike starts beyond this first 0.7 mile.

Finding the Trail

From the intersection of US 19 and US 441 South in Cherokee, North Carolina, head east on US 19 to Bryson City, North Carolina. After 10 miles, turn right just after the Swain County Courthouse onto Everett Street. In 0.2 mile, a couple of blocks after you cross the Tuckasegee River, turn right onto Depot Street. In 0.2 mile, turn left onto Ramseur Street at the brown DEEP CREEK CAMPGROUND sign, and then make an immediate right onto Deep Creek Road. In 0.3 mile, veer left (north) onto West Deep Creek Road at another brown campground sign. (The route is well signed throughout.) In about 2 miles, reach the park entrance—you'll see a snack bar and tubing rentals on your right. A short

TRAIL USE
Day Hiking,
Backpacking, Horses

LENGTH
12.0 miles, 6–7½ hours

VERTICAL FEET
±1,900

DIFFICULTY
– 1 2 **3** 4 5 +

TRAIL TYPE
Loop

FEATURES
Ridgeline
Stream
Waterfall
Autumn Colors
Wildflowers
Backcountry Camping
Secluded
Historical Interest

FACILITIES
Campground
Picnic Tables
Restrooms
Water

distance later, veer left toward the sign reading TRAILHEAD, WATERFALLS. The Deep Creek Trail starts just north of the picnic area, 0.6 mile from the park entrance.

From Exit 27 off I-40 west of Asheville, head west on US 74 for 40 miles to Exit 67 in Bryson City. Turn right (west) onto Veterans Boulevard and, after 0.6 mile, turn right on Main Street. In 0.2 mile, turn left on Everett Street and follow the directions above to the campground.

Sunkota **is the pioneer interpretation of the Cherokee word for "apple."**

Trail Description

You can appreciate the biological diversity of the Smokies on this valley and ridge trek. This circuit follows Deep Creek to Indian Creek, past Tom Branch Falls then Indian Creek Falls before you've gone a mile. Leave any crowds behind to climb to Martins Gap and return via the quiet Sunkota Ridge Trail, with its drier forest, then along Deep Creek and its accompanying riverine habitat.

Stream

Waterfall

The Deep Creek Trail ►1 makes a wide track as it passes the spur trail to Juney Whank Falls. It reaches Tom Branch Falls at 0.2 mile. Tom Branch spills in four stages over rock slabs to fill Deep

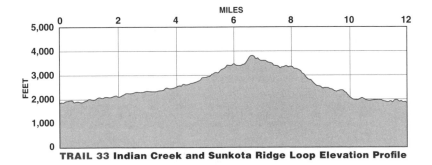

TRAIL 33 Indian Creek and Sunkota Ridge Loop Elevation Profile

A hiker checks out *trail signs at Martins Gap.*

Creek, as Deep Creek in turn rushes over gray rocks, sometimes mossy, sometimes not, then slows in still pools. Bridge Deep Creek at 0.4 mile, just below an alluring pool.

Reach the Indian Creek Trail junction at 0.7 mile. ▶2 Turn right on the Indian Creek Trail, coming to Indian Creek Falls at 0.8 mile. ▶3 A short side trail on your left leads to the base of the falls, which slopes 25 feet over a fanlike rock face into a large pool.

Gain a top-down view of Indian Creek Falls as you continue on up the trail, bridging Indian Creek at 0.9 mile. At 1.2 miles, the Stone Pile Gap Trail leaves right for Thomas Divide. ▶4 This hike keeps up the moist valley amid everywhere-you-look beauty. Notice shiny mica rock at your feet. At 1.5 miles, the Loop Trail heads up Sunkota Ridge. ▶5

Stay north on the Indian Creek Trail. Look for remnants of clearings and nonnative trailside bushes. Locust and tulip trees are reclaiming the homesites. At 2.0 miles, bordering hills squeeze Indian Creek into a tight valley. At 2.2 miles, a spur trail leads to a pioneer cemetery. The valley widens again. At 2.9 miles, bridge Indian Creek. Bridge it again at 3.3 miles, then pass a second spur to

> A series of pioneer homesites appears on the creek sides.

❋ **Wildflowers**

🏠 **Historical Interest**

A Shorter, Easier Trek

To cut 8.8 miles from your hike, use the Loop Trail. Start this hike as described, but at 1.5 miles, leave the Indian Creek Trail left on the Loop Trail, climbing 400 feet in a half mile to a gap on Sunkota Ridge. From here, continue tracing the Loop Trail downhill to the flat at Jenkins Place on Deep Creek. The wide Deep Creek Trail allows you to watch the delightful creek splash down the valley while you return to the trailhead.

Stream

another pioneer graveyard. At mile 3.6, bridge the creek again just before meeting the Deeplow Gap Trail. ▶6 *Bicycles are not allowed beyond this point.*

Continue up Indian Creek, bridging it at 4.0, 4.3, and 4.5 miles to its end at 4.6 miles, in an old road turnaround near Estes Branch and backcountry campsite #46. ▶7

Backcountry Camping ⚠

Here, the park service arbitrarily starts the Martins Gap Trail. Cross now-smaller Indian Creek three times in a half mile on slim footbridges before switchbacking up Sunkota Ridge. Arrive at Martins Gap, a sag on Sunkota Ridge, at 6.0 miles. ▶8 Turn left on the serene singletrack Sunkota Ridge Trail.

Climb 450 feet to the loop's high point of 3,800 feet at 6.7 miles. ▶9 Begin a slow descent, winding along the ridgetop and its flanks. Enjoy your well-earned downgrade under oaks, maples, and pines. The higher Thomas Divide and Noland Divide are visible beyond the trees. A watery symphony from Indian Creek and Deep Creek drifts into your ears.

Autumn Colors 🍁

At 9.7 miles, meet the Loop Trail. ▶10 Turn right on the Loop Trail, descending to a flat and the old Jenkins Place, another pioneer homestead, to intersect Deep Creek Trail at 10.3 miles. ▶11 Follow the wide Deep Creek Trail downstream over three bridges to meet the Indian Creek Trail at 11.3 miles. ▶12 Return to the trailhead on the short section of the Deep Creek Trail you traversed earlier. Complete your loop at 12.0 miles. ▶13

🚶 MILESTONES

▶1	0.0	Deep Creek Trailhead
▶2	0.7	Right on Indian Creek Trail
▶3	0.8	Indian Creek Falls
▶4	1.2	Pass Stone Pile Gap Trail
▶5	1.5	Pass Loop Trail
▶6	3.6	Pass Deeplow Gap Trail
▶7	4.6	Campsite #46; join Martin Gap Trail
▶8	6.0	Martins Gap, and left on Sunkota Ridge Trail
▶9	6.7	High point of hike
▶10	9.7	Right on Loop Trail
▶11	10.3	Left on Deep Creek Trail at Jenkins Place
▶12	11.3	Pass Indian Creek Trail
▶13	12.0	Deep Creek Trailhead

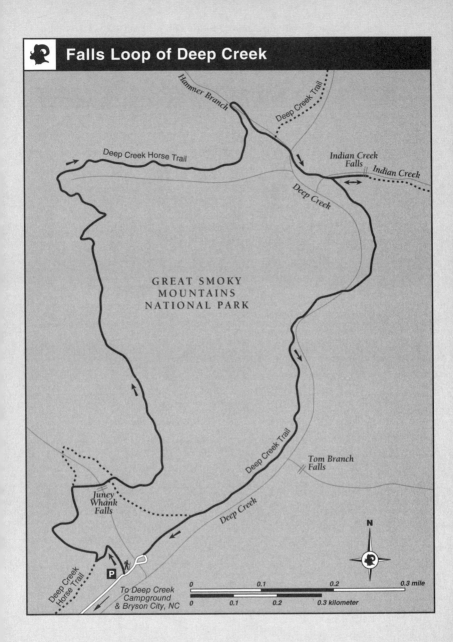

Falls Loop of Deep Creek

Hammer Branch

Deep Creek Trail

Deep Creek Horse Trail

Indian Creek
Falls

Indian Creek

Deep Creek

GREAT SMOKY
MOUNTAINS
NATIONAL PARK

Deep Creek Trail

Tom Branch
Falls

Juney
Whank
Falls

Deep Creek

Deep Creek

N

Deep Creek
Horse Trail

P

To Deep Creek
Campground
& Bryson City, NC

| 0 | | 0.1 | | 0.2 | | 0.3 mile |

| 0 | 0.1 | 0.2 | 0.3 kilometer |

Falls Loop of Deep Creek

This great family day hike has numerous rewards. Visit Juney Whank Falls, then cruise hills above Deep Creek before returning to visit a cataract on Indian Creek. Enjoy a streamside cruise on lower Deep Creek, passing Tom Branch Falls.

Best Time

Winter and spring are best for seeing these waterfalls at their boldest; you'll also find solitude then. Water lovers will want to come here during summer, but many others will enjoy the aquatic features with you then.

Finding the Trail

From the intersection of US 19 and US 441 South in Cherokee, North Carolina, head east on US 19 to Bryson City, North Carolina. After 10 miles, turn right just after the Swain County Courthouse onto Everett Street. In 0.2 mile, a couple of blocks after you cross the Tuckasegee River, turn right onto Depot Street. In 0.2 mile, turn left onto Ramseur Street at the brown DEEP CREEK CAMPGROUND sign, and then make an immediate right onto Deep Creek Road. In 0.3 mile, veer left (north) onto West Deep Creek Road at another brown campground sign. (The route is well signed throughout.) In about 2 miles, reach the park entrance—you'll see a snack bar and tubing rentals on your right. A short distance later, veer left toward the sign reading TRAILHEAD, WATERFALLS. The Juney Whank Falls Trail heads northwest from the upper

TRAIL USE
Day Hiking,
Child Friendly

LENGTH
2.4 miles, 1–2 hours

VERTICAL FEET
±390

DIFFICULTY
– **1 2** 3 4 5 +

TRAIL TYPE
Loop

FEATURES
Stream
Waterfall
Autumn Colors
Wildflowers
Photo Opportunity
Swimming
Historical Interest

FACILITIES
Campground
Picnic Tables
Water
Restrooms

end of the trail parking area, just before the auto turnaround and the Deep Creek Trailhead, 0.6 mile from the park entrance.

From Exit 27 off I-40 west of Asheville, head west on US 74 for 40 miles to Exit 67 in Bryson City. Turn right (west) onto Veterans Boulevard and, after 0.6 mile, turn right on Main Street. In 0.2 mile, turn left on Everett Street and follow the directions above to the campground.

Trail Description

This hike begins at the developed Deep Creek area, ▶1 with its campground and picnic facilities, located on the park's edge near Bryson City. The Juney Whank Falls Trail leads uphill in rich woods, climbing along Juney Whank Branch. It isn't long before you reach the slender two-tier cataract that spills in a slender ribbon over a rock face, then under the trail before making a second dive toward Deep Creek.

Beyond here, the hike wanders back to Deep Creek before it travels up another tributary, Indian Creek. Indian Creek Falls is a larger, wider waterfall

This family day hike is great for anybody who loves a waterfall. It has three, centered on Deep Creek and its tributaries.

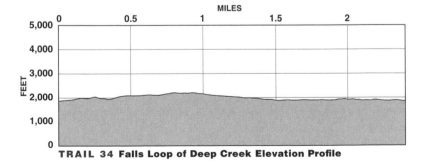

TRAIL 34 Falls Loop of Deep Creek Elevation Profile

that spills into a large pool. Next you return to Deep Creek, enjoying its everywhere-you-look beauty before coming to yet another tributary, Tom Branch. It makes a dramatic rocky plunge as it meets Deep Creek. A little more waterside walking returns you to the parking area.

Avoid this hike in the summertime if you disdain crowds. Lower Deep Creek can be crazy with tubers floating from the confluence of Indian Creek and Deep Creek through the Deep Creek Campground and beyond the park border.

The Juney Whank Falls Trail starts out as a wide gravel path leading from the parking area. Juney Whank Branch flows calmly to your right after pouring off Beaugard Ridge. Shortly veer away from the watercourse, climbing to meet the Deep Creek Horse Trail at 0.1 mile. Watch for horses here, as a concessionaire operates nearby, using this route for a short distance. Stay right with the equestrian path in the second-growth woods of maple, pine, buckeye, beech, and tulip trees.

Reach the spur trail to Juney Whank Falls after a quarter mile. ▶2 Turn right here and descend a hill to reach a bridge and the falls. The low-flow cascade spills close enough to the bridge with a built-in observation deck and seat that you can nearly touch the water.

Leave Juney Whank Falls, rejoining the Deep Creek Horse Trail, after you pass a shortcut leading right, down to Deep Creek. Travel in pine–oak woods, turning up a quiet hollow. Dogwoods are plentiful here. The short tree with scaly brown bark and a widespread crown is easy to identify. It is widely regarded as one of the most beautiful trees in the Southeast. Dogwoods range from the eastern Texas north to Michigan, east to Massachusetts, and south to Florida. It grows in both moist and dry soils below 3,000 feet in the Smokies. In the spring, dogwoods offer showy white or pinkish blooms.

The waterfalls are at their most dramatic during winter, when they're frozen, and spring, when they flow strongest.

Waterfall

Tom Branch Falls *spills into Deep Creek.*

 Autumn Colors

After greening up, dogwoods produce a shiny red fruit in fall. These small, berrylike fruits taste bitter to humans but are an important food for birds. Dogwood is extremely hard and is used to make mallet heads, jeweler's blocks, and spools. The Cherokee used dogwood roots to make a red dye. Dogwoods growing in shady woods, such as these, are susceptible to a fungus known as dogwood anthracnose.

Reach a high point and a gap at 0.8 mile. ▶3
The Deep Creek Trail drifts toward Hammer Branch,
following a trickling tributary. Curve to step over
fast-flowing Hammer Branch, as a spur trail leaves for
a pioneer cemetery. This hike then bridges Hammer
Branch to meet the Deep Creek Trail at 1.4 miles. ▶4
Watch for bicycles in the next section, primarily during summer. Deep Creek flows broad and boisterous
as you cross the stream on a wide bridge. Span Indian
Creek to meet the Indian Creek Trail at 1.5 miles.

Your second waterfall ▶5 stands a football field
distant, up the Indian Creek Trail. An access path
leads to the base of this broad, tumbling froth of
whitewater. Indian Creek Falls plunges over a rock
face into a pool open to the sky overhead. While
here, grab a top-down view from the Indian Creek
Trail, too.

Your return trip leads down Deep Creek. The
trail travels well above the creek, where you can
look directly into the water. The path drops creekside, then bridges Deep Creek. At 2.2 miles, reach
your final fall. ▶2 Here, repose benches make a perfect observation point to see Tom Branch stairstep
over a series of rock ledges, finally meeting Deep
Creek. From here, your trip returns to the parking
area after 0.2 mile. ▶7

 **Historical
Interest**

**Photo
Opportunity**

Waterfall

🚶	MILESTONES		
▶1	0.0	Deep Creek Trailhead	
▶2	0.1	Deep Creek Horse Trail and Juney Whank Falls	
▶3	0.8	High point at gap	
▶4	1.4	Deep Creek Trail	
▶5	1.6	Indian Creek Falls	
▶6	2.2	Tom Branch Falls	
▶7	2.4	Deep Creek Trailhead	

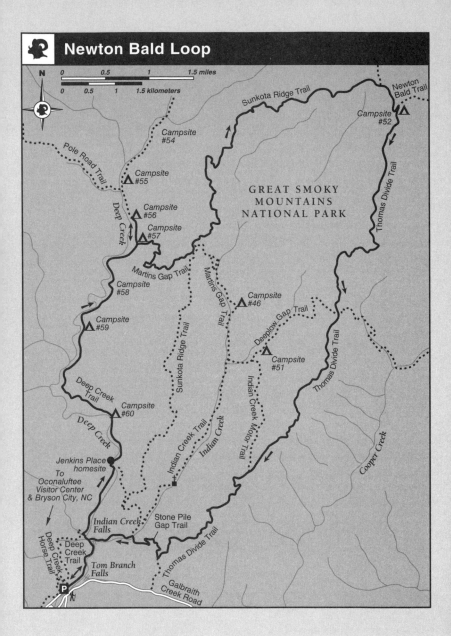

Newton Bald Loop

N

| 0 | 0.5 | 1 | 1.5 miles |
| 0 | 0.5 | 1 | 1.5 kilometers |

Sunkota Ridge Trail

Newton Bald Trail

Campsite #52

Campsite #54

Pole Road Trail

GREAT SMOKY MOUNTAINS NATIONAL PARK

Thomas Divide Trail

Campsite #55

Deep Creek

Campsite #56

Campsite #57

Martins Gap Trail

Martins Gap Trail

Campsite #58

Campsite #46

Deeplow Gap Trail

Campsite #59

Sunkota Ridge Trail

Campsite #51

Deep Creek Trail

Indian Creek Motor Trail

Thomas Divide Trail

Campsite #60

Deep Creek

Indian Creek

Cooper Creek

Jenkins Place homesite

To Oconaluftee Visitor Center & Bryson City, NC

Indian Creek Trail

Indian Creek

Indian Creek Falls

Stone Pile Gap Trail

Deep Creek Horse Trail

Deep Creek Trail

Tom Branch Falls

Thomas Divide Trail

Galbraith Creek Road

P

Newton Bald Loop

Head up the famed fishing waters of Deep Creek to a streamside camp beneath white pines. Next, climb to a backcountry campsite 5,000 feet high on Thomas Divide. Follow the quiet Thomas Divide Trail back to Deep Creek.

Best Time

Summer and early fall are ideal for fishing and swimming. Even during hot spells, Deep Creek and Newton Bald will still be cool. Winter is a good option, too, because the trip requires no fords, even though it offers miles of streamside trekking in addition to high-country action.

Finding the Trail

From the intersection of US 19 and US 441 South in Cherokee, North Carolina, head east on US 19 to Bryson City, North Carolina. After 10 miles, turn right just after the Swain County Courthouse onto Everett Street. In 0.2 mile, a couple of blocks after you cross the Tuckasegee River, turn right onto Depot Street. In 0.2 mile, turn left onto Ramseur Street at the brown DEEP CREEK CAMPGROUND sign, and then make an immediate right onto Deep Creek Road. In 0.3 mile, veer left (north) onto West Deep Creek Road at another brown campground sign. (The route is well signed throughout.) In about 2 miles, reach the park entrance—you'll see a snack bar and tubing rentals on your right. A short distance later, veer left toward the sign reading TRAILHEAD, WATERFALLS. The Deep Creek Trail

TRAIL USE
Backpacking, Horses
LENGTH
22.5 miles,
11–13½ hours
VERTICAL FEET
±3,100
DIFFICULTY
– 1 2 3 4 **5** +
TRAIL TYPE
Loop

FEATURES
Ridgeline
Stream
Waterfall
Autumn Colors
Wildflowers
Wildlife
Backcountry Camping
Swimming
Secluded
Historical Interest
FACILITIES
Campground
Picnic Tables
Restrooms
Water

starts just north of the picnic area, 0.6 mile from the park entrance.

From Exit 27 off I-40 west of Asheville, head west on US 74 for 40 miles to Exit 67 in Bryson City. Turn right (west) onto Veterans Boulevard and, after 0.6 mile, turn right on Main Street. In 0.2 mile, turn left on Everett Street and follow the directions above to the campground.

Trail Description

Expect to see bear scat, if not bears, on Sunkota Ridge and Thomas Divide.

Enjoy an archetypal Smoky Mountain stream, and camp beside its singing waters. Next, loop into the high country and overnight at 5,000 feet on this two-night backpacking adventure. First you'll head up the famed waters of Deep Creek, where many a fishing exploit has taken place (then exaggerated about). Camp at a streamside site on a carpet of pine needles beneath a white pine grove.

Next, leave the Deep Creek watershed via the steep Martins Gap Trail. Hike Sunkota Ridge, where a ridgetop trek leads to lesser-used Newton Bald backcountry campsite on Thomas Divide. Finally, head south on Thomas Divide Trail back to Deep

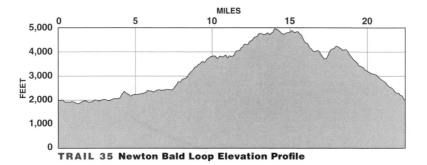

TRAIL 35 Newton Bald Loop Elevation Profile

Creek, completing the circuit, but not before passing Indian Creek Falls.

Begin the hike on the wide Deep Creek Trail, ▶1 humming with hikers, bikers, and tubers in the summertime, to pass Tom Branch Falls at 0.2 mile. The tributary spills over rock ledges into Deep Creek. Pass the Indian Creek Trail junction at 0.7 mile. ▶2 Bridge Indian Creek and continue up Deep Creek Trail. The wide track continues upstream, crossing three bridges to meet the Loop Trail at the Jenkins Place homesite at 1.7 miles. ▶3 The graded trail narrows some, and summertime crowds thin out. Wander alongside Deep Creek, which is following gravity's orders as it drains the Carolina side of Mount Collins, as well as the streams flowing down Noland Divide and Thomas Divide. Cross Bumgardner Branch, reaching Bumgardner Branch backcountry campsite #60 at 2.9 miles. ▶4 Stay on the east bank of Deep Creek, rising far above the stream while surmounting Bumgardner Ridge. The creek sounds fade.

Waterfall

Backcountry Camping

Drop to McCracken Branch backcountry campsite #59 at mile 4.2. ▶5 Repeat the pattern of rise and fall to make Nicks Nest Branch backcountry campsite #58 at mile 5.5 ▶6 Trace the right bank of Deep Creek, coming to historic Bryson Place and the Martins Gap Trail, at 5.9 miles. ▶7 Once the site of a backwoods cabin and a hunting lodge, this piney place was a favorite haunt of famed outdoors writer and national park proponent Horace Kephart. Today, the locale hosts Bryson Place backcountry campsite #57.

Backcountry Camping

Fishing continues to be a recreational pastime of many Smokies visitors. A monument to Mr. Kephart is just off the trail, on the Deep Creek side of the path before you reach the small stream at Bryson Place campsite. The monument spot was the location of Kephart's last camp in the Smokies before he perished in an automobile crash near Bryson City.

Historical Interest

Food-storage cables, *such as this one at campsite #56, keep food safely out of bears' reach.*

Leave Bryson Place on the Deep Creek Trail and meet Burnt Spruce backcountry campsite #56, elevation 2,405 feet, at mile 6.2. ▶8 This is your first night's destination, under big white pines with Deep Creek rushing nearby. A wide streamside rock slab allows easy access to Deep Creek. Burnt Spruce campsite is situated between two campsites, Bryson Place and Pole Road, that receive heavier usage and thus remains a fine creekside camp.

Day two begins by returning to Bryson Place, 0.3 mile back down Deep Creek Trail. ▶9 Turn left up the Martins Gap Trail, rising along a streamlet before bridging the watercourse. Wind up a galax-lined path under pines. Views of Deep Creek Valley open before you reach Martins Gap on Sunkota Ridge at mile 8.0 of your loop hike. ▶10 Turn left on infrequently trod singletrack Sunkota Ridge Trail, gently ascending out of Martins Gap under oaks, maples, and sourwood. Pass a spring seep at 8.4 miles. Continue ascending, passing another seep at 9.2 miles. It seems the trail will top out, yet it keeps gaining elevation in moderate increments between gaps. Occasional glimpses of Noland Divide and Thomas Divide open beyond the trees. Break the 4,000-foot barrier at 10.4 miles, in a mix of oaks and northern hardwoods.

Intersect the Thomas Divide Trail at 12.5 miles. ▶11 It has come 4.6 miles from Newfound Gap Road. Turn right on the Thomas Divide Trail and walk 0.4 mile to arrive at Newton Bald Trail junction. Turn left on the Newton Bald Trail, ▶12 following it to Newton Bald backcountry campsite #52, your second night's destination, at 13.0 miles. ▶13

This 5,000-foot-high campsite, located in a sag on Thomas Divide near what once was an open meadow, is a favorable place to escape the heat in summer and crowds anytime. During winter, Newton Bald campsite is susceptible to strong winds. Understory grasses are all that remain of the former

▲ **Backcountry Camping**

👤 **Secluded**

🍁 **Autumn Colors**

▲ **Backcountry Camping**

meadow, which stretched easterly. Nowadays, white oaks, yellow birch, cherry, and red spruce shade the small camp. A cold, clear spring, accessed on a foot trail dropping off the east side of the gap, is the headwaters of Cooper Creek.

Start day three by backtracking to the Thomas Divide Trail. ▶14 Turn left and begin a southwesterly course toward Deep Creek Campground on a less-used path. Walk among wooded knolls at around 4,700-foot elevation for 1.5 miles, then begin a prolonged descent to reach Deeplow Gap and a trail junction at 16.0 miles of your loop hike. ▶15 Climb out of Deeplow Gap, still on Thomas Divide Trail, to soon pass a spring seep.

Secluded

Autumn Colors

Top out at 17.0 miles. The downhill becomes relentless. Intersect the Indian Creek Motor Trail at 18.5 miles. ▶16 The Thomas Divide Trail turns left here and traces a wide track that was originally designed to be an auto touring route. Public outcry stopped it in the late 1960s and early 1970s, but not before the route was graded for car use. Enjoy easy walking as you continually lose elevation. Meet the Stone Pile Gap Trail and the park boundary at 20.6 miles. ▶17 Turn right here, back on a singletrack path, and continue your descent along a pine ridge, then repeatedly crisscross a small tributary of Indian Creek that often muddies the trail.

A footbridge leads over swift Indian Creek at 21.2 miles. Turn downstream to shortly intersect the Indian Creek Trail. ▶18 Turn left onto the wide, roadlike path that's open to bikes. Pass Indian Creek

Waterfall

Falls, ▶19 a 25-foot cascade that fans over a rock slab into a mountain pool. Continue downhill to meet the Deep Creek Trail at 21.8 miles. ▶20 Turn left on the Deep Creek Trail, and follow it 0.7 mile to complete your backpacking circuit. ▶21

🚶 MILESTONES

▶1   0.0   Deep Creek Trailhead

▶2   0.7   Stay left with Deep Creek Trail

▶3   1.7   Loop Trail leaves right

▶4   2.9   Bumgardner Branch campsite #60

▶5   4.2   McCracken Branch campsite #59

▶6   5.5   Nicks Nest Branch campsite #58

▶7   5.9   Bryson Place campsite #57 and Martins Gap Trail

▶8   6.2   Burnt Spruce campsite #56

▶9   6.5   Backtrack to reach Bryson Place campsite #57
          and Martins Gap Trail

▶10 8.0   Reach Martins Gap; left on Sunkota Ridge Trail

▶11 12.5 Right on Thomas Divide Trail

▶12 12.9 Left on Newton Bald Trail

▶13 13.0 Newton Bald campsite #52

▶14 13.1 Backtrack and turn left on Thomas Divide Trail

▶15 16.0 Pass Deeplow Gap Trail

▶16 18.5 Intersect Indian Creek Motor Trail, and stay left

▶17 20.6 Right on Stone Pile Gap Trail

▶18 21.3 Left on Indian Creek Trail

▶19 21.7 Indian Creek Falls

▶20 21.8 Left on Deep Creek Trail

▶21 22.5 Deep Creek Trailhead

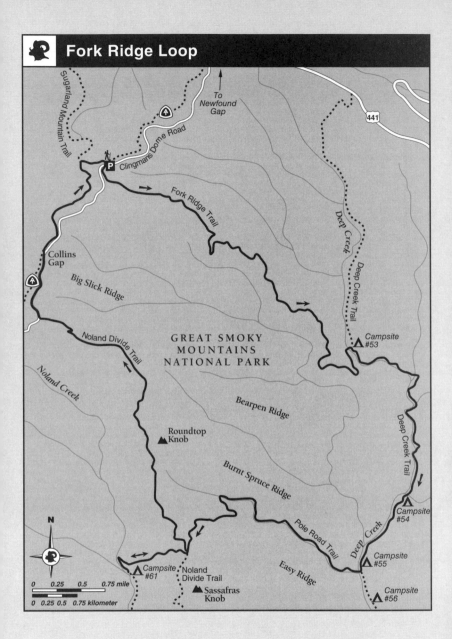

Fork Ridge Loop

Fork Ridge Loop

This challenging backpack loop has major elevation changes. Explore spruce–fir ridges and camp near high-elevation streams. Descend beneath big spruce and yellow birch trees on Fork Ridge to junglelike Deep Creek. Climb to the Appalachian Trail (AT) with views from Mount Collins.

Best Time

Clingmans Dome Road, the trail access and where this hike begins, is open from April through November. Spring and fall have the clearest skies for stupendous views. Call ahead about road conditions if you want to hike during the shoulder seasons. Midsummer through fall is best for fishing. Autumn offers color, solitude, and drier trails.

Finding the Trail

From the junction of US 321 and US 441/Parkway in Gatlinburg, Tennessee (signed traffic light #3), head south on US 441 for 2.7 miles into the park. With the Sugarlands Visitor Center on your right, keep south on US 441/Newfound Gap Road for 13.1 miles. Turn right on Clingmans Dome Road, passing shortly into North Carolina, and follow it 3.5 miles to the Fork Ridge Trailhead, on your left.

Trail Description

Enjoy highland-stream camping along with many miles of rare spruce–fir forest. You will also experience ample solitude on this elevation-changing

TRAIL USE
Backpacking, Horses

LENGTH
20.1 miles, 12–14 hours

VERTICAL FEET
-4,300/+4,300

DIFFICULTY
– 1 2 3 4 **5** +

TRAIL TYPE
Loop

FEATURES
Ridgeline
Stream
Autumn Colors
Wildflowers
Spruce–Fir
Great Views
Backcountry Camping
Swimming
Secluded
Steep

FACILITIES
None

weekend loop. Take Fork Ridge Trail and amble beneath big spruce and yellow birch trees. Descend through transitioning forest types before reaching Deep Creek Valley and the Poke Patch backcountry campsite. Poke Patch is not nearly as notable as the big trees, but it will do. Keep descending in attractive Deep Creek Valley to reach the Pole Road Creek Trail. *Note that the bridge over Deep Creek periodically washes out; if hiking during the cold season, check backcountry trail park alerts at nps.gov/grsm.* Climb to Noland Divide, only to drop to Noland Creek and Bald Creek campsite. On the final day, backtrack to Noland Divide, then climb into evergreens near Clingmans Dome Road. Follow the road a short piece to intersect the AT, then trace the AT over Mount Collins. Enjoy the view from 6,000-plus feet before completing the loop.

Secluded

Old-Growth

Start the overnight loop ▶1 on the singletrack hiker-only Fork Ridge Trail. This trail is also part of North Carolina's Mountains-to-Sea Trail, which accounts for the circular white blazes. Cruise a narrow path where sturdy old-growth red spruce hold sway overhead, complemented by yellow birches, Fraser firs, and ferns aplenty. Partial vistas open to the east. Curve toward a feeder stream of Keg Drive Branch at 1.6 miles. The stream was named for

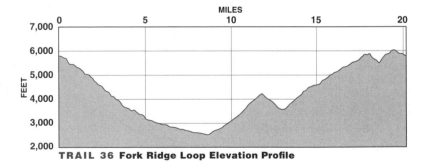

TRAIL 36 Fork Ridge Loop Elevation Profile

Spruce trees *reach for the sky on Noland Divide.*

Cherokee hunter Jim Keg. As the trail drops, cherry, beech, and other deciduous trees rise in the forest. Giant trailside hemlock trunks still stand, waiting for a big storm to blow them down.

Autumn Colors

Rejoin the slender ridgecrest at 2.6 miles. Dry environment species, such as chestnut oak, sourwood, and mountain laurel, appear. Views into Left Fork Deep Creek open. Fork Ridge is the divide between the forks of Deep Creek. The sounds of both forks drift upward on your downgrade. Reach Deep Creek Gap at 4.6 miles. ▶2 The trail makes an abrupt left turn and plunges toward Deep Creek on a sheer slope. Just before reaching Deep Creek, look left at a switchback for a faint trail leading left 40 yards to a huge tulip tree. The circumference of this ancient poplar will amaze you.

Return to the main trail and soon come to Deep Creek. This is usually a wet crossing. Just across the stream, at 5.2 miles, is the junction with the Deep Creek Trail and the Poke Patch backcountry campsite #53. ▶3 The camping flat, open to the sky overhead, has been used for a long time and shows signs of wear. This is your first night's destination.

Backcountry Camping

Stream

Wildflowers

Start the second day by heading downstream on the Deep Creek Trail, laid out by the Civilian Conservation Corps in the 1930s. Walk beneath a cathedral of more large trees. Rhododendron and doghobble create an incredibly dense eye-level cavalcade of greenery. Deep Creek is sometimes seen but always heard. At mile 5.9 of your loop hike, step over Cherry Creek. Climb away from the stream, only to drop directly alongside Deep Creek among rocks. The trail here was blasted out of the mountainside to avoid a ford. Beetree Creek falls in from your left at 6.3 miles. Wind deeper into luxuriant Deep Creek Valley to reach Nettle Creek and backcountry campsite #54 at mile 7.5. ▶4 Beyond this campsite, sycamores appear in the forest. Open to a flat rife with white pines, reaching Pole Road

Backcountry Camping

backcountry campsite #55, with a horse-hitching rack and picnic tables, at mile 8.5. ▶5

⚠ **Backcountry Camping**

Intersect the Pole Road Creek Trail just ahead. Cross Deep Creek on a footbridge high above Deep Creek. ▶6 Soon step over Pole Road Creek. When the Deep Creek Valley was selectively logged, timber men placed poles at intervals to slide felled trees down Pole Road Creek Valley to Deep Creek where they were amassed at splash dams, then floated downstream after heavy rains.

Cross Pole Road Creek at 9.4 miles. The trail steepens a bit and crosses the stream again at miles 9.7, 10.0, and 10.1. Pass a huge tulip tree just before the final crossing at 10.6 miles. ▶7 Swing around a rib ridge of Noland Divide. Keep ascending in oaks and mountain laurel to reach Upper Sassafras Gap on Noland Divide at mile 11.8. ▶8

🧍 **Steep**

Catch your breath at the gap, then drop into rhododendron, now on the Noland Creek Trail. The roar of Noland Creek hastens your step. Watch for views of nearby Forney Ridge. Reach Noland Creek then turn downstream to meet Bald Creek campsite #61 at mile 12.8. ▶9 This two-tiered campsite is your second night's destination.

Start day three of your hike by backtracking to Noland Divide, reaching Upper Sassafras Gap at mile 13.8 ▶10 of your loop hike. Turn left in an oak forest on the Noland Divide Trail, and begin a steady uptick to a small knob. Catch your breath in rhododendron thickets on a level stretch at 14.5 miles. Circle Roundtop Knob to level out at 5,200 feet at 15.8 miles.

Stairstep in primeval spruce, fir, and yellow birch woodland to reach a grassy road at mile 17.0. ▶11 This closed road accesses a water source and acid rain–monitoring stations, one of which you pass. Reach Clingmans Dome Road at mile 17.5. ▶12 Turn right here and descend Clingmans Dome Road for 0.7 mile. Dip left into the woods, reaching

The Smokies *is known for its deep forests and vast wildlands.*

the AT at Collins Gap. If you come to a parking area on the right with 11 spaces in it, you have gone a little too far.

Once on the AT, turn right, northbound. ►13 Climb 500 feet from Collins Gap and over Mount Collins, reaching 6,188 feet and a Carolina view at 19.5 miles. ►14 Drop to intersect Sugarland Mountain Trail at mile 19.9. ►15 Stay on the AT and intersect Fork Ridge Connector Trail at mile 20.1. ►16 Turn right here, and walk a few steps to Clingmans Dome Road, completing your loop.

Great Views 🔭

🚶 MILESTONES

▶1	0.0	Fork Ridge Trailhead
▶2	4.6	Left at Deep Creek Gap
▶3	5.2	Poke Patch campsite #53
▶4	7.5	Nettle Creek campsite #54
▶5	8.5	Pole Road Creek campsite #55
▶6	8.6	Cross Deep Creek on Pole Road Creek Trail
▶7	10.6	Leave Pole Road Creek
▶8	11.8	Upper Sassafras Gap; descend Noland Creek Trail
▶9	12.8	Bald Creek campsite #61
▶10	13.8	Upper Sassafras Gap, and left on Noland Divide Trail
▶11	17.0	Reach a grassy roadbed
▶12	17.5	Right on Clingmans Dome Road
▶13	18.2	Join Appalachian Trail northbound from Collins Gap
▶14	19.5	View into Carolinas from atop Mount Collins
▶15	19.9	Pass Sugarland Mountain Trail
▶16	20.1	Right on Fork Ridge Connector to reach trailhead

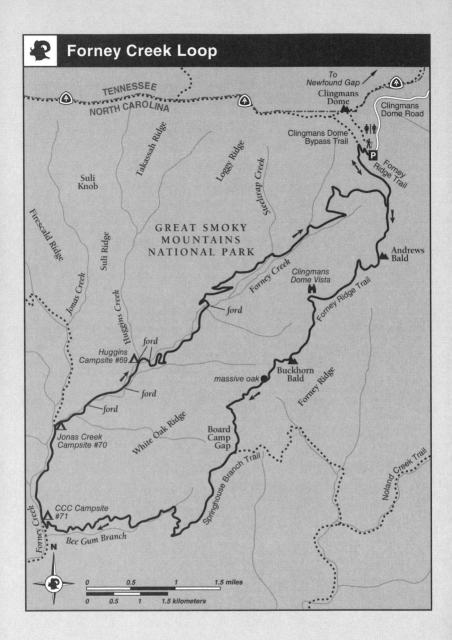

Forney Creek Loop

To Newfound Gap

Clingmans Dome

Clingmans Dome Road

TENNESSEE

NORTH CAROLINA

Clingmans Dome Bypass Trail

P

Forney Ridge Trail

Takassah Ridge

Loggy Ridge

Steeltrap Creek

Suli Knob

Andrews Bald

Firescald Ridge

Suli Ridge

GREAT SMOKY MOUNTAINS NATIONAL PARK

Forney Creek

Clingmans Dome Vista

Forney Ridge Trail

Jonas Creek

Huggins Creek

ford

ford

Huggins Campsite #69

ford

massive oak

Buckhorn Bald

Forney Ridge

ford

White Oak Ridge

Jonas Creek Campsite #70

Board Camp Gap

Springhouse Branch Trail

Noland Creek Trail

Forney Creek

CCC Campsite #71

Bee Gum Branch

N

0   0.5   1   1.5 miles

0   0.5   1   1.5 kilometers

Forney Creek Loop

This tough but rewarding backpacking trek involves numerous creek fords and an elevation change of more than 4,000 feet one-way! Travel Forney Ridge, passing Andrews Bald, to make Forney Creek. Ascend Forney Creek and visit Forney Creek Cascades on your return trip.

Best Time

Clingmans Dome Road, the trail access and where this hike begins, is open from April through November; check ahead if you'll be hiking during the shoulder seasons. June features great rhododendron and flame azalea blooms. Midsummer through fall is best for swimming and fishing Forney Creek. Fording the streams is safer then, because the waterways are at their lowest.

Finding the Trail

From the junction of US 321 and US 441/Parkway in Gatlinburg, Tennessee (signed traffic light #3), head south on US 441 for 2.7 miles into the park. With the Sugarlands Visitor Center on your right, keep south on US 441/Newfound Gap Road for 13.1 miles. Turn right on Clingmans Dome Road, passing shortly into North Carolina, and follow it about 6.9 miles to its dead end. The Forney Ridge Trail heads briefly west from the parking area, then south, away from Clingmans Dome.

TRAIL USE
Backpacking, Horses
LENGTH
19.4 miles, 11–13 hours
VERTICAL FEET
±4,200
DIFFICULTY
– 1 2 3 4 **5** +
TRAIL TYPE
Loop

FEATURES
Ridgeline
Stream
Waterfall
Autumn Colors
Wildflowers
Spruce–Fir
Great Views
Photo Opportunity
Backcountry Camping
Swimming
Steep
Historical Interest
FACILITIES
Bookstore
Restrooms
Water

Trail Description

This is a tough but rewarding two-night backpacking trip, involving numerous creek fords, an elevation change of more than 4,000 feet, and a long first day. Leave Clingmans Dome and travel Forney Ridge, passing Andrews Bald with its wonderful views. Continue down Forney Ridge to reach Civilian Conservation Corps (CCC) backcountry campsite #71. Turn up Forney Creek, ascending a wild valley along a scintillating mountain stream capped with a visit to Forney Creek Cascades, one of the best rock slides in the entire Southern Appalachians.

Along Forney Creek, logging and settler relics can be spotted by observant hikers. Remember to leave artifacts for others to discover and enjoy. Be apprised that Forney Creek Trail has several fords, which are challenging at high water. For your second night's destination of Steeltrap campsite, camp in a less-used clearing or beside Forney Creek Cascades. Your final day climbs back into the spruce–fir high country.

Leave the Clingmans Dome/Forney Ridge parking area ▶1 on the Forney Ridge Trail, bordered by big boulders, Fraser fir, and mountain ash. Bear left after meeting the Clingmans Dome Bypass Trail. The rough, rocky track winds in and out of shade.

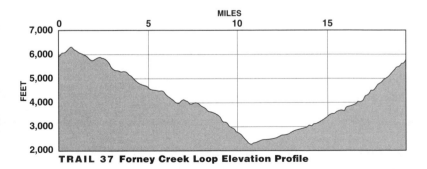

TRAIL 37 Forney Creek Loop Elevation Profile

Parts of Forney Creek Cascades *are a vast waterslide over naked rock.*

Great Views Open areas allow southwesterly views. Spruce and fir grow in dense thickets elsewhere, along with yellow birch. Meet the Forney Creek Trail, your return route, at 1.1 miles. ▶2 At 1.8 miles, open onto the upper end of Andrews Bald. ▶3 Blueberries, azaleas, **Wildflowers** and rhododendron bushes dot the meadow, which yields views south to Fontana Lake and waves of Carolina mountains beyond.

Beyond the bald, the trail receives much less use. Work downhill, under partial tree canopy. Brambles and briars crowd the path during summertime. Occasional spinelike rock protrusions emerge from the trailside. At 3.1 miles, while the trail curves around a knob, a view of Clingmans Dome opens to the right. Keep descending, leaving the high-country evergreens, now in oak woods. The trail rambles either the crest or the right-hand **Ridge** side of Forney Ridge while trending downhill amid occasional pockets of rhododendron.

In a gap, at 4.5 miles, the trail passes a massive oak tree. From here, the Forney Ridge Trail gently undulates beneath now-wooded Buckhorn Bald. Reach Board Camp Gap and join the Springhouse Branch Trail at 5.8 miles. ▶4 The junction is a nice place for a break, with a level area and trees against which to lean. From Board Camp Gap, the trail undulates on a narrow wooded ridge, then makes a hard switchback right at 7.1 miles, ▶5 leaving Forney Ridge. Wind in and out of hollows, crossing the headwaters of Bee Gum Branch at 7.7 miles. Keep westerly in this valley, staying well above Bee Gum Branch, alternately entering moist hollows and drier mountain laurel, oak, and sassafras woods.

You keep hearing water, thinking you're almost there. Make a couple of last switchbacks, then open **Backcountry Camping** onto CCC campsite #71, elevation 2,160 feet, at 9.9 miles. ▶6 This former homesite and CCC workers' camp has a large chimney and metal artifacts. The **Historical Interest** CCC boys who built the trail you just walked were headquartered here. This busy campsite is your first night's destination. Forney Creek rumbles nearby, providing fishing and swimming venues. Follow the railroad grade upstream from the camp to an old stone trestle at the creek's edge. There you will find two large pools.

Swimming

Start your 6-mile second day, turning up Forney Creek Trail as it veers away from the stream to avoid fords, then descends to reach a former logging railroad grade at 10.7 miles of your loop hike. The trail becomes quite rocky before intersecting the Jonas Creek Trail at 11.1 miles. ▶7 Jonas Creek backcountry campsite #70 is across the bridge from the Forney Creek Trail. The Forney Creek Trail is open only to hikers from this point forward. Continue up the lush valley bordered by doghobble, mountain laurel, and rhododendron, passing through huge forested flats.

Make the first and second fords of Forney Creek at 11.6 miles and 12.1 miles. These are wet fords under normal flows, though late summer and fall may allow a nimble rock-hopper dry passage. Continue up the right bank, reaching the third ford and Huggins campsite #69 at 12.4 miles. ▶8 This backcountry campsite was historically known as Monteith Camp. Metal logging relics lie about. After the fourth ford, just beyond Huggins, the trailbed becomes wet and rocky. Switchback past an enormous rock retaining wall, left over from the railroad days. The trail is well above the stream after making another switchback.

Backcountry Camping

Reach the fifth ford at 14.0 miles. This crossing takes you to the left-hand bank. More switchbacks lie ahead as you enter vast cove hardwood forests, where tulip trees grow straight and tall. This railroad grade was made gentle enough for tree-loaded flatcars to ascend these mountains; therefore, a backpacker loaded with camping gear should be able to make it as well.

Backcountry Camping

Historical Interest

Waterfall

Spruce–Fir

Steep

Reach Lower Steeltrap campsite #68B at 15.9 miles, ▶9 a short ways after stepping over Steeltrap Creek. A clearing has a single fire ring. Upper Steeltrap campsite #68B, elevation 4,250 feet, is up the trail 0.4 mile at 16.3 miles, ▶10 near Forney Creek Cascades. That site has old railroad artifacts including wheels and rail. The cascades are a wide rock slide about 50–60 feet high, with another fall above it. Interestingly, quartz striations run through the cascade rocks. Either campsite is your second night's destination.

Start your 3-mile third day by crossing uppermost Forney Creek one last time, an easy step over. Railroad artifacts continue amid a northern hardwood forest of beech, sugar maple, and yellow birch. Spruce and fir trees mix in as you climb. Curve into a watery rock garden, making a big switchback away from the water. Ascend a wet, rocky track, making a last hard switchback to the right before reaching the Forney Ridge Trail at 18.3 miles. ▶11 From here, backtrack 1.1 miles to Clingmans Dome, ▶12 completing your two-night backpack loop.

🚶 MILESTONES

►1	0.0	Clingmans Dome Trailhead
►2	1.1	Straight on Forney Ridge Trail
►3	1.8	Andrews Bald
►4	5.8	Join Springhouse Branch Trail at Board Camp Gap
►5	7.1	Leave Forney Ridge on hard switchback
►6	9.9	Reach Civilian Conservation Corps campsite #71
►7	11.1	Pass Jonas Creek Trail
►8	12.4	Huggins campsite #69
►9	15.9	Lower Steeltrap campsite #68B
►10	16.3	Upper Steeltrap campsite #68A
►11	18.3	Left on Forney Ridge Trail
►12	19.4	Clingmans Dome Trailhead

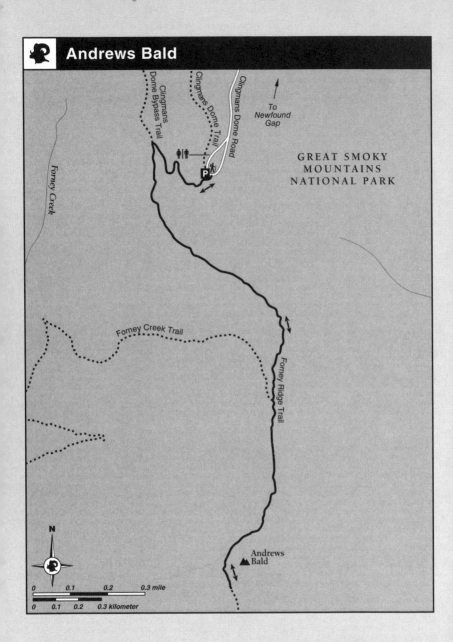

Andrews Bald

Clingmans Dome Bypass Trail

Clingmans Dome Trail

Clingmans Dome Road

To Newfound Gap

P

Forney Creek

GREAT SMOKY MOUNTAINS NATIONAL PARK

Forney Creek Trail

Forney Ridge Trail

N

Andrews Bald

0   0.1   0.2   0.3 mile
0   0.1   0.2   0.3 kilometer

Andrews Bald

From the park's highest trailhead, explore the extraordinary spruce–fir forest community on the way to the meadow of Andrews Bald, resplendent with stunning views.

Best Time

Clingmans Dome Road, the trail access and where this hike begins, is open from April through November; check ahead if you'll be hiking during the shoulder seasons. June features great Catawba rhododendron blooms, as well as flame azaleas. August is good for blueberry picking, and fall is best for views. In midsummer, the bald is sometimes enshrouded in fog and mist.

Finding the Trail

From the junction of US 321 and US 441/Parkway in Gatlinburg, Tennessee (signed traffic light #3), head south on US 441 for 2.7 miles into the park. With the Sugarlands Visitor Center on your right, keep south on US 441/Newfound Gap Road for 13.1 miles. Turn right on Clingmans Dome Road, passing shortly into North Carolina, and follow it about 6.9 miles to its dead end. The Forney Ridge Trail heads briefly west from the parking area, then south, away from Clingmans Dome.

Trail Description

This is one of the Smokies' finest hikes. The trip passes through an extraordinary spruce–fir forest

TRAIL USE
Day Hiking,
Child Friendly

LENGTH
3.6 miles, 1½–2½ hours

VERTICAL FEET
±150

DIFFICULTY
– 1 **2** 3 4 5 +

TRAIL TYPE
Out-and-back

FEATURES
Summit
Ridgeline
Autumn Colors
Wildflowers
Spruce–Fir
Great Views
Photo Opportunity

FACILITIES
Bookstore
Restrooms
Water

to the grassy field of Andrews Bald. Resplendent with stunning views, the mountain meadow is the ideal backdrop for a picnic in the sky. The origin of these fields is not clear, although natural fires, clearing by Indians, and grazing cattle possibly kept the fields clear. Balds once stretched along many ridges in the Smokies and throughout the Southern Appalachians. In summer, residents of the nearby lowlands would drive their cattle up to these balds to graze, which certainly helped keep the balds open; when the practice ceased trees began reclaiming the meadows. Now, only names recall the balds of the Smokies, save for this one and Gregory Bald. Outside the park, on nearby lands, national forests are keeping other balds open.

> Andrews Bald is one of only two grassy fields in the Smokies that the park service maintains in their open state.

Those who want to restore the Southern Appalachians to their "original" state find the question about preserving the balds a vexing one. Are the historic vistas worth keeping, or should they keep the balds for their natural qualities? Or allow them to disappear? Hikers are lured to the balds. Most are glad the balds are kept open. Views in this verdant, mountainous forest are limited.

After leaving the busy Clingmans Dome parking area ▶1 on the Forney Ridge Trail, descend a gravel

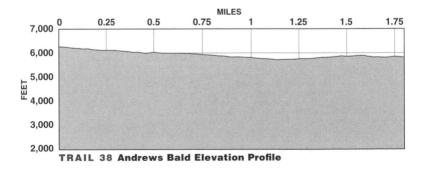

TRAIL 38 Andrews Bald Elevation Profile

Bluets brighten *the trailside on the way to Andrews Bald.*

track bordered by boulders to reach a trail junction at 0.1 mile. The Clingmans Dome Bypass Trail heads right, but you stay left with the Forney Ridge Trail, which drops along a rocky section that allows views to the south. Closed-in areas are inhabited by an evergreen forest reminiscent of Maine or Canada. The smell of red spruce and Fraser fir wafts into your nostrils while northern red squirrels, also known as boomers, scold you from cone-laden green boughs. This area receives upward of 90 inches of rain per year, and the trail is built with water bars of stone and wood, along with steps and even boardwalks, to minimize erosion and allow hikers to focus on the unique surroundings. At 1.1 miles, intersect the Forney Creek Trail. ▶2 It leads right and downhill 10-plus miles to Fontana Lake.

    This hike continues along the undulating and rocky Forney Ridge to arrive at the northern end of Andrews Bald at mile 1.8. ▶3 The highland

Great Views

Spruce–Fir

Ridge

meadow, dotted with bushes and occasional trees, stands at an elevation of 5,800 feet. The lush grass beckons you to lie down and cool off. But that would deny you the expansive views of the southern range of the Smokies and beyond, as far south as the clarity of the sky allows. Fontana Lake is plainly visible on a clear day. Cool breezes drift in from the woods, countering a warm summer sun. This bald, the Smokies' highest, offers marvelous flower displays in June, plus blueberries and blackberries in late summer.

Trees border the meadow as it drops off Forney Ridge, and the Forney Ridge Trail disappears into the woods, aiming for Forney Creek. Most hikers find a grassy seat and enjoy the scene before backtracking to the Clingmans Dome Trailhead.

> Andrews Bald was historically known as Anders Bald until an errant mapmaker renamed it Andrews Bald, which stuck.

🚶 MILESTONES

▶1	0.0	Clingmans Dome Trailhead
▶2	1.1	Straight on Forney Ridge Trail
▶3	1.8	Andrews Bald

Flame azaleas *dot the open grasses of Andrews Bald.*

Smokemont, Cataloochee, and Big Creek Area

Smokemont, Cataloochee, and Big Creek Area

Smokemont, Cataloochee, and Big Creek together make up the most easterly North Carolina section of the park. Top to bottom, the area contains some of the highest terrain in the entire park. Newfound Gap Road and the Oconaluftee River form the western boundary of the area. The state-line ridge dividing North Carolina and Tennessee creates the northern border. On this crest, elevations remain above 5,000 feet for more than 20 miles. Spruce–fir forests cloak this division between the states. Evergreens also run atop spur ridges, including high and wild Balsam Mountain, which roughly divides Smokemont from Cataloochee and Big Creek.

Several big streams drain southward from the mountain crests. The streams west of Balsam Mountain—Oconaluftee River and Raven Fork—flow beyond the park and through the adjacent Cherokee Indian Reservation and into the Tuckasegee River. The streams east of Balsam Mountain—Cataloochee Creek and Big Creek—pour into the Pigeon River.

Elevations range from higher than 6,500 feet along the state-line ridge and Appalachian Trail (AT) to 1,600 feet where Big Creek exits the park. However, the area is far more high elevation than not and has the highest average elevation of any park segment. Most of these highest points remained wild until the park was established. The lowest elevations, primarily Bradley Fork, a tributary of the Oconaluftee River, and the lower Cataloochee Valley, were settled by pioneers, but much of this was Indian country. The ultra-rugged Raven Fork valley was where many Cherokees hid during the westward Indian removal of the 1830s. The remaining band then successfully petitioned to have their own reservation. It now borders the park.

Opposite and overleaf: Evergreens rise *near and far from the perch atop* *Mount Sterling (Trail 48).*

Cataloochee is a bucolic valley tucked away in the southeastern corner of the park. It is home to pioneer settler structures as well as wild elk that roam green meadows from which rise the great mountaintop evergreen forests. Although lower Big Creek was headquarters for a lumber operation, the forest has regrown to such a state that most visitors can't tell it was ever logged. Big Creek, a gorgeous mountain stream with big boulders and bigger pools, is a gateway for entering the spruce–fir forest that virtually encircles it.

Thanks to a favorable trail network, there are plenty of loop hikes in this area, ranging from shorter day hikes to overnight backpacks. If you like streams, there's also plenty of waterside walking—miles and miles of it. But this is also where hikers can and should explore the high country. One major reason: these high ridges exhibit the same characteristics as the state-line ridge upon which the busy AT travels. Here, you can enjoy high-country ridge walking in solitude. Flat Creek Falls and Vista (Trail 42) combines high-country views with one of the highest-elevation streams in the park.

Smokemont, Cataloochee, and Big Creek each have a primary trailhead at their respective campgrounds. Balsam Mountain Campground is accessed off the Blue Ridge Parkway. Each campground has at least one hike nearby campers can enjoy. Numerous other entry points exist, and the hikes here take advantage of them. Highlights of this area are historic—pioneer homes and churches of Cataloochee, for instance. They are also watery—Chasteen Creek Cascades, Gunter Fork Falls, and Mouse Creek Falls. They are natural—the Big Poplars—huge old-growth tulip trees, miles of spruce–fir atop Balsam Mountain, and majestic Mount Sterling. And they are eye-opening: the extensive views from Hemphill Bald and 360-degree vistas from the historic fire towers atop Mount Sterling and Mount Cammerer.

Permits

Permits are *not* required for day hiking. Backpackers must get a backcountry permit to stay at one of the 15 designated backcountry campsites and trail shelters in this area. All campsites require a reservation, which you can make online at smokiespermits.nps.gov, then print at home.

Maps

For the Smokemont, Cataloochee, and Big Creek area, you will need the following USGS 7.5-minute (1:24,000-scale) topographic quadrangles, listed in geographic order as you hike along your route:

(Continued on page 304)

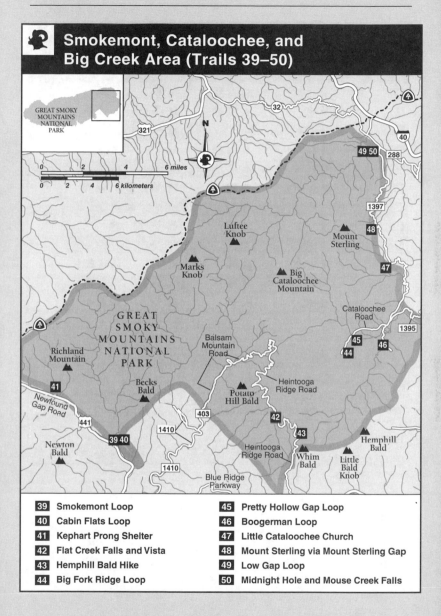

Smokemont, Cataloochee, and Big Creek Area (Trails 39–50)

GREAT SMOKY MOUNTAINS NATIONAL PARK

0   2   4   6 miles
0   2   4   6 kilometers

32

321

40

288

49 50

1397

N

Luftee Knob

48

Mount Sterling

47

Marks Knob

Big Cataloochee Mountain

Cataloochee Road

1395

GREAT SMOKY MOUNTAINS NATIONAL PARK

Richland Mountain

Balsam Mountain Road

45

44

46

41

Becks Bald

Heintooga Ridge Road

Newfound Gap Road

Potato Hill Bald

441

403

42

Newton Bald

1410

43

Hemphill Bald

39 40

Heintooga Ridge Road

Whim Bald

Little Bald Knob

1410

Blue Ridge Parkway

39 Smokemont Loop		**45** Pretty Hollow Gap Loop	
40 Cabin Flats Loop		**46** Boogerman Loop	
41 Kephart Prong Shelter		**47** Little Cataloochee Church	
42 Flat Creek Falls and Vista		**48** Mount Sterling via Mount Sterling Gap	
43 Hemphill Bald Hike		**49** Low Gap Loop	
44 Big Fork Ridge Loop		**50** Midnight Hole and Mouse Creek Falls	

Smokemont, Cataloochee, and Big Creek Area

TRAIL	DIFFICULTY	LENGTH	TYPE	USES & ACCESS	TERRAIN	FLORA & FAUNA	OTHER
39	2	6.0	Loop	Day Hiking	Summit, Ridge, Stream	Autumn Colors, Wildflowers	Secluded, Historical Interest
40	4	17.4	Loop	Horses, Backpacking	Ridge, Stream, Waterfall	Autumn Colors, Wildflowers	Backcountry Camping, Swimming, Historical Interest
41	2	4.0	Out-and-back	Day Hiking, Horses, Backpacking	Stream	Autumn Colors, Wildflowers	Backcountry Camping
42	2	3.8	Point-to-point	Day Hiking, Child Friendly	Ridge, Stream, Waterfall	Autumn Colors, Spruce–Fir	Great Views, Photo Opportunity
43	3–4	9.6	Out-and-back	Day Hiking	Ridge	Autumn Colors, Wildflowers, Spruce–Fir	Great Views, Photo Opportunity, Secluded
44	3	9.1	Loop	Horses, Backpacking	Ridge, Stream	Autumn Colors, Wildflowers, Wildlife, Old-Growth	Backcountry Camping, Swimming, Historical Interest
45	4–5	19.1	Loop	Horses, Backpacking	Ridge, Stream	Autumn Colors, Wildflowers, Wildlife, Spruce–Fir	Great Views, Backcountry Camping, Secluded, Historical Interest
46	3	7.5	Loop	Day Hiking	Ridge, Stream	Autumn Colors, Wildflowers, Old-Growth	Historical Interest
47	2	4.0	Out-and-back	Horses, Backpacking	Stream	Autumn Colors, Wildflowers	Secluded, Historical Interest
48	3	5.4	Out-and-back	Day Hiking, Backpacking	Summit, Ridge	Autumn Colors, Spruce–Fir	Great Views, Photo Opportunity, Backcountry Camping, Secluded
49	5	17.2	Loop	Day Hiking, Horses	Ridge, Stream, Waterfall	Autumn Colors, Wildflowers, Wildlife	Great Views, Backcountry Camping, Historical Interest
50	2	4.0	Out-and-back	Day Hiking, Horses	Stream, Waterfall	Autumn Colors, Wildflowers	Photo Opportunity, Backcountry Camping, Swimming

USES & ACCESS	TYPE	TERRAIN	FLORA & FAUNA	OTHER
Day Hiking	Loop	Summit	Autumn Colors	Great Views
Backpacking	Out-and-back	Ridge	Wildflowers	Photo Opportunity
Horses	Point-to-point	Lake	Wildlife	Backcountry Camping
Child Friendly		Stream	Spruce–Fir	Swimming
	DIFFICULTY −1 2 3 4 5 + less more	Waterfall	Old-Growth	Secluded
				Steep
				Historical Interest
				Geologic Interest

(Continued from page 302)

Trail 39: Smokemont

Trail 40: Smokemont, Mount Guyot

Trail 41: Smokemont

Trail 42: Bunches Bald

Trail 43: Bunches Bald

Trail 44: Dellwood, Bunches Bald

Trail 45: Cove Creek Gap, Luftee Knob

Trail 46: Dellwood

Trail 47: Cove Creek Gap

Trail 48: Cove Creek Gap, Luftee Knob

Trail 49: Waterville, Cove Creek Gap, Luftee Knob, Hartford

Trail 50: Waterville, Cove Creek Gap, Luftee Knob

Smokemont, Cataloochee, and Big Creek Area

Smokemont Loop 309

This classic day hike starts at Smokemont Campground. Enjoy riparian woodland, wildflowers, and pioneer homesites along Bradley Fork. Climb into dry ridgetop terrain on Richland Mountain, with partial views and vivid fall colors.

Day Hiking
6.0 miles, Loop
Difficulty: 1 **2** 3 4 5

Cabin Flats Loop 315

This water-based trek has a little high country mixed in. Travel up Bradley Fork to dead-end at a streamside flat deep in the mountains. Leave the valley and climb to quiet Hughes Ridge where northern hardwoods and evergreens await. Descend to a streamside camp along upper Chasteen Creek. Your return route leads past Chasteen Creek Cascades.

Backpacking, Horses
17.4 miles, Loop
Difficulty: 1 2 3 **4** 5

Kephart Prong Shelter 321

This historic hike leads from the Oconaluftee River past the site of a Civilian Conservation Corps Camp—great for exploring. Ahead, cross gorgeous Kephart Prong four times on footlogs to reach the Kephart Prong trail shelter, perfect for a picnic or a quick overnight adventure.

Day Hiking, Horses
4.0 miles,
Out-and-back
Difficulty: 1 **2** 3 4 5

Flat Creek Falls and Vista 327

This great family day hike first passes an overlook, then travels along a high-elevation stream to reach a waterfall and second vista. One of the highest-water treks in the park, the hike travels near a picnic area and campground.

Day Hiking,
Child Friendly
3.8 miles,
Out-and-back
Difficulty: 1 **2** 3 4 5

Mount Sterling via
Mount Sterling Gap 363

This steep trail starts high and gets higher as it enters spruce–fir forest, culminating atop 5,842-foot Mount Sterling. A fire tower stands atop the mountain, where those who climb its heights are rewarded with an eye-popping 360-degree view of the Smoky Mountains and beyond.

TRAIL 48

Day Hiking,
Backpacking, Horses
5.4 miles,
Out-and-back
Difficulty: 1 2 **3** 4 5

Low Gap Loop 369

This highlight-laden stream-and-ridge loop starts at Big Creek, then heads up that scenic waterway past waterfalls and swimming holes to reach a pair of backcountry campsites. From there, climb to the state-line ridge, taking the Appalachian Trail to Mount Cammerer and its historic observation tower. A prolonged descent returns you to the trailhead.

TRAIL 49

Day Hiking,
Backpacking, Horses
17.2 miles, Loop
Difficulty: 1 2 3 4 **5**

Midnight Hole and
Mouse Creek Falls 377

This hike travels up the Big Creek watershed, past swimming holes, cascades, and a waterfall amid all-encompassing stream beauty. Big Creek valley has been a recreation destination since before the inception of the national park.

TRAIL 50

Day Hiking, Horses
4.0 miles,
Out-and-back
Difficulty: 1 **2** 3 4 5

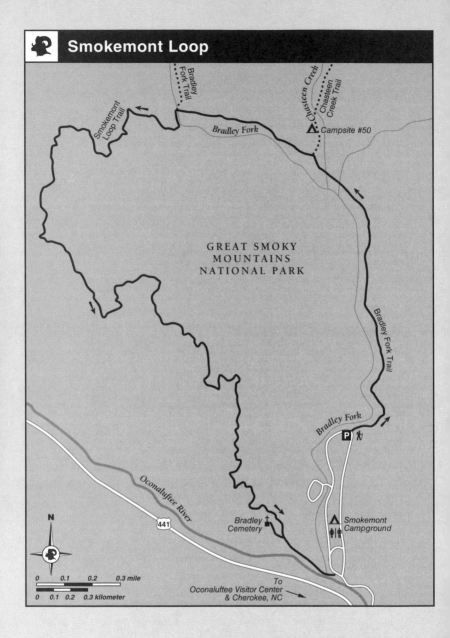

Smokemont Loop

Bradley Fork Trail

Chasteen Creek

Chasteen Creek Trail

Smokemont Loop Trail

Bradley Fork

△ Campsite #50

GREAT SMOKY
MOUNTAINS
NATIONAL PARK

Bradley Fork Trail

Bradley Fork

P 🚶

Oconaluftee River

441

Bradley
Cemetery

△ Smokemont
Campground

N

0   0.1   0.2   0.3 mile
0   0.1 0.2   0.3 kilometer

To
Oconaluftee Visitor Center →
& Cherokee, NC

Smokemont Loop

This classic day hike starts at Smokemont Campground. Enjoy riparian woodland, wildflowers, and pioneer homesites along Bradley Fork. Climb into dry ridgetop terrain on Richland Mountain, with partial views and vivid fall colors.

Best Time

Fall hikers can enjoy the variety of tree species along moist Bradley Fork and yet more species on Richland Mountain. The tree variety adds up to a cornucopia of autumn color. Spring reveals wildflowers along Bradley Fork and views from Richland Mountain before the trees leaf out.

Finding the Trail

From the intersection of US 19 and US 441 South in Cherokee, North Carolina, drive north 3.4 miles into the park. With the Oconaluftee Visitor Center on your right, drive 3.2 miles farther on Newfound Gap Road. Turn right, cross the Oconaluftee River, and make a hard left (north) toward Smokemont Campground. In 0.2 mile, bear right onto the campground loop, passing the check-in station. In another 0.5 mile, reach the Bradley Fork Trailhead, at the far north end of the campground. In winter, parts of the campground may be gated, in which case you may have to park a bit closer to the check-in station.

TRAIL USE
Day Hiking

LENGTH
6.0 miles, 3½–4½ hours

VERTICAL FEET
±1,390

DIFFICULTY
– 1 **2** 3 4 5 +

TRAIL TYPE
Loop

FEATURES
Summit
Ridgeline
Stream
Autumn Colors
Wildflowers
Secluded
Historical Interest

FACILITIES
Water
Restrooms
Campground

Trail Description

The 1931 USGS survey map of the Smokies shows seven homes on both sides of the Bradley Fork between Smokemont and its confluence with Chasteen Creek.

Stream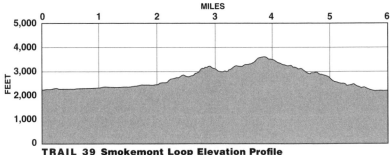

Wildflowers

This loop hike leads from Smokemont Campground, open year-round. It travels along Bradley Fork, once home to pioneers eking out a living on streamside flats. The creek displays superlative mountain-stream scenery. The second part of the loop climbs dry pine and oak ridges of Richland Mountain. Partial views extend across the Oconaluftee Valley. The trail winds down to the Oconaluftee River, returning to Smokemont. Extend your trek with a side trip to Bradley Cemetery, where Smoky Mountain pioneers are interred.

Start your loop hike on Bradley Fork Trail, ▶1 at the far north end of Smokemont Campground. Work around a pole gate on a wide track, making a gentle climb. The ultraclear swirling waters of Bradley Fork wear incessantly away at whitish-gray time-worn stones, stalling where gravity and depth allow pools to form. Riparian woodland of witch hazel, sycamore, black birch, and ironwood, along with rhododendron, rises from mossy banks. Wildflowers carpet the valley in spring. Summer wildflowers are fewer but showier.

TRAIL 39 Smokemont Loop Elevation Profile

A streamside view *of beautiful Bradley Fork*

Scant trailside forest cover indicates former homesites along the trail. A concessionaire horse trail merges on your right. Cross a wide wooden bridge over Chasteen Creek, then meet Chasteen Creek Trail at 1.2 miles. ▶2 Press forward through the junction, enjoying more Bradley Fork stream panoramas and intonations to reach the Smokemont Loop Trail junction at 1.7 miles. ▶3

Turn left on the Smokemont Loop Trail, spanning Bradley Fork on a long footbridge. Stop to look upstream and downstream on Bradley Fork, marveling at water so clear it seems as if you are peering through air. Turn downstream to cross a smaller branch on a smaller footbridge.

The narrow hiker-only path makes a hard switchback to the left at 2.0 miles, gaining ground on Richland Mountain. Water sounds fade. Level off in a gap at mile 2.7, ▶4 then resume your climb, now on the west side of Richland Mountain. Fragmented pine, oak, and hickory woods allow westerly views of Thomas Divide. The white noise of the Oconaluftee River drifts uphill.

Autumn Colors

Summit ▲

The trail reaches its high point, 3,640 feet, at 3.5 miles. ▶5 Well-used downed logs invite a rest. The trail then winds down the slope of Richland Mountain, alternately flanked by open woods and thick rhododendron where trickling springs dribble across the path. The downgrade is continuous and regular.

Bradley Cemetery appears on your right, farther along the trail, but don't use the erosive paths shortcutting down to it. Continue a short piece to reach a jeep road and flats along Oconaluftee River at 5.2 miles. ▶6 A right turn here leads up a small hill to graves of settlers, whose names are lost to time, standing beside some gravestones whose names are still legible.

Historical Interest 🏠

Stream

Return to the jeep road and follow it along the big Oconaluftee River. Wide streamside boulders offer a chance to relax and absorb the scene. Ahead, an old stone bridge spans Bradley Fork at 5.5 miles. ▶7

The trail dumps you out on the lower end of Smokemont Campground. Check out the campers on your half-mile walk through the campground back to the trailhead. ▶8 This extra distance *is* counted in the total mileage, though occasional campground section closures during winter may alter exactly where you park.

🚶 MILESTONES

▶1 0.0 Bradley Fork Trailhead
▶2 1.2 Chasteen Creek Trail
▶3 1.7 Left on Smokemont Loop Trail
▶4 2.7 Unnamed gap
▶5 3.5 High point of hike
▶6 5.2 Spur trail to cemetery
▶7 5.5 Smokemont Campground
▶8 6.0 Bradley Fork Trailhead

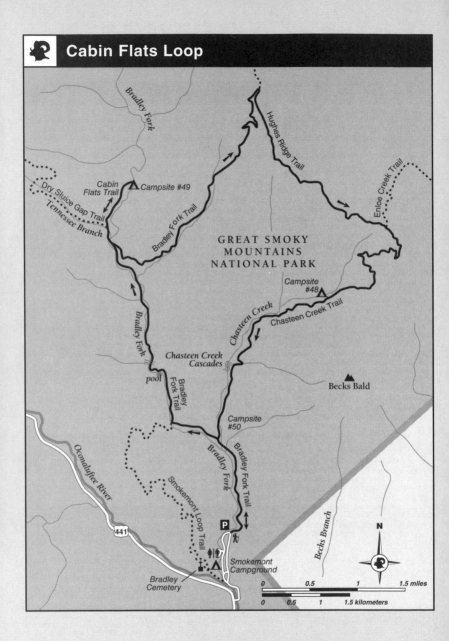

Cabin Flats Loop

Bradley Fork

Hughes Ridge Trail

Enloe Creek Trail

Cabin Flats Trail

△ Campsite #49

Dry Sluice Gap Trail

Tennessee Branch

Bradley Fork Trail

GREAT SMOKY
MOUNTAINS
NATIONAL PARK

Campsite #48 △

Chasteen Creek

Chasteen Creek Trail

Bradley Fork

Chasteen Creek Cascades

pool

Bradley Fork Trail

▲ Becks Bald

Campsite #50

Bradley Fork

Bradley Fork Trail

Oconaluftee River

Smokemont Loop Trail

Becks Branch

N

P

441

Smokemont Campground

Bradley Cemetery

0   0.5   1   1.5 miles

0   0.5   1   1.5 kilometers

Cabin Flats Loop

This water-based trek has a little high country mixed in. Travel up Bradley Fork to dead-end at a streamside flat deep in the mountains. Leave the valley and climb to quiet Hughes Ridge where northern hardwoods and evergreens await. Descend to a streamside camp along upper Chasteen Creek. Your return route leads past Chasteen Creek Cascades.

Best Time

Summer is good for swimming and fishing. In June, backpackers can achieve a big bloom "triple crown," as flame azalea, mountain laurel, and rhododendron color the trails. The spring wildflowers along Bradley Fork are stunning. The elevation variation is sure to bring autumn splash anytime during the fall. Crowds aren't much of an issue here, though Cabin Flats backcountry campsite #49 sees summer weekend use.

Finding the Trail

From the intersection of US 19 and US 441 South in Cherokee, North Carolina, drive north 3.4 miles into the park. With the Oconaluftee Visitor Center on your right, drive 3.2 miles farther on Newfound Gap Road. Turn right, cross the Oconaluftee River, and make a hard left (north) toward Smokemont Campground. In 0.2 mile, bear right onto the campground loop, passing the check-in station. In another 0.5 mile, reach the Bradley Fork Trailhead, at the far north end of the campground. In winter, parts of the campground may be gated, in which case you may have to park closer to the check-in station.

TRAIL USE
Backpacking, Horses
LENGTH
17.4 miles, 10–12 hours
VERTICAL FEET
±2,850
DIFFICULTY
– 1 2 3 **4** 5 +
TRAIL TYPE
Loop

FEATURES
Ridgeline
Stream
Waterfall
Autumn Colors
Wildflowers
Backcountry Camping
Swimming
Historical Interest
FACILITIES
Campground
Restrooms
Water

Trail Description

This loop travels the watercourses and ridges of the Bradley Fork watershed. Leave Smokemont Campground and make your way up Bradley Fork. Continue to the upper reaches of the stream and overnight at Cabin Flats, formerly one of the Smokies most notorious campsites because of frequent bear encounters. Worry not, as bearproof food storage cables have been installed here, as at all other Smokies campsites. Beautiful Bradley Fork is great for wading, fishing, or simply peering into the crystalline waters.

The next day, climb along Taywa Creek, in places falling steeply, creating a cavalcade of cascades. Switchback up dry mountainside woodlands to reach Hughes Ridge. Here, rhododendrons and altitude-loving spruce trees line the trail. Make a pleasant cruise in the high country before dropping to Chasteen Creek and a second campsite. Your final day takes you past Chasteen Creek Cascades before returning to Bradley Fork.

Leave Smokemont Campground. ▶1 Bradley Fork flows, dashes, and splashes along the Bradley Fork Trail, where mossy boulders and ferns lie beneath the forest with many locust and tulip trees taking over formerly inhabited clearings. Cross a wooden bridge over Chasteen Creek. Beyond this

---

Try to imagine the homesites that once occupied these flats along Bradley Fork.

Stream

Historical Interest

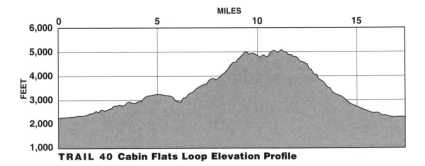

TRAIL 40 Cabin Flats Loop Elevation Profile

crossing, at 1.2 miles, ►2 is the Chasteen Creek Trail junction, your return route.

Keep straight on the Bradley Fork Trail, rambling through a temperate jungle thick with dog-hobble and rhododendron. Tiny tributaries trickle toward translucent Bradley Fork, which crashes alongside the trail between sporadic gray rock bars. At 1.7 miles, the Smokemont Loop Trail leaves left. ►3 Keep straight to reach a spur trail leading left to a deep pool at 2.3 miles. Here, a series of rapids slows to a crystalline reservoir that begs a swim. Look for trout facing upstream in its depths.

 Swimming

At 2.6 miles, come to a repose bench and horse-hitching post. Look across the stream to see a low-flow tributary plummeting 40 feet into Bradley Fork. At 3.2 miles, bridge Bradley Fork as it splits around an island. The gentle ascent continues. At 3.7 miles, the trail bridges Bradley Fork again. The bridge makes for an ideal vantage to view Taywa Creek dashing among mossy rocks to meet Bradley Fork.

Waterfall

Pick up the Cabin Flats Trail in a traffic circle at 4.2 miles. ►4 Immediately cross Bradley Fork on an impressive iron trestle bridge. Span Tennessee Branch on a footbridge, just beyond which lies the Dry Sluice Gap Trail junction at mile 4.4. The Cabin Flats Trail winds along the west side of the Bradley Fork valley before descending into Cabin Flats proper, at mile 5.0, after a sharp right turn. ►5 This is the location of Cabin Flats backcountry campsite #49. In the days before bearproof food-storage cables, this campsite used to be regularly closed because of bear activity, but not these days. Whether you be man or beast, I understand coming here to enjoy the beauty of the stream and woods.

The Hughes Ridge Trail used to continue straight here, but it was abandoned because it bisected Cherokee land.

Start the second day of the overnight loop by backtracking to Bradley Fork Trail, ►6 this time taking the path as it heads into the Taywa Creek valley. The narrow footbed, overlain on a wide track, first curves around a dry ridge before entering a sharply

Rhododendron *and other wildflowers abound along the trail in spring and summer.*

Stream

cut valley with rock protrusions aplenty. Bridge the stream at 6.8 and 7.0 miles of your loop hike. Note the small but incessant tumbling cascades shaded by buckeye and yellow birch. Bridge Taywa Creek at 7.8 miles. ►7 This is your last easy water, so fill up. Several switchbacks ease the ascent, and you drift into a pretty gap with a shady spruce grove and the Hughes Ridge Trail junction at 9.3 miles. ►8

Ridge ▲

Turn right on Hughes Ridge Trail, walking the crest amid northern hardwoods and spruce. Bisect obvious gaps at 10.1 and 10.4 miles before making a long climb, then drop to meet Enloe Creek Trail at 11.8 miles. ►9 Keep straight on Hughes Ridge Trail to reach Chasteen Creek Trail at 12.2 miles. ►10 This loop descends Chasteen Creek Trail via switchbacks to enter wide coves full of ruler-straight tulip trees. Come to your second night's destination and Upper Chasteen backcountry campsite #48 at 13.8 miles. ►11 Small streams seemingly encircle the tiered camp, shaded by preserved hemlock and tulip trees.

Backcountry Camping ⚠

Your final day continues down Chasteen Creek Trail. You stay way above Chasteen Creek. Watch for a low-flow sliding rock cascade at 14.8 miles. The descent steepens, and you can see Chasteen Creek Cascades. Be patient and continue down-trail to meet a spur trail and horse-hitching post at 15.4 miles. ►12 Here, Chasteen Creek tumbles 20 feet over a rock face. Depending on the flow, the waterfall sometimes splits into separate ribbons as it pours over the rock. The trail widens below the falls because of horse use.

Waterfall

Bridge Chasteen Creek just before passing Lower Chasteen backcountry campsite #50 at 16.1 miles. ►13 Continue down-trail to meet Bradley Fork and complete the loop portion of the hike at 16.2 miles. ►14 If you prefer a longer exit route instead, take the Smokemont Loop Trail and add 2.9 miles to your final day. Retrace your steps along Bradley Fork, appreciating more of this superlative watercourse on an easy, moderate downgrade. Reach Smokemont Campground ►15 and the end of the hike at 17.4 miles.

MILESTONES

►1	0.0	Smokemont Campground Trailhead
►2	1.2	Straight on Bradley Fork Trail
►3	1.7	Smokemont Loop leaves left
►4	4.2	Join the Cabin Flats Trail
►5	5.0	Cabin Flats campsite #49
►6	5.8	Resume Bradley Fork Trail
►7	7.8	Final bridging of Taywa Creek
►8	9.3	Right on Hughes Ridge Trail
►9	11.8	Pass Enloe Creek Trail
►10	12.2	Right on Chasteen Creek Trail
►11	13.8	Chasteen Creek campsite #48
►12	15.4	Spur to Chasteen Creek Cascades
►13	16.1	Lower Chasteen campsite #50
►14	16.2	Left on Bradley Fork Trail
►15	17.4	Smokemont Campground Trailhead

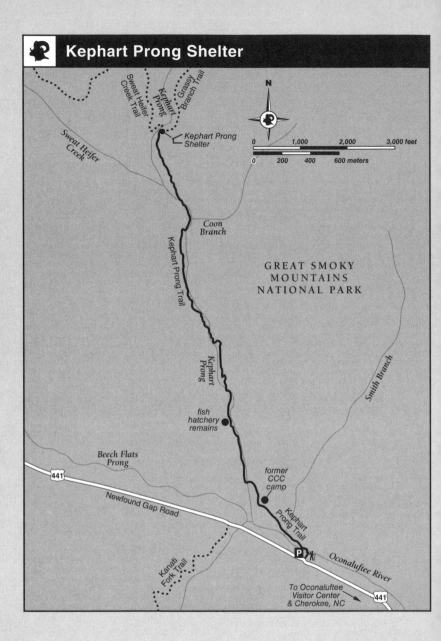

Kephart Prong Shelter

N

| 0 | 1,000 | 2,000 | 3,000 feet |

| 0 | 200 | 400 | 600 meters |

Sweat Heifer Creek Trail

Kephart Prong

Grassy Branch Trail

Kephart Prong Shelter

Sweat Heifer Creek

Coon Branch

GREAT SMOKY MOUNTAINS NATIONAL PARK

Kephart Prong Trail

Kephart Prong

Smith Branch

fish hatchery remains

Beech Flats Prong

441

former CCC camp

Newfound Gap Road

Kephart Prong Trail

P

Oconaluftee River

Kanati Fork Trail

To Oconaluftee Visitor Center & Cherokee, NC

441

Kephart Prong Shelter

Best Time

This is a good hike year-round. Spring will have wildflowers, summer will have swimming near the trailhead, and fall will have color. In winter, the trail shelter is a preferred overnighting option.

Finding the Trail

From the intersection of US 19 and US 441 South in Cherokee, North Carolina, drive north 3.4 miles into the park. With the Oconaluftee Visitor Center on your right, drive 6.8 miles farther on Newfound Gap Road to the trailhead, on your right.

Description

The Kephart Prong Trail is one of those paths that some Smokies visitors end up on by accident, starting as it does on the park's transmountain highway, Newfound Gap Road. That need not be so—the trail deserves better.

First, you cross the Oconaluftee River on a wide bridge at a popular water-play area. Then the Kephart Prong Trail heads past a former Civilian Conservation Corps (CCC) camp located along Kephart Prong. Here, young men lived and worked, helping the Smokies park come to be.

The area is fun to explore—don't expect to stay on the trail. Spur trails aplenty branch off to these historic sites. Still farther ahead, you'll come upon the remains of a fish hatchery that operated during this same time. After the Smokies were heavily logged in pre-park days, the water became silted

TRAIL USE
Day Hiking, Backpacking, Horses

LENGTH
4.0 miles, 2½–3 hours

VERTICAL FEET
+800/–800

DIFFICULTY
– 1 **2** 3 4 5 +

TRAIL TYPE
Out-and-back

FEATURES
Stream
Autumn colors
Wildflowers
Backcountry Camping
Historical Interest

FACILITIES
None

and warm, killing off native trout. Replacement fish were reared here and reintroduced to the streams. Unfortunately, that was a big mistake: most of the fish were rainbow trout that have since been displacing the native brook trout that once inhabited the entire Smokies.

Beyond the hatchery, four hiker bridges span Kephart Prong, making for exhilarating crossings and giving you a different perspective of the clear-as-air creek. Your final destination is the Kephart Prong shelter, a trail wayside for overnight campers.

Leave the parking area ►1 stretched along Newfound Gap Road, and cross the Oconaluftee River on a wide, roadlike wooden bridge. Enjoy views up and down the waterway. Walk a wide, gravelly track up **Stream** the Oconaluftee River. Spur paths lead to the water, where visitors will be playing in the summer.

The first part of the hike is maintained for casual walkers. Smith Branch comes in on your right, tiny in comparison to the Oconaluftee. By 0.3 mile, you've reached the site of the ►2 former CCC camp, as the stone sign makes evident. The camp operated **Historical Interest** from 1933 to 1942. Young men worked on roads, trails, and other infrastructure of Great Smoky Mountains National Park. Numerous spur trails lead in both directions away from the maintained

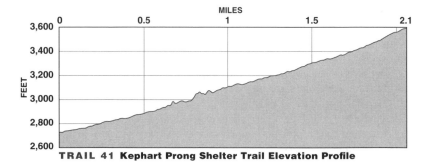

TRAIL 41 Kephart Prong Shelter Trail Elevation Profile

path. Explore to your heart's content, finding pipes, metal relics, even an old water fountain. The area is a fun place for kids to explore rather than trudging up a trail.

At 0.5 mile, make your ►3 first of four bridged crossings of Kephart Prong. Each crossing is accompanied by a ford for equestrians. The elevated span—with a handrail—allows for excellent views into the mountain stream. Continue upstream in rich hardwoods with plenty of yellow birch, reflecting the cool climate of this highland valley. At 0.7 mile on the left, you can see the concrete remains of the fish hatchery that once operated here.

Autumn Colors

Cross back over to the other side of Kephart Prong at 0.9 mile. ►4 This bridge is perched particularly high above the watercourse. Kephart Prong cascades below you, skirting around water-worn boulders while rhododendron, buckeye, and yellow birch line the stream. You are on the right bank, heading upstream. Pass an old trailside metal rail from the days when this area was logged—and timber hauled out on trains—before crossing back over to the left bank on yet another footlog. Hikers must continue up the valley a bit beyond the horse ford to make this third crossing at 1.0 mile. ►5

 Stream

At one time, Smokies trail shelters were fronted by metal fencing to keep bears out.

Ahead, bluffs rise above the trail, which is more primitively maintained this far above Newfound Gap Road. Most strollers have turned back. The path is quite rocky in places, but wildflowers find their way out in spring. Occasional small tributaries feed Kephart Prong. Cross back over to the right bank on a footbridge ►6 at 1.6 miles; this is the last of the log bridges. Coon Branch comes in on your right at 1.7 miles, draining Richland Mountain above. The valley widens as you continue to climb. Here, Sweat Heifer Creek and Kephart Prong converge, creating a vale.

Wildflowers

At 2.0 miles, the Grassy Branch Trail leaves right for the high country. You stay straight, joining the

The Kephart Prong shelter *is a cozy place to spend the night or just relax awhile.*

Backcountry Camping

Sweat Heifer Creek Trail and walk just a few feet to reach the ►7 Kephart Prong trail shelter. This structure stands in a clearing fairly close to Kephart Prong. It includes an inside fireplace and a fire ring nearby outside. I have camped here in rain and fog and have always been glad for the refuge.

Historical Interest

The stone part was built long ago, but the additional fronting and wooden built-in benches and tables were added more recently. Almost all of the Smokies' historic trail shelters are located along the Appalachian Trail, with the exception of this one and the one atop Mount Le Conte. Most shelters in the park are heavily used, the Kephart Prong shelter a bit less so; if you stay here during the week, odds are you'll have the place to yourself, especially in winter. Even if you're not overnighting, the shelter makes a good stopping point and is fun for a picnic or trail snack. The seating is convenient, and on a clear day you can look up and see the state-line ridge dividing North Carolina and Tennessee. Enjoy those bridges on your return trip. ▶8

⬩	MILESTONES	
▶1	0.0	Newfound Gap Road Trailhead
▶2	0.3	Historic Civilian Conservation Corps campsite
▶3	0.5	Bridge crossing
▶4	0.9	Bridge crossing
▶5	1.0	Bridge crossing
▶6	1.6	Bridge crossing
▶7	2.0	Kephart Prong shelter
▶8	4.0	Newfound Gap Road Trailhead

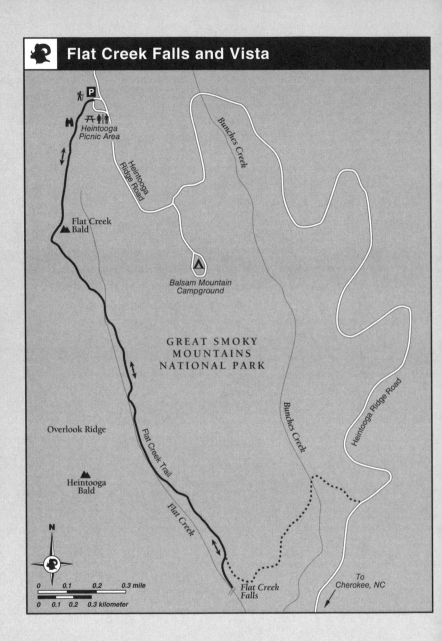

Flat Creek Falls and Vista

Heintooga Picnic Area

Heintooga Ridge Road

Bunches Creek

Flat Creek Bald

Balsam Mountain Campground

GREAT SMOKY MOUNTAINS NATIONAL PARK

Overlook Ridge

Flat Creek Trail

Bunches Creek

Heintooga Ridge Road

Heintooga Bald

Flat Creek

N

0   0.1   0.2   0.3 mile

0   0.1   0.2   0.3 kilometer

Flat Creek Falls

To Cherokee, NC

Flat Creek Falls and Vista

This great family day hike first passes an overlook, then travels along a high-elevation stream to reach a waterfall and second vista. One of the highest-water treks in the park, this hike is convenient to a picnic area and campground.

Best Time

The access, Heintooga Ridge Road, is generally open from mid-May through October. Enjoy a respite from the broiling lowlands during summer. June offers the most water in Flat Creek and a more robust falls. Fall has colors that contrast with the spruce trees, plus clear skies for awesome views.

Finding the Trail

From the intersection of US 19 and US 441 South in Cherokee, North Carolina, drive north 2.8 miles into the park and bear right at the intersection onto the Blue Ridge Parkway. Follow the parkway 10.9 miles to Heintooga Ridge Road, and turn left (north). Turn left on Heintooga Ridge Road and continue 8.7 miles to the Heintooga Picnic Area, on your left. The Flat Creek Trail starts at the end of the auto turnaround near the picnic area.

Trail Description

You may wonder why more people don't hike this trail—maybe it's because the Flat Creek Trail begins on a less-traveled road or because it doesn't connect to other trails. But for Smoky Mountains enthusiasts,

TRAIL USE
Day Hiking,
Child Friendly

LENGTH
3.8 miles, 2–3 hours

VERTICAL FEET
±470

DIFFICULTY
– 1 **2** 3 4 5 +

TRAIL TYPE
Out-and-back

FEATURES
Ridgeline
Stream
Waterfall
Autumn Colors
Spruce–Fir
Great Views
Photo Opportunity

FACILITIES
Campground
Picnic Tables
Restrooms
Water

there are no maybes about hiking this path. It starts above 5,300 feet and passes a wonderful view of the Smokies crest before entering high-country forest of spruce and yellow birch. The path then descends to the perched watershed of Flat Creek and makes its way to the highest-elevation falls accessible by trail in the park.

Photo Opportunity

The Flat Creek Trail swings around Heintooga Picnic Area. ►1 At 0.1 mile, near a water fountain, come to a cleared view, Heintooga Ridge Overlook. The crest of the Smokies stands north. Field glasses reveal a view of the Clingmans Dome tower.

Great Views

Soon reach a trail junction. The wide track continuing forward heads to the picnic area restrooms. Drop right on a narrow hiker-only path. Overhead are regal straight spruces with their reddish trunks supporting boughs of evergreen, complemented by yellow birch, with its trademark horizontal peeling bark. Cherry, beech, and maple trees add to the woodland mix. Powerful winter winds can twist and distort these deciduous tree trunks. Blackberry bushes grow wherever the sun penetrates the tree cover. Ferns and grasses scatter on the forest floor.

Spruce–Fir 🌲

At 0.5 mile, work around the knob where Flat Creek Bald once was. It is forested now, though the

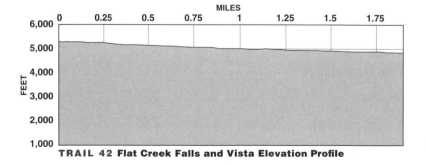

TRAIL 42 Flat Creek Falls and Vista Elevation Profile

OPTIONS

Island Forests

Thousands of years ago, when glaciers covered much of the United States, a forest much more reminiscent of Canada existed here. When the glaciers retreated, this forest—the southern limit of this ice age relic—survived on the highest points of the Smokies, creating "island" forests. Spruce–fir forests have many more ecologically important components than just red spruce and Fraser fir trees. Boreal plants and animals of the north, such as Canada mayflower, red squirrel, and saw-whet owl, reflect the chilly climes of these high-country "sky islands." Balsam Mountain Campground is located in a swath of this rare forest. Not only does it offer the highest camping within the confines of the Great Smoky Mountains National Park at 5,300 feet, it also offers camp-ers a chance to experience this remarkable forest firsthand.

understory remains grassy. Reach Flat Creek at 0.8 mile. ▶2 The small highland stream is easily crossed on a footbridge. Keep a fairly level course through pleasant woodland, crossing a tributary on a footlog at 0.9 mile. Rock-hop Flat Creek twice in succession at 1.1 miles.

The surroundings change minute to minute. First you may be in grassy deciduous woods, then under tall spruce, then in a rhododendron thicket. All of it is striking. More wet-weather drainages bisect the trailbed from the left as the path gets away from the creek. Reach the side trail for Flat Creek Falls at 1.8 miles. ▶3 Turn right here on a faint spur as the main track continues toward Hein-tooga Ridge Road. Descend to Flat Creek. *Keep kids under close supervision in this area,* because Flat Creek puts gravity to work on its way to meet Bunches Creek in the valley below. ▶4 Views of the Bunches Creek watershed open near Flat Creek. The cut of ◤ **Waterfall**

Bunches Creek Valley *as seen from a vista on Flat Creek*

Heintooga Ridge Road is visible. Side trails spur on both sides of the creek to the steep, narrow fall. It is challenging to get a complete view of the entire cascade, as the fall is narrow and drops down a heavily vegetated rock chute. When you're ready, find your way back to the trailhead. ▶5

Consider combining your hike with a picnic or camp out at nearby Balsam Mountain Campground.

The rare spruce–fir forests atop ol' Smoky were important reasons these mountains were chosen as a national park.

Balsam Mountain Campground stands between the headwaters of Flat Creek and Bunches Creek. The campsites are small, discouraging most of today's RV campers. Even with the small sites relatively close together, you will find ample privacy—the campground rarely fills. Since it opens and closes around the same time as Heintooga Ridge Road, it should be open any time you choose to hike the Flat Creek Trail.

Spruce–fir forests cover just 13,000 of the park's 500,000 acres.

🚶	**MILESTONES**	
▶1	0.0	Heintooga Picnic Area Trailhead
▶2	0.8	Flat Creek
▶3	1.8	Spur to Flat Creek Falls
▶4	1.9	Flat Creek Falls
▶5	3.8	Heintooga Picnic Area Trailhead

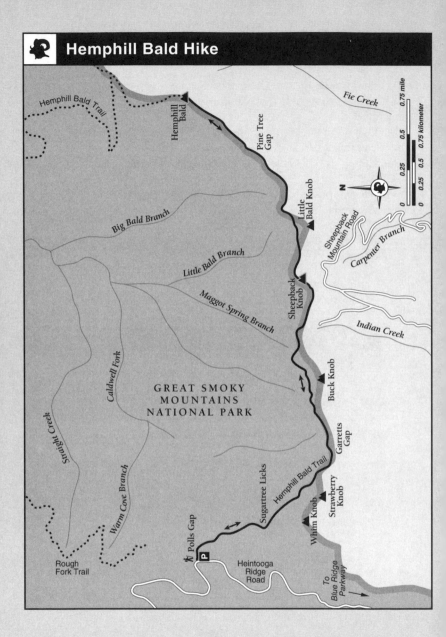

Hemphill Bald Hike

Hemphill Bald Trail

Hemphill Bald

Pine Tree Gap

Fie Creek

Big Bald Branch

Little Bald Branch

Little Bald Knob

Sheepback Mountain Road

Carpenter Branch

Maggot Spring Branch

Sheepback Knob

Indian Creek

Caldwell Fork

GREAT SMOKY MOUNTAINS NATIONAL PARK

Buck Knob

Straight Creek

Garretts Gap

Warm Cove Branch

Sugartree Licks

Hemphill Bald Trail

Strawberry Knob

Whim Knob

Rough Fork Trail

Polls Gap

P

Heintooga Ridge Road

To Blue Ridge Parkway

N

0.75 mile

0.5

0.75 kilometer

0.25

0.5

0.5

0.75

0

0

0.25

Hemphill Bald Hike

This high-country ramble travels the backbone of Cataloochee Divide, on the park boundary. Cross knob and gap, reaching the hike's highest point, Hemphill Bald. Take in sweeping vistas of meadows and mountains.

Best Time

The access for this hike, Heintooga Ridge Road, is open from mid-May through October. Spring can be cool and wet, but when the skies clear, you will enjoy magnificent vistas. Summer can be hazy. Fall is the best choice, with open roads, clear skies, and good weather.

Finding the Trail

From the intersection of US 19 and US 441 South in Cherokee, North Carolina, drive north 2.8 miles into the park and bear right at the intersection onto the Blue Ridge Parkway. Follow the parkway 10.9 miles to Heintooga Ridge Road, and turn left (north). Continue 6 miles to Polls Gap, on your right. The Hemphill Bald Trail leaves right.

Trail Description

This hike stays above 5,000 feet the entire trek, as it travels along Cataloochee Divide, which forms the park border at this point, southeast of Cataloochee Valley. Because this trail runs along a ridge that forms the park border, much of the private land along the boundary has been kept as open pasture.

TRAIL USE
Day Hiking

LENGTH
9.6 miles, 5–6 hours

VERTICAL FEET
±1,300

DIFFICULTY
– 1 2 **3** 4 5 +

TRAIL TYPE
Out-and-back

FEATURES
Ridgeline
Autumn Colors
Wildflowers
Spruce–Fir
Great Views
Photo Opportunity
Secluded

FACILITIES
Campground nearby
Picnic Area

This area resembles the Smokies a century ago, when Cataloochee Valley farmers would send their livestock to the hills to graze during the summer. These open mountaintop meadows, or "balds," as they are called, allowed for extensive vistas. The park service has let most of the balds within the Smokies reforest. The contrast is striking, as you discover along this first ridge-running segment of the Hemphill Bald Trail.

The Hemphill Bald Trail leaves Polls Gap ►1 southeasterly on a singletrack path overlain on a wide railroad grade. Beech, birch, and cherry trees accompany the trail as it begins to work around Strawberry Knob south of Polls Gap. Vistas open through the trees, where Cataloochee Divide forms a rampart to the south. To the east, wave upon wave of Carolina mountains meld into the distance. Below you, the depths of Caldwell Fork Valley confirm your perched elevation.

Reach the gap known as Sugartree Licks, then curve below Whim Knob. Occasional views open in briery areas along the path. Look for misshapen old-growth yellow birch trees in the adjacent woods. Large quartz boulders rise from the ground at 0.9 mile. By now, the old railroad grade has been left behind. The trail reaches Garretts Gap and a fence

Photo Opportunity 📷

Autumn Colors 🍁

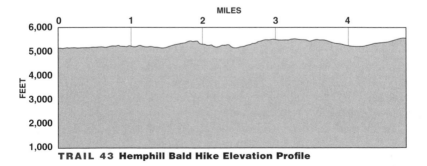

TRAIL 43 Hemphill Bald Hike Elevation Profile

line at 1.4 miles. ►2 This wooden split-rail fence delineates the park border for miles.

From here, the Hemphill Bald Trail turns east and joins Cataloochee Divide, making a steady climb to level off in an alluring flat below Buck Knob. The path becomes rocky before reaching the unappetizingly named Maggot Spring Gap. It then ascends from the gap along the fence line, making several switchbacks to reach the ridgecrest and the top of Sheepback Knob at 3.1 miles. ►3 The walking is easy in the bushy, oak-topped crest, where upthrusted rocks point skyward.

The trail descends to an unnamed gap. A grassy road ends at the gap on the private-land side of the fence. The trail angles up the north side of no longer bald Little Bald Knob to regain the crest of Cataloochee Divide past the knob. Now, the Hemphill Bald Trail makes a prolonged moderate downgrade in a young forest toward Pine Tree Gap. The private side of the ridge, just across the fence from you, becomes open and grassy. The pastureland presents previews of Hemphill Bald ahead, perfectly divided by the park border. The park side of the fence is wooded, and the private side is open.

The private land is part of Cataloochee Ranch, originally in Cataloochee before the park came to be. After the park was established, the tourist operation moved just outside the boundaries. Today, their land is a conservation easement and is partly managed by the Southern Appalachian Highlands Conservancy. It will remain as you see it.

Reach Pine Tree Gap at 4.1 miles, ►4 where there are no pine trees. Begin the 300-foot climb to the top of Hemphill Bald. The trail straddles the park borderline. Views open to the southeast. The area is a study in reforestation and land management. Where there is no grazing or mowing, the mountain has grown up with trees, despite the short growing season at this altitude. And with grazing

Photo Opportunity

▲ **Ridge**

Great Views

Standing higher than 5,500 feet, Hemphill Bald presents panoramic views south beyond the park.

Open meadows *border the trail. Photo: Bryan Delay*

and mowing, the bald of Hemphill Bald stays open and offers wonderful vistas.

Reach the top of Hemphill at 4.8 miles. ▶5 A stone table, a hitching rack, and some benches are located on the ranch. A kiosk detailing all the mountains and towns to the east of Hemphill Bald is embedded into the table. It displays exactly what you are looking at.

Great Views

Photo Opportunity 📷

🚶 MILESTONES

▶1   0.0   Polls Gap Trailhead
▶2   1.4   Garretts Gap
▶3   3.1   Sheepback Knob
▶4   4.1   Pine Tree Gap
▶5   4.8   Hemphill Bald

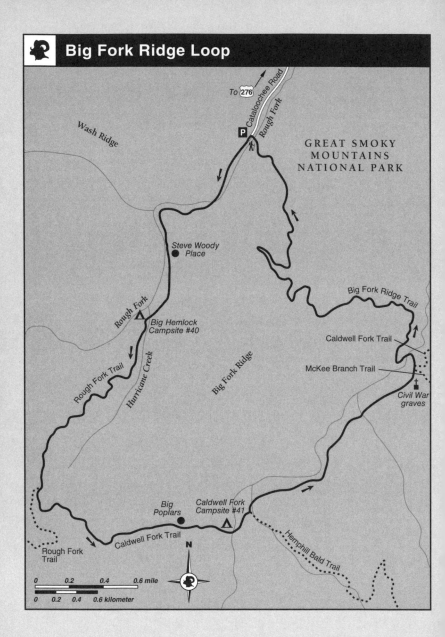

Big Fork Ridge Loop

To 276

Cataloochee Road

Rough Fork

P

GREAT SMOKY
MOUNTAINS
NATIONAL PARK

Wash Ridge

Steve Woody
Place

Rough Fork

Big Fork Ridge Trail

Big Hemlock
Campsite #40

Caldwell Fork Trail

McKee Branch Trail

Rough Fork Trail

Hurricane Creek

Big Fork Ridge

Civil War
graves

Big
Poplars

Caldwell Fork
Campsite #41

Rough Fork
Trail

Caldwell Fork Trail

Hemphill Bald Trail

N

| 0 | 0.2 | 0.4 | 0.6 mile |
| 0 | 0.2 | 0.4 | 0.6 kilometer |

Big Fork Ridge Loop

Visit a homesite and huge trees on this loop. Follow Rough Fork through old-growth northern red oak, climbing up and over Big Fork Ridge to Caldwell Fork, a gorgeous stream. Pass the "Big Poplars," massive tulip trees. Complete the circuit with a second climb of Big Fork Ridge.

TRAIL USE
Day Hiking,
Backpacking, Horses
LENGTH
9.1 miles, 5 hours
VERTICAL FEET
±1,940
DIFFICULTY
– 1 2 **3** 4 5 +
TRAIL TYPE
Loop

FEATURES
Ridgeline
Stream
Autumn Colors
Wildflowers
Wildlife
Old-Growth
Backcountry Camping
Swimming
Historical Interest
FACILITIES
Camping

Best Time

Because this watery loop requires no wet fords, winter is a great time to enjoy it. That's when the large forest trees really stand out. During the warm season, anglers can fish and hikers can take a dip in the creek. The big trees display their colors in autumn. Two backcountry campsites make for a good one-night starter loop or an extended backpack fishing foray.

Finding the Trail

From Exit 20 on I-40, head south a short distance on US 276. Turn right (north) onto Cove Creek Road and follow it nearly 6 miles into the park. Two miles beyond the park boundary, turn left at the intersection onto Cataloochee Entrance Road. Follow it 5.6 miles to its dead end at the Rough Fork Trail, at the end of the parking area.

Trail Description

Start on the Rough Fork Trail, tracing a clear mountain stream. Stop by the interesting Woody Place, then enter the land of the giants, where stately oak trees form a forest cathedral. Climb away from Rough Fork to meet the Caldwell Fork Trail. Descend past the "Big Poplars," huge tulip trees, then walk along Caldwell Fork Valley and return over Big Fork Ridge back to Cataloochee. This loop has two climbs, but is neither overly long nor difficult. If you're looking for a 2-mile, family-friendly walk, head to the Woody Place and back.

Wildlife

The Rough Fork Trail ►1 leaves the uppermost end of Cataloochee Valley. Watch for elk here. You will have added appreciation for this path when you consider that a road was once going to roughly follow it to reach Polls Gap and Balsam Mountain Road. Back in the 1960s, park personnel worried that Cataloochee Valley would become so popular that it would need an outlet instead of the current dirt-road entry setup. No doubt, the arrival of elk in the valley has increased Cataloochee's popularity, but hopefully its reputation will never warrant the abolition of this trail.

Stream

Cruise the wide, nearly level track under maple, white pine, and yellow birch. The valley soon narrows. Cross Rough Fork on a footbridge, then twice more in short order. The trailbed between the second and third crossings is very wet.

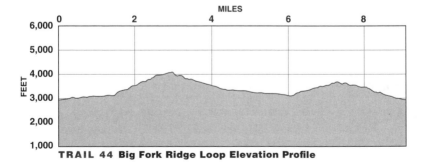

TRAIL 44 Big Fork Ridge Loop Elevation Profile

Open to a clearing and make the Steve Woody Place at 1.0 mile. ►2 The wood clapboard structure is worth a tour. A cedar tree stands in the front yard. Note the differing ceiling heights, indicating that the structure was built in stages over time. It was once a one-room log cabin. A total of 14 kids lived here, headed by Steve Woody's father, Jonathan Woody, after he married a widower with her own children. A springhouse is nearby. The open, level area near the house was the garden. Fields once extended far behind the house, and there were many out-buildings. In the 1920s, as tourists came from the outside to fish and sightsee in Cataloochee, the Woody family hosted them. Steve stocked Rough Fork with rainbow trout and charged fishermen for their catches.

The Rough Fork Trail enters old-growth woodland of northern red oak. You'll see the skeletons of giant hemlocks, victims of the hemlock woolly adelgid. Cross Hurricane Creek and come to Big Hemlock backcountry campsite #40 at 1.5 miles. ►3 Camping nooks and crannies are situated between the rhododendron and doghobble. Rough Fork flows nearby.

The hike, which has been nearly level to this point, now climbs away from Big Hemlock onto Little Ridge. The rocky, root-covered trail, open to horses and hikers, makes a steady climb. The sounds of Hurricane Creek disappear. Big tulip trees grow trailside. Top out on Little Ridge near two large chestnut oak trees. The trail bumps up a few more times before intersecting the Caldwell Fork Trail at mile 3.0. ►4

Turn left here on the Caldwell Fork Trail and descend through more big trees, mostly northern hardwoods such as cherry and buckeye, into the Caldwell Fork Valley. Pass through a prominent gap, then drift into shallow coves.

 Old-Growth

Backcountry Camping

▲ Ridge

 Old-Growth

Elk in Cataloochee *are monitored by the park service.*

 Old-Growth

**Backcountry
Camping**

At 4.1 miles, reach the spur accessing the "Big Poplars." ▶5 These are actually tulip trees, not poplars, as they were once called. The closest one is huge; it takes many outstretched arms to encircle it. Descend to reach Caldwell Fork backcountry campsite #41 at mile 4.4. ▶6 The site is set in a flat along Caldwell Fork.

Bridge Caldwell Fork on a footlog, and rise to a homestead that was open country not too long ago. Pass the Hemphill Bald Trail at 4.5 miles. ▶7 Keep descending the valley of Caldwell Fork, mostly on a slope well above the stream. Reach a side trail leading right to a gravesite at mile 5.9. ▶8 Up this trail are the bodies of three former Union soldiers buried in two graves. They were killed just before the end of the Civil War by fellow Union thugs, who actually claimed no side but used the war as an excuse to pillage local residents. Meet the McKee Branch Trail not far beyond here. Keep straight in very level land growing up with the usual species—locust, tulip, and cherry—that reclaim old farm fields.

Historical Interest

Turn left on the Big Fork Ridge Trail at mile 6.0. ▶9 Make a dry crossing via footbridge over Caldwell Fork on the Big Fork Ridge Trail. Ascend on a pre-park path shaded by oaks. Make a big switchback to the left, heading to Rabbit Ridge. Continue climbing to Big Fork Ridge, reaching a gap at mile 7.5. ▶10 It's all downhill from here into the Rough Fork valley.

Come to a cove and a pioneer homesite, as evidenced by fields being reclaimed by forest. Pass a spot that was an acclimation pen for elk but has now been removed. Cross Rough Fork on a footbridge. You just descended 750 feet. Complete your loop at 9.1 miles. ▶11

MILESTONES

▶1	0.0	Rough Fork Trailhead
▶2	1.0	Woody Place
▶3	1.5	Big Hemlock campsite #40
▶4	3.0	Left on Caldwell Fork Trail
▶5	4.1	Spur trail to Big Poplars
▶6	4.4	Caldwell Fork campsite #41
▶7	4.5	Hemphill Bald Trail
▶8	5.9	Spur to Civil War gravesite
▶9	6.0	Left on Big Fork Ridge Trail
▶10	7.5	Gap in Big Fork Ridge
▶11	9.1	Rough Fork Trailhead

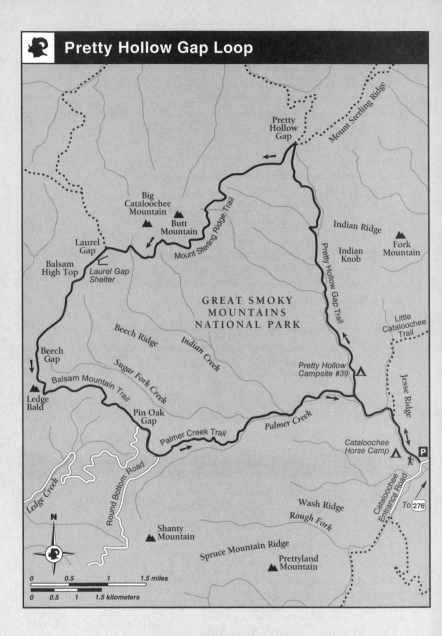

Pretty Hollow Gap Loop

Pretty Hollow Gap

Mount Sterling Ridge

Big Cataloochee Mountain

Butt Mountain

Indian Ridge

Fork Mountain

Laurel Gap

Balsam High Top

Laurel Gap Shelter

Indian Knob

Mount Sterling Ridge Trail

GREAT SMOKY MOUNTAINS NATIONAL PARK

Pretty Hollow Gap Trail

Beech Ridge

Indian Creek

Little Cataloochee Trail

Beech Gap

Pretty Hollow Campsite #39

Ledge Bald

Balsam Mountain Trail

Sugar Fork Creek

Pin Oak Gap

Palmer Creek Trail

Palmer Creek

Jesse Ridge

Cataloochee Horse Camp

P

Ledge Creek

Round Bottom Road

N

Wash Ridge

Rough Fork

Cataloochee Entrance Road

To 276

Shanty Mountain

Spruce Mountain Ridge

Prettyland Mountain

| 0 | 0.5 | 1 | 1.5 miles |
| 0 | 0.5 | 1 | 1.5 kilometers |

Pretty Hollow Gap Loop

Explore highlands above scenic Cataloochee Valley on this two-night backpacking circuit. An easy first day leads to Pretty Hollow campsite. The next day, ascend a deeply cut gorge, reaching spruce forest at Pretty Hollow Gap. Join Mount Sterling Ridge and cruise the high country to camp at Laurel Gap Shelter, over a mile high. From there, follow Balsam Mountain and finally dip into the lowlands via the lush Palmer Creek Trail.

TRAIL USE
Backpacking, Horses

LENGTH
19.1 miles, 10–11 hours
over 3 days

VERTICAL FEET
±2,600

DIFFICULTY
– 1 2 3 **4 5** +

TRAIL TYPE
Loop

FEATURES
Ridgeline
Stream
Autumn Colors
Wildflowers
Wildlife
Spruce–Fir
Great Views
Backcountry Camping
Historical Interest

FACILITIES
Horse Camp

Best Time

Late spring to early summer is the best time to make this loop. The high country is relatively warm but still feels springlike. Fall presents great color. Winter can be harsh and snowy up high.

Finding the Trail

From Exit 20 on I-40, take US 276 south a short distance to Cove Creek Road. Turn right on Cove Creek Road and follow it nearly 6 miles to enter the park. Two miles beyond the park boundary, turn left onto Cataloochee Entrance Road and follow it 4.1 miles until it becomes gravel. The Pretty Hollow Gap Trail starts 0.6 mile ahead on the right in a parking area, just before the gravel road crosses Palmer Creek.

Trail Description

Cataloochee Valley is enjoying increased popularity these days because of the reintroduction of the

Wildlife 🦌 majestic elk that now roam the area. You may see elk pellets along the path. Leave Cataloochee Road ▶1 on the wide roadbed of the easy-walking Pretty Hollow Gap Trail. Palmer Creek rushes by to your left. Pass the Cataloochee Horse Camp at 0.2 mile, and then pass the Little Cataloochee Trail at 0.7 mile. ▶2

Here, the Pretty Hollow Gap Trail veers left, nearing rock walls and other settlement evidence before intersecting the Palmer Creek Trail, your return route, at 1.6 miles. ▶3 Keep straight, beginning your journey into Pretty Hollow. The ascent is minimal and soon the path reaches Pretty Hollow

Backcountry Camping ⚠ backcountry campsite #39. This is your first night's destination. The sloped camping area has four designated sites. A pine overstory shades other smaller trees. The uppermost campsite is in oak woods. A horse-hitching rack is located just up the trail from the campsite.

Stream 🏞 The next day, ascend from the camp, coming alongside Pretty Hollow Creek. Cross it by footlog at 3.1, ▶4 3.4, and 3.8 miles. Span Onion Bed Branch at 4.1 miles. The canopied forest gives way to gorgeous open woodland of beech, buckeye, yellow birch, spruce, and fir with a grassy carpet for a floor.

Wildflowers 🌸

Reach Pretty Hollow Gap, elevation 5,179 feet, at 5.5 miles. ▶5 Pretty Hollow Gap forms a grassy

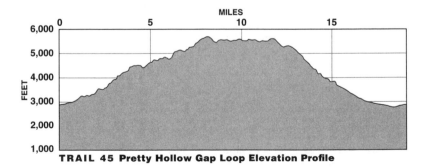

TRAIL 45 Pretty Hollow Gap Loop Elevation Profile

break in Mount Sterling Ridge. Head left on the level Mount Sterling Ridge Trail. Here, the Benton MacKaye Trail runs in conjunction with the Mount Sterling Ridge Trail. Make a gentle climb amid more grassy woods.

▲ **Ridge**

The trail shortly reaches the 5,500-foot level and stays at this elevation for miles, offering perhaps the easiest high-country walking in the park. The slope to your right rises high to Big Cataloochee Mountain, at 6,155 feet. Several spring branches flow over the path. The levelness of the trail causes drainage problems in some areas. The track can be muddy in spots as it wanders through thick stands of red spruce and Fraser fir. Bisect occasional open grassy slopes pocked with wind-stunted birch and maple stands, allowing intermittent views to the south and east. Still other trail sections travel beneath rhododendron.

 Spruce–Fir

Reach the Balsam Mountain Trail at 9.6 miles. ▶6 Veer left on Balsam Mountain, walking 0.3 mile to reach the Laurel Gap trail shelter ▶7 and your second night's destination. A clearing enhances the highland setting. Dark-eyed juncos flitter about the vicinity in summer. This little gray bird returns to the high country during the spring warm-up, then stays in the spruce–fir woods until fall, when it heads to the park's lowlands. This so-called "vertical migration" is its most notable characteristic.

▲ **Backcountry Camping**

Start day three by continuing on the Balsam Mountain Trail, rising past Balsam High Top before descending through grassy forest to meet the Beech Gap Trail at 11.3 miles of your loop hike. ▶8 Stay with the Balsam Mountain Trail as it heads more down than up, leaving the spruce–fir high country for deciduous woodlands, meeting gravel Round Bottom Road at Pin Oak Gap at 13.6 miles. ▶9

 Autumn Colors

Turn left, walking Round Bottom Road to meet the Palmer Creek Trail at 14.3 miles. ▶10 Begin descending the deep forest path on Trail Ridge for

A backpacker crosses *aptly named Pretty Hollow Creek on a footlog.*

Stream

a half mile to drop into the steep Palmer Creek watershed, crossing tributary Beech Creek on a footlog at 15.9 miles. ►11 Palmer Creek's steep slopes prevented the heavy settlement that other parts of Cataloochee Valley saw.

Historical Interest

The name "Palmer" could've derived from any number of Palmers who settled in Cataloochee Valley, starting with George Palmer in the 1840s. He had many descendants also named George, so you can safely say that the creek is named for George Palmer and leave it at that. At one time, there were so many George Palmers in Cataloochee that they had to have nicknames.

Stay along the precipitous mountainside above Palmer Creek, crossing Indian Creek at 16.3 miles. ▶12 Keep downhill to reach the bottomland along Palmer Creek, where red maple, birch, beech, and scads of rhododendron thrive. Cross Palmer Creek on a footlog before meeting Pretty Hollow Gap Trail at 17.5 miles. ▶13 From here, backtrack 1.6 miles to complete the circuit. ▶14

❈ **Wildflowers**

🚶	**MILESTONES**	
▶1	0.0	Pretty Hollow Gap Trailhead
▶2	0.7	Pass Little Cataloochee Trail
▶3	1.6	Pretty Hollow campsite #39
▶4	3.1	First crossing of Pretty Hollow Creek
▶5	5.5	Pretty Hollow Gap; left on Mount Sterling Ridge Trail
▶6	9.6	Left on Balsam Mountain Trail
▶7	9.9	Laurel Gap Shelter
▶8	11.3	Pass the Beech Gap Trail
▶9	13.6	Join Round Bottom Road
▶10	14.3	Left on Palmer Creek Trail
▶11	15.9	Cross Beech Creek
▶12	16.3	Cross Indian Creek
▶13	17.5	Right on Pretty Hollow Gap Trail; backtrack
▶14	19.1	Pretty Hollow Gap Trailhead

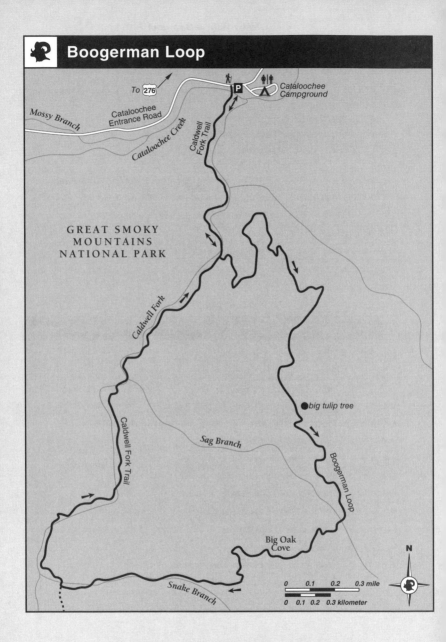

Boogerman Loop

To (276)

Mossy Branch

Cataloochee Entrance Road

Cataloochee Creek

Caldwell Fork Trail

Cataloochee Campground

GREAT SMOKY
MOUNTAINS
NATIONAL PARK

Caldwell Fork

Caldwell Fork Trail

Sag Branch

big tulip tree

Boogerman Loop

Big Oak Cove

Snake Branch

| 0 | 0.1 | 0.2 | 0.3 mile |
| 0 | 0.1 0.2 | 0.3 kilometer | |

N

Boogerman Loop

This hike appropriately starts with a footlog crossing. You'll be quite familiar with these narrow bridges before this loop is over. Along the way, enjoy huge trees, homesites, and mountain streams. There is quite a bit of up and down, but the trail makers were simply visiting the biggest trees in the area.

Best Time

Winter is a good time, since the elevations aren't high and the lack of leaves allows views of big trees and historic homesites. Spring reveals copious wildflowers along Caldwell Fork. Summer could be warm. The trails are their driest in fall.

Finding the Trail

From Exit 20 on I-40, take US 276 south a short distance to Cove Creek Road. Turn right on Cove Creek Road and follow it nearly 6 miles to enter the park. Two miles beyond the park boundary, turn left onto Cataloochee Entrance Road and follow it 2.6 miles to Caldwell Fork Trail, on your left just after you pass Cataloochee Campground.

Trail Description

Leave Cataloochee Valley, immediately spanning Palmer Creek on a long footbridge. Enter a homesite just to the right of the trail. White pines are reclaiming the former residence. This boggy but scenic flat has been improved with wooden planks for

TRAIL USE
Day Hiking

LENGTH
7.5 miles, 3½–4½ hours

VERTICAL FEET
±1,020

DIFFICULTY
– 1 2 **3** 4 5 +

TRAIL TYPE
Loop

FEATURES
Ridgeline
Stream
Autumn Colors
Wildflowers
Old-Growth
Historical Interest

FACILITIES
(SEASONAL)
Campground
Restrooms
Water

hikers. Caldwell Fork flows to your left. Doghobble lines the trail. Make your first footlog crossing of Caldwell Fork at 0.8 mile. Reach the lower end of the Boogerman Trail. Turn left and join it.

The main part of Cataloochee Valley was a little too crowded for Robert "Boogerman" Palmer, so he decided to make his homestead away from others. The first half of the Boogerman Trail roughly follows the road that Palmer built to reach his back of beyond. There is quite a bit of up and down on Boogerman Trail, and the trail doesn't always go where you think it will or should go, but the trail makers, while often using old roads, make a few twists and turns to visit the biggest trees. Toward the trail's end, along Snake Branch, the path rejoins another pioneer road.

Leave Cataloochee Road on the Caldwell Fork Trail, ▶1 ambling up a green mountain valley. The Boogerman Trail, open to hikers only, leaves Caldwell Fork ▶2 and winds up the slope of Den Ridge after crossing a streamlet. Gray-trunked **Old-Growth** 🌳 tulip trees tower overhead. Continue ascending beneath other giants. Come near Palmer Branch, but turn away, instead climbing by switchback. Curve around the side slope of Den Ridge, full of maple,

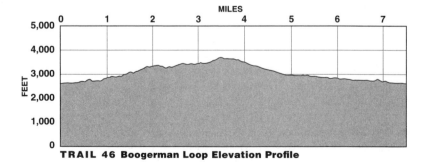

TRAIL 46 Boogerman Loop Elevation Profile

pine, oak, and mountain laurel. Mount Sterling is visible through the trees.

Turn into the Den Branch valley, where you can hear Den Branch rushing to meet Caldwell Fork. Pine needles carpet the trailbed in gold. More switchbacks lead atop Den Ridge. Cruise along, passing big oaks on a now-easy trail to reach Boogerman's homestead. He thought this place sufficiently desolate for a man named Boogerman. Ol' Palmer did clear a few trees for his farm, but as you have seen, he left plenty of big trees for us to enjoy today. Palmer became known for not allowing his property to be logged.

A wooden bridge spans shallow and rocky Palmer Branch. Hike away from the homestead and curve into the next drainage, which was also farmsteaded. An old metal wheel lies beside the trail. Just ahead, at 2.6 miles, stands an enormous tulip tree. ▶3 A short path leads left to this forest giant.

The path passes through another gap into the Sag Branch watershed, curving along the mountainside and dipping to cross Sag Branch at 3.2 miles. ▶4 Sag Branch flows off the slopes of Cataloochee Divide. Enter formerly cultivated timber just past Sag Branch. Note the younger pole trees. The Boogerman Trail climbs very steeply, only to dip into Big Oak Cove at 3.6 miles. Take note of the double-trunked tulip tree left of the trail: there is enough board feet in those connected trunks and the trees around it to fill a lumberyard.

The path leaves the cove and winds along low ridges, looking for Snake Branch. It eventually reaches Snake Branch valley and an elaborate, squared-off rock wall in the middle of the woods. The trail makes its way downstream in formerly settled country. Snake Branch, flowing off to your left, used to have four homesteads along it. Step over Snake Creek at 4.3 miles, ▶5 and soon cross it a second time. The trail joins an old farm road.

🏠 **Historical Interest**

This trail is named for shy Robert "Boogerman" Palmer. When asked his name in school, he purportedly hid his face and said, "Boogerman." It stuck for life.

🌳 **Old-Growth**

🏠 **Historical Interest**

Hand-laid stone walls *serve as reminders of the park's pioneer heritage.*

Rock walls and lightly wooded, elevated land to your right bear testimony of formerly plowed lands. Look right for a trail leading acutely right to a stone wall and homesite, still with rotting logs.

Cross Snake Branch a last time, now on your right. Pass more stone walls, metal relics, and the carved-out basement of a homestead. Make a final descent through white pine woods. Meet Caldwell Fork Trail at 4.8 miles. ▶6

Stream Turn right and head down picturesque Caldwell Fork valley. Cross Snake Branch on a footlog, and soon start the nine crossings of Caldwell Fork on footbridges underneath rich riparian woodlands.

The Caldwell Fork Trail can be muddy and confusing; at the stream crossings, the trail splits. Hikers go one-way over footbridges, and horses ford the creek—always take the trail headed for higher, drier ground. Handrails attached to footlogs aid hiker crossings. Because this trail is also open to horses, an accompanying horse ford is adjacent to each footlog, but often the footlog trail and horse ford trail diverge near the creek. Other path improvements, such as waterbars (logs or rocks embedded to channel water off sloped trail sections), have been added. Note where the footlogs have been elevated with rocks to keep them anchored during floods. Short footlogs cross tributaries.

These footbridges are a dry way to appreciate the crystal-clear creek, with its alternating deep pools, falls, and riffles clamoring as you descend the valley. At mile 6.7, ▶7 come again to the northern junction of the Boogerman Loop Trail. Continue down the Caldwell Fork Trail, backtracking to finish the loop at 7.5 miles. ▶8

🚶 MILESTONES

▶1	0.0	Caldwell Fork Trailhead
▶2	0.8	Boogerman Trail
▶3	2.6	Huge tulip tree
▶4	3.2	Sag Branch
▶5	4.3	Snake Creek
▶6	4.8	Caldwell Fork Trail
▶7	6.7	Pass Boogerman Trail
▶8	7.5	Caldwell Fork Trailhead

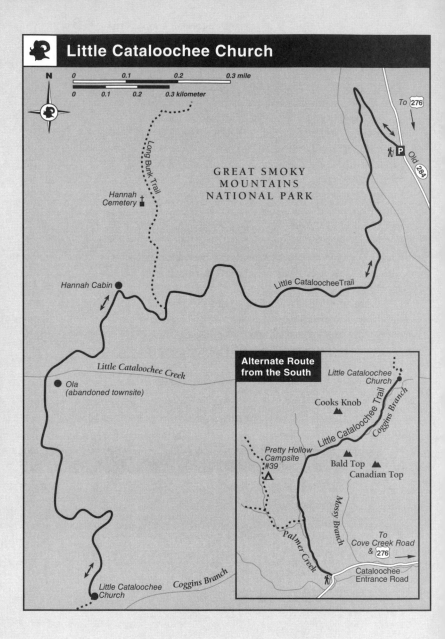

Little Cataloochee Church

N

0   0.1   0.2   0.3 mile
0   0.1   0.2   0.3 kilometer

Long Bunk Trail

GREAT SMOKY MOUNTAINS NATIONAL PARK

Hannah Cemetery

To 276

P

Old 284

Hannah Cabin

Little Cataloochee Trail

Little Cataloochee Creek

Ola
(abandoned townsite)

Alternate Route from the South

Little Cataloochee Church

Cooks Knob

Little Cataloochee Trail

Coggins Branch

Pretty Hollow Campsite #39

Bald Top

Canadian Top

Mossy Branch

Palmer Creek

To Cove Creek Road & 276

Cataloochee Entrance Road

Little Cataloochee Church

Coggins Branch

Little Cataloochee Church

The secluded hike is a trip back in time. Pass a preserved pioneer cabin on your rolling trek into the Little Cataloochee valley. View more homesites and farmsteads to finally end up at pastoral Little Cataloochee Church, built in 1890 and maintained to this day.

Best Time

This low-elevation hike is best enjoyed from late fall through early spring, when the leaves are off and you can more clearly see the outlines of old homesites and other evidence of pre-park settlers. Spring offers wildflowers aplenty. Summer could be muggy.

Finding the Trail

From Exit 20 on I-40, take US 276 south a short distance to Cove Creek Road. Turn right (north) on Cove Creek Road and follow it nearly 6 miles to enter the park. Two miles beyond the park boundary, reach an intersection with paved Cataloochee Entrance Road, but keep straight (north) and look for a sign for BIG CREEK, COSBY, joining gravel Old NC 284.

Follow the road for 2.1 miles, then come to another split. Keep right, still on gravel Old NC 284, and follow it 3.5 miles to the Little Cataloochee Trail, on your left. *Do not block the gate at the trailhead.*

TRAIL USE
Day Hiking, Horses

LENGTH
4.0 miles, 2–3 hours

VERTICAL FEET
±700

DIFFICULTY
− 1 **2** 3 4 5 +

TRAIL TYPE
Out-and-back

FEATURES
Stream
Autumn Colors
Wildflowers
Secluded
Historical Interest

FACILITIES
None

Trail Description

Secluded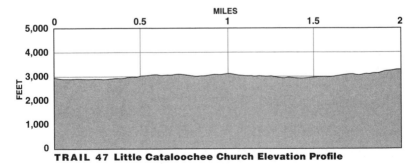

You will likely have this hike to yourself. It has a remote trailhead, and the few people who hike to Little Cataloochee Church do it from Cataloochee Valley. You will be surprised at the ups and downs—never steep—that travel through what was one of the most heavily settled areas in the pre-park Smoky Mountains.

Stream

From the trailhead, ▶1 the wide roadbed of a trail leaves Old NC 284 and curves down to Correll Branch in moist, rich woods. Cross Correll Branch on a road bridge. Big trees shade the path as it climbs, then curves into the Little Cataloochee Creek valley, high on a side slope.

Historical
Interest

The Little Cataloochee Trail cruises through pine and oak woods with mountain laurel aplenty to intersect the Long Bunk Trail at 1.0 mile. ▶2 The Long Bunk leaves right and climbs to reach the Mount Sterling Trail near Mount Sterling Gap after 3.3 miles. Reach the spur trail to the Hannah Cabin at 1.2 miles. ▶3 This cabin was built in the 1860s and restored by the park service. A brick chimney adds color to the weathered wood building. Look uphill from the cabin for rock piles from when the tulip tree woods were cornfields. Apple orchards once stretched up and down the hills, too.

TRAIL 47 Little Cataloochee Church Elevation Profile

OPTIONS

Cataloochee Valley

You can also start this hike from Cataloochee Valley, on the Pretty Hollow Trail, a wide roadbed (see the alternate route on the trail map). Palmer Creek rushes by to your left. Pass the Turkey George horse camp at 0.2 mile. The valley tightens before reaching a trail junction at 0.7 mile. Turn right here, joining the Little Cataloochee Trail. Soon step over Little Davidson Branch, which drains the now-forested Bald Top. The trail keeps up the narrowing Davidson Branch hollow.

The ascent steepens and heads directly for Davidson Gap, which you reach at 2.4 miles. The gap splits Cooks Knob to your left and Bald Top to your right. Descend into the Little Cataloochee Valley, passing remnants of former settlements, which were strung all along Little Cataloochee Creek and its tributaries. Reach restored Dan Cook Place at 3.1 miles. Climb a bit from Coggins Branch to reach Little Cataloochee Baptist Church at 3.9 miles.

The Little Cataloochee Trail keeps forward on a well-maintained roadbed, descending to bridge Little Cataloochee Creek at 1.4 miles. ▶4 You are now at the former mountaineer community of Ola. Look for persistent apple trees and dying locusts. Home-site evidence is all over the south side of the creek. Explore the mountain place that once had enough settlers to warrant its own post office. Remember that the remnants are a living archaeological exhibit of life in the Smokies, and *leave artifacts where you find them.*

Begin climbing past the settlement toward the ridge dividing Little Cataloochee Creek from Coggins Branch. Reach Little Cataloochee Baptist Church at 2.0 miles. ▶5 After you've passed many dilapidated remnants, the well-maintained white church on the hilltop looks even more impressive. An accompanying graveyard lies nearby. Local

Preacher's-eye view *of historic Little Cataloochee Church*

families keep up the church. Walk inside the church, and see the white wooden pews and the old pot-bellied stove used to heat it.

Interestingly, the 400-pound church bell was used to inform the community when someone passed away. The bell would be rung several times followed by a period of silence. The bell ringer would then ring the bell once for each year of the person's life. Locals could surmise by the number of tolls the identity of the deceased person.

🚶 MILESTONES

▶1	0.0	Little Cataloochee Trailhead
▶2	1.0	Long Bunk Trail leaves right
▶3	1.2	Hannah Cabin
▶4	1.4	Little Cataloochee Creek
▶5	2.0	Little Cataloochee Church

OPTIONS

Dan Cook Place

If you want to see another intact structure, continue 0.6 mile beyond the church to the Dan Cook Place. Originally built in 1856, the cabin features a stone fireplace, a wraparound porch, and a wooden shingle roof. A short set of stairs leads to a small second floor. The stone remnants of the Cooks' apple barn remain intact across Coggins Branch. (Little Cataloochee was a big apple-growing place in its latter days.) Apples were stored in the stone basement, which you can still see. Overhead was a storage building.

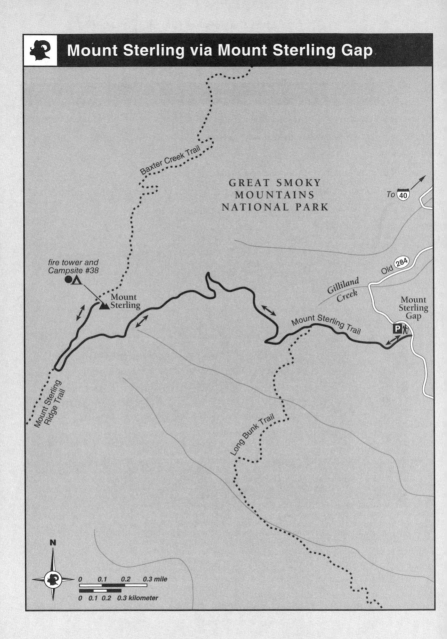

Mount Sterling via Mount Sterling Gap

GREAT SMOKY
MOUNTAINS
NATIONAL PARK

Baxter Creek Trail

To 40

Old 284

Gilliland Creek

fire tower and
Campsite #38

Mount
Sterling

Mount
Sterling
Gap

Mount Sterling Trail

Mount Sterling Ridge Trail

Long Bunk Trail

N

0   0.1   0.2   0.3 mile
0 0.1 0.2 0.3 kilometer

Mount Sterling via Mount Sterling Gap

This steep trail starts high and gets higher as it enters spruce–fir forest, culminating atop 5,842-foot Mount Sterling. A fire tower stands atop the mountain, where those who climb its heights are rewarded with an eye-popping 360-degree view of the Smoky Mountains and beyond.

TRAIL USE
Day Hiking,
Backpacking, Horses

LENGTH
5.4 miles, 2½–3 hours

VERTICAL FEET
+1,950/–1,950

DIFFICULTY
– 1 2 **3** 4 5 +

TRAIL TYPE
Out-and-back

Best Time

Anytime the skies are clear is a good time to go to Mount Sterling, with its fire tower affording a 360-degree view. Winter can be windy and snowy. Also, Old NC 284 can be closed during inclement weather. Spring has clear periods. Summer can be hazy and stormy. Autumn is a great time, with clear skies and fall colors.

FEATURES
Summit
Ridgeline
Autumn Colors
Spruce–Fir
Great Views
Photo Opportunity
Backcountry Camping
Steep

FACILITIES
None

Finding the Trail

From Exit 451 on I-40, just west of the North Carolina state line, head west across the Pigeon River on Tobes Creek Road. Just across the bridge, turn left (south) on Waterville Road to follow the Pigeon upstream. Come to a four-way intersection 2.3 miles after crossing the Pigeon—turn left here onto Old NC 284/Mount Sterling Road, and follow it south 6.7 winding miles to Mount Sterling Gap. The Mount Sterling Trail starts on the right (west) side of the gap.

Trail Description

Short and steep, with a fantastic view: that describes the Mount Sterling Trail in a nutshell. Leave Mount Sterling Gap and soon pass the Long Bunk Trail before entering Smokies spruce–fir forest, found only atop the park's highest points. Reach Mount Sterling Ridge, and then make a final push for the mountaintop and tower. Mount Sterling Gap, at an elevation of 3,890 feet, offers a leg up to the high country.

The Mount Sterling Trail leaves west from Mount Sterling Gap. ▶1 Pass around a pole gate, and begin climbing steeply up a wooded mountainside on the jeep road formerly used to maintain the tower atop the mountain. Hardwoods cloak the ridgeline that wends westerly from the Mount Sterling Gap. Larger oaks border the pathway. Begin to run beneath a power line that is going the same place you are but by a more direct route. The trailside trees are kept small here to accommodate it. The result is an open sky and a warm pathway when the sun is out.

In winter, Mount Sterling and its evergreen canopy are visible through the deciduous trees. The path levels and reaches the Long Bunk Trail at 0.5 mile. ▶2 The Mount Sterling Trail resumes climbing

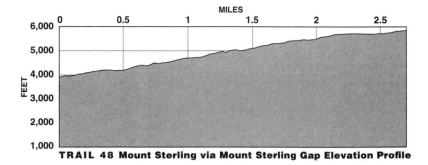

TRAIL 48 Mount Sterling via Mount Sterling Gap Elevation Profile

Mount Sterling *on a winter day as seen from Cataloochee*

and paralleling the power line. The southern exposure of the ridgeline allows mountain laurel to thrive along the trailside here, despite the elevation.

The path makes a sharp switchback to the right at 0.7 mile. Galax lines the trail. The first spruce trees begin to appear, especially when the trail curves around to the north side of the ridge. Craggy yellow birches enjoy this cool microclimate, too. Spruce dominates the north-facing landscape above 4,800 feet, standing straight and tall above the splayed rhododendron that drapes the steep slopes. Beech trees join the ranks of the northern trees after another switchback. But when the trail exposure curves to the south again, mountain laurel and oaks still hold sway, along with a scraggly pine or two. The forests on the lower slopes of Mount Sterling are heavily influenced by exposure.

Higher up, in the dim of regal evergreens, small Fraser fir trees grow atop mossy rocks, forming **Spruce–Fir** a green understory beneath tall spruce overhead.

Mount Sterling *offers 360-degree vistas of the Smoky Mountains.*

Ridge ▲

Spring seeps dribble across the path, which passes under the power line at 1.8 miles. The clearing underneath the power line opens views of grassy ridges in the distance. The trail then curves right and eases its ascent to reach a clearing and a trail junction at 2.3 miles. ▶3 Here, the Mount Sterling Ridge Trail leaves to the left for Pretty Hollow Gap in 1.4 miles.

Stay with the Mount Sterling Trail as it turns right and heads north for the summit. Cruise a grassy ridgeline bordered by thick Fraser fir trees. The path is mostly level before rising to reach a horse-hitching post. Soon open onto the summit of Mount Sterling and backcountry campsite #38, also named Mount Sterling. ▶4 The grassy mountaintop is surrounded by evergreens.

The tower stands at the very crest of the summit. The Baxter Creek Trail, coming 6 steep miles from the Big Creek Ranger Station, ends at the tower. The park's eastern swath is the featured view from the tower. The main crest of the Smokies lies to your north and west. I-40 and its road-cut in the Pigeon River gorge lie to your east. Beyond the park, the meadow of Max Patch stands clear.

 Summit

 Great Views

Towers such as these were once used during fire season. Nowadays, planes are used for fire watching. This tower, along with Shuckstack, are the last remaining metal towers in the park once used for fire patrol.

 Historical Interest

Backcountry campsite #38 is popular. The favored campsite is in the grassy area below the tower. More-sheltered campsites are situated in the surrounding woods. If you're thirsty, there's a spring to your left, a half mile down the Baxter Creek Trail.

 Backcountry Camping

MILESTONES

►1	0.0	Mount Sterling Gap Trailhead
►2	0.5	Pass Long Bunk Trail
►3	2.3	Stay right as Mount Sterling Ridge Trail leaves left
►4	2.7	Mount Sterling tower and backcountry campsite #38

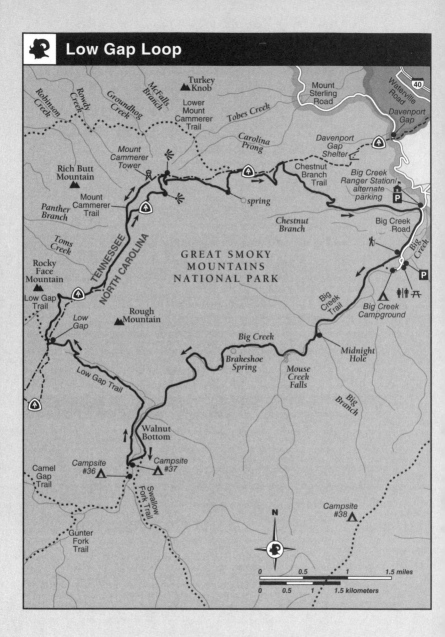

Low Gap Loop

Turkey Knob

Robinson Creek

Rowdy Creek

Groundhog Creek

McFalls Branch

Lower Mount Cammerer Trail

Tobes Creek

Mount Sterling Road

Waterville Road

40

Davenport Gap

Carolina Prong

Davenport Gap Shelter

Rich Butt Mountain

Mount Cammerer Tower

Chestnut Branch Trail

Big Creek Ranger Station/ alternate parking

P

Mount Cammerer Trail

Panther Branch

spring

Chestnut Branch

Big Creek Road

Toms Creek

TENNESSEE

NORTH CAROLINA

GREAT SMOKY MOUNTAINS NATIONAL PARK

Big Creek

P

Rocky Face Mountain

Low Gap Trail

Low Gap

Rough Mountain

Big Creek Trail

Big Creek Campground

Low Gap Trail

Big Creek

Brakeshoe Spring

Mouse Creek Falls

Midnight Hole

Big Branch

Walnut Bottom

Camel Gap Trail

Campsite #36

Campsite #37

Swallow Fork Trail

Campsite #38

Gunter Fork Trail

N

0   0.5   1   1.5 miles

0   0.5   1   1.5 kilometers

Low Gap Loop

This highlight-laden stream-and-ridge loop starts at Big Creek, then heads up that scenic waterway past waterfalls and swimming holes to reach a pair of backcountry campsites. From there, climb to the state-line ridge, taking the Appalachian Trail (AT) to Mount Cammerer and its historic observation tower. A prolonged descent returns you to the trailhead.

Best Time

This long loop is excellent for backpacking year-round. If you're doing it as a day hike, shoot for spring through fall for longer days.

Finding the Trail

From Exit 451 on I-40, just west of the North Carolina state line, head west across the Pigeon River on Tobes Creek Road. Just across the bridge, turn left (south) on Waterville Road to follow the Pigeon upstream. Come to a four-way intersection 2.3 miles after crossing the Pigeon, proceed forward on Old NC 284/Mount Sterling Road through the intersection to enter the park, passing the Big Creek Ranger Station on your right. Drive 0.9 mile to the end of the gravel road and the group parking area. The Big Creek Trail starts on the right (west) side of the road, just before the parking area.

Trail Description

This hike covers a lot of ground, and a lot of beautiful places, as it makes a classic stream-and-ridge circuit. Start by following Big Creek into one of the

TRAIL USE
Day Hiking,
Backpacking
LENGTH
17.2 miles, 9–11 hours
VERTICAL FEET
±3,280
DIFFICULTY
– 1 2 3 4 **5** +
TRAIL TYPE
Loop

FEATURES
Ridgeline
Stream
Waterfall
Autumn Colors
Wildflowers
Wildlife
Great Views
Backcountry Camping
Swimming
Historical Interest
FACILITIES
Campground
Picnic Area
Restrooms

Smokies' most scenic valleys, visiting the swimming spot known as the Midnight Hole as well as Mouse Creek Falls. Reach Walnut Bottom, where two backcountry campsites await for those who want to overnight it.

From there, the hike makes its way to the state-line ridge at Low Gap, to join the AT. Next, trek out to Mount Cammerer and garner spectacular views from a historic fire tower. Beyond the tower, return to the AT and begin a long descent through rich woods and past rock outcrops where more views can be had. Finally, leave the AT, taking the Chestnut Branch Trail back to Big Creek.

This can be done as a very long day hike, but explorers would be better served to turn this into a one-night backpacking trip, staying at Walnut Bottom. Or you could easily turn it into a two-nighter by continuing on the AT beyond Mount Cammerer and overnighting at Davenport Gap Shelter, then backtracking and returning to Big Creek by Chestnut Branch Trail.

Keep your batteries charged—there will be ample photo opportunities along Big Creek and on the AT, plus just about everywhere else, as this circuit is ensconced in near-continuous beauty.

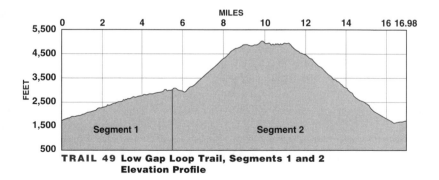

TRAIL 49 Low Gap Loop Trail, Segments 1 and 2 Elevation Profile

The hike's beginning ►1 is easy, as the Big Creek Trail gently works up a flowery valley under an overarching tree canopy through which courses a crystal-clear stream. Stay on the valley side slope, passing a spur trail leading down to Big Creek Campground at 0.2 mile. The path comes alongside Big Creek at 0.9 mile. The valley was blasted to make room for the path, as boulder fields rise from the stream.

 Wildflowers

 Stream

Big Creek is quite a sight, its colorations ranging from clear to tropical blue-green. Find ►2 Midnight Hole at 1.5 miles. Here, a fall splits two boulders and flows into a swimming pool that is quite a summer attraction. Note the smooth, timeworn boulders through which Big Creek flows.

Rhododendron borders the pathway. Reach Mouse Creek Falls at 2.0 miles. ►3 There is a horse hitching post here. This cataract, located across Big Creek, is Mouse Creek's last hurrah before it joins the waters of Big Creek. Here, Mouse Creek emerges as a narrow flow in a rhododendron thicket, then makes a tiered descent. The cataract widens on its first drop, forms a pool, and then falls one more time before meeting its mother stream.

 Waterfall

Most day hikers turn around here. At 2.3 miles, ►4 bridge Big Creek above alluring pools. Gaze down to see trout swimming. The next segment offers everywhere-you-look beauty, save for brushy areas recovering from a storm back in 2013. Intersect the Swallow Fork Trail at 5.1 miles, ►5 then bridge Big Creek to reach Walnut Bottom and campsite #37 at 5.2 miles. It and companion campsite #36 are set in a wooded flat through which Big Creek sings.

 Photo Opportunity

 Wildlife

Meet and join the Low Gap Trail at 5.3 miles. ►6 You're prepared to climb, but instead the singletrack path rolls downstream parallel to Big Creek. At 6.3 miles, the path turns up the hollow of Low Gap Branch and begins the expected ascent. Continue

The Midnight Hole *is an alluring swimming spot.*

in rich woods, occasionally winding through rocky coves. At 7.4 miles, ▶7 cross Low Gap Branch. This is your last chance for water for a good while, so fill up. Climb away from the stream, then angle back to reach Low Gap and the AT at 7.9 miles. This now-scruffy spot suffered damage from the same 2013 storm.

Ridge ▲

Head right, northbound on the AT, continuing the climb. You are well above 4,000 feet in elevation. Look for red spruce trees dotting the woods. At 8.6 miles, curve sharply right around the ridge of Rocky Face Mountain. Gain glimpses into the hills of East Tennessee. At 9.1 miles, cruise below Sunup Knob. The walking is easy, but then you reach the Mount Cammerer Trail at 10.0 miles. ▶9 Dip, then

Summit ◬

work up a bit to reach the outcrop and ▶10 tower at mile 10.6. Exhilarating vistas open before you enter the tower, but you must enter the restored historic fire lookout. The rock cut of I-40, which follows the Pigeon River, a whitewater destination, is visible to your east. Mount Sterling and its metal fire tower rise to your south. Stone Mountain rises north, and beyond East Tennessee rolls as far as the eye can see. *Wow!*

Photo Opportunity

Great Views

Backtrack to rejoin the AT ▶11 at 11.2 miles. Begin a prolonged downgrade on the North Carolina side of the ridge, stepping often off wood and earth steps. Take your time. Come to a view at 11.8 miles as you curve around and along a severe rock outcrop. Below, Chestnut Branch and Big Creek cut swaths through the thick woods. The Mount Sterling tower is still visible above.

Geologic Interest

At 12.2 miles, open onto a north view into the Volunteer State, then switchback, keeping downhill. Transition into a lower-elevation forest of oak, mountain laurel, and pine, along with galax. Watch for trailside quartz. The descent passes a spur right to a small, somewhat iffy spring at 13.1 miles. The relentless drop continues through the intersection with the ▶12 Lower Mount Cammerer Trail at 13.4 miles. Meet and join the Chestnut Branch Trail in a gap at 14.3 miles. ▶13 (Those wanting to make a two-night trip can continue on the AT for another mile to reach the Davenport Gap trail shelter, then backtrack the next day.)

Great Views

Rest a minute, because the drop sharpens on Chestnut Branch Trail. Cut through a hollow created by a tributary of Chestnut Branch before turning away and making a switchback right at 15.2 miles. Return to the tributary, then saddle alongside much-bigger Chestnut Branch, which resembles a mini–Big Creek.

The valley opens, and you enter formerly settled terrain and a homesite at 15.7 miles. Look for rusted relics. Watch for a huge old trailside oak tree at 15.9 miles. The valley widens, and then you meet Big

Looking toward Mount Sterling *from a rock outcrop on the AT at mile 11.8 of this hike*

Creek Road at 16.4 miles. ▶14 The Big Creek Ranger Station and alternate parking are a short ways to the left, but you most likely parked at the Big Creek trailhead and picnic area, so follow Big Creek Road right, uphill, to reach the parking area and trailhead at 17.2 miles, ▶15 completing the circuit.

🚶 MILESTONES

▶1　0.0　Big Creek Trailhead and Picnic Area
▶2　1.5　Midnight Hole
▶3　2.0　Mouse Creek Falls
▶4　2.3　Bridge Big Creek
▶5　5.1　Swallow Fork Trail
▶6　5.3　Walnut Bottom, Low Gap Trail
▶7　7.4　Cross Low Gap Branch
▶8　7.9　Low Gap, Appalachian Trail
▶9　10.0　Mount Cammerer Trail
▶10　10.6　Mount Cammerer Tower
▶11　11.2　Back on AT
▶12　13.4　Lower Mount Cammerer Trail
▶13　14.3　Right on Chestnut Branch Trail
▶14　16.4　Big Creek Road
▶15　17.2　Big Creek Trailhead and Picnic Area

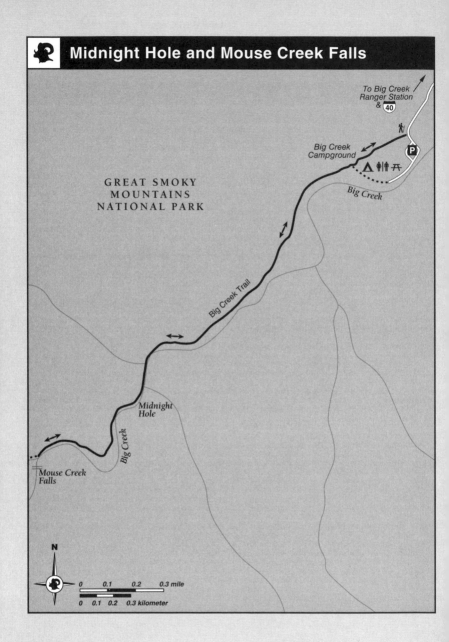

Midnight Hole and Mouse Creek Falls

To Big Creek
Ranger Station
& 40

Big Creek
Campground

Big Creek

GREAT SMOKY
MOUNTAINS
NATIONAL PARK

Big Creek Trail

Midnight
Hole

Big Creek

Mouse Creek
Falls

N

0   0.1   0.2   0.3 mile

0   0.1   0.2   0.3 kilometer

Midnight Hole and Mouse Creek Falls

This hike travels up the Big Creek watershed, past swimming holes, cascades, and a waterfall amid all-encompassing stream beauty. Big Creek valley has been a recreation destination since before the inception of the national park.

Best Time

Spring through summer is the best period for this trek. In spring, Big Creek and Mouse Creek Falls are at their boldest, complementing the wide-ranging wildflower displays. In summer, water enthusiasts can swim in Midnight Hole and fish Big Creek.

Finding the Trail

From Exit 451 on I-40, just west of the North Carolina state line, head west across the Pigeon River on Tobes Creek Road. Just across the bridge, turn left (south) on Waterville Road to follow the Pigeon upstream. Come to a four-way intersection 2.3 miles after crossing the Pigeon, proceed forward on Old NC 284/Mount Sterling Road through the intersection to enter the park, passing the Big Creek Ranger Station on your right. Drive 0.9 mile to the end of the gravel road and the group parking area. The Big Creek Trail starts on the right (west) side of the road, just before the parking area.

Trail Description

Big Creek Valley has returned to its original state of forest primeval. Before our time, this area was

TRAIL USE
Day Hiking, Horses

LENGTH
4.0 miles, 2–2½ hours

VERTICAL FEET
±530

DIFFICULTY
– 1 **2** 3 4 5 +

TRAIL TYPE
Out-and-back

FEATURES
Stream
Waterfall
Autumn Colors
Wildflowers
Photo Opportunity
Swimming

FACILITIES
Campground
Picnic Tables
Water

home to settlers, then a timber source and camp for loggers, and then a place where young men of the Civilian Conservation Corps built trails. Now only the trail, the Big Creek Ranger Station, a picnic area, a small campground, and a trailhead reveal the human touch on this valley.

The Big Creek Trail makes a gentle but steady ascent, gaining an average of 240 feet per mile. This grade enables you to look up at the rich forest, out to a spring carpet of wildflowers and into the ultra-crystalline creek—possibly the clearest in the Smokies, if there is such a beast. Avid anglers can vie for Smoky Mountain trout.

Wildflowers

Proceed up the Big Creek Trail, ▶1 passing around a metal gate, and follow parts of what has been an Indian path; a settlers' wagon road; a logging railroad; an auto road; and now, coming full circle, a horse and footpath again. The pea gravel track stays a good 200 feet above the stream. After a quarter mile, pass a spur trail leading into the valley below and down to the Big Creek Campground.

Stream

Saddle alongside Big Creek at 0.9 mile. ▶2 Notice the trailside blasted rock where the gorge pinches the path against the steep mountainside, broken by impressive boulder fields rising up the mountainside. One thing you surely won't miss is

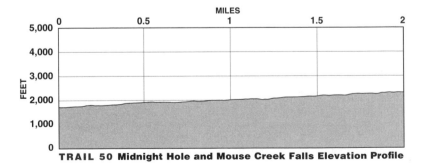

TRAIL 50 Midnight Hole and Mouse Creek Falls Elevation Profile

the color of Big Creek: depending on the depth and time of year, it displays an array of blues and greens that can look almost tropical. Reach Midnight Hole at 1.5 miles. ▶3 Here, a fall splits two boulders and flows into a swimming pool big enough for an army of sweaty hikers. It's deep, too. This locale draws swimmers during the warm season.

Autumn Colors

Swimming

Continue upstream. Small rivulets flow under the trail and into Big Creek. Small wooden bridges allow dry passage for hikers and horsemen. Flanks of rhododendron border the pathway. Take a second to look over now-nearby Big Creek. Midstream boulders have been worn smooth by thousands upon thousands of years of Big Creek following gravity's downward pull.

Reach the short spur trail leading left to Mouse Creek Falls and a horse-hitching post at 2.0 miles. ▶4 This falls, located across Big Creek, is Mouse Creek's last hurrah before joining the waters of Big Creek. Here, Mouse Creek emerges as a narrow flow in a rhododendron thicket, then makes a two-tiered descent. The cataract widens on its first drop, forms a pool, and then falls one more time before meeting its mother stream. Mouse Creek drains the highlands of Mount Sterling Ridge above.

Waterfall

Photo Opportunity

Backpackers can hike 3 additional, fairly easy miles to reach Lower Walnut Bottom backcountry campsite #37, elevation 3,000 feet. This popular campsite was once one of the most troublesome locales for human–bear interactions. Food-storage cables are provided to help keep the bears wild and hikers stocked with the provisions they've brought. Before the park service installed the cables, they put up metal poles with hooks atop them for campers to hang their packs . . . but the bears would just shimmy up the poles. (That prompted the park to grease the poles, but that didn't work either!) Happily, times are much better at Walnut Bottom for man and beast.

Backcountry Camping

Midnight Hole *in winter*

Campers can also consider Big Creek Campground, located near the trailhead for this hike. It is the Smokies' smallest campground and its sole one that's tent-only. This walk-in campground is set deep in the woods adjacent to Big Creek. A small footpath leaves the parking area and loops the 12 campsites in the shade of tall hardwoods. Because it's a walk-in campground, you must tote your camping supplies anywhere from 100 to 300 feet. But after that, you'll be hearing only the intonations of Big Creek instead of car engines and smelling the wildflowers instead of exhaust fumes.

MILESTONES

▶1   0.0   Big Creek Trailhead
▶2   0.9   Come alongside Big Creek
▶3   1.5   Midnight Hole
▶4   2.0   Mouse Creek Falls

Appendix 1

Local Resources

National Park Service
Great Smoky Mountains National Park
107 Park Headquarters Road
Gatlinburg, TN 37738
865-436-1200, nps.gov/grsm

Plentiful information is available at the park's website. Can't find something online? Call the number above and follow the prompts.

Other Smoky Mountains National Park Area Resources
Fontana Marina
300 Woods Road/PO Box 68
Fontana Dam, NC 28733
828-498-2129, fontanavillage.com/shuttle-services

Access the south side of the Smokies using shuttles from this marina. Fontana Village also offers varied overnight accommodations.

Gatlinburg Visitors and Convention Bureau
811 E. Parkway/PO Box 527
Gatlinburg, TN 37738
800-588-1817, gatlinburg.com

Learn everything you ever wanted to know about the Tennessee Smokies gateway town.

Cherokee, North Carolina, Information

498 Tsali Blvd.
Cherokee, NC 28719
800-438-1601, visitcherokeenc.com

The website details the myriad indoor and outdoor recreation activities at the Cherokee Indian Reservation, on the south side of the park.

Nantahala National Forest

1070 Massey Branch Road
Robbinsville, NC 28771
828-479-6431, www.fs.usda.gov/nfsnc

Smokies visitors often base-camp at this national forest, which borders the Smokies on its south side, across from Fontana Lake.

Smokies Partnership Groups

Great Smoky Mountains Association

115 Park Headquarters Road
Gatlinburg, TN 37738
865 436-7318
smokiesinformation.org

Established in 1953, this group helps the park "through sales, labor, donations, and volunteer efforts, and provides the National Park Service with additional tools for fulfilling its mission." The group supports the park's educational, scientific, and historical programs, enhancing public enjoyment and understanding of Great Smoky Mountains National Park.

Friends of the Smokies

PO Box 1660
Kodak, TN 37764
865-932-4794, friendsofthesmokies.org

Friends of the Great Smoky Mountains National Park assists the National Park Service in its mission to preserve and protect Great Smoky Mountains National Park by raising funds and public awareness and providing volunteers for needed projects. They work closely with the park service to bring desired projects to reality.

Appendix 2

Useful Sources

Books

The Great Smoky Mountains Association produces a wide variety of books on specific subjects pertaining to the park. Browse the selection at smokiesinformation.org/all-products; part of your purchase goes to support the park. Titles cover just about every park-related subject you can imagine. Here's a sampling: *Smokies Road Guide, Mountain People & Life, Place Names of the Smokies, Wildflowers of the Smokies, Ferns of the Smokies* and *Churches of the Smokies.*

Maps

Great Smoky Mountains National Park produces a paper trail map for a nominal fee. Buy it at the visitor centers, ranger stations, and select trail-heads. You can also download it from the park website, nps.gov/grsm.

Trails Illustrated (natgeomaps.com) produces maps of the Smokies. They sell a single map of the park, *229–Great Smoky Mountains National Park,* along with a pair of more detailed maps, *316–Cades Cove, Elkmont* and *317– Clingmans Dome, Cataloochee.*

Index

Check out this great title from
Menasha Ridge Press!

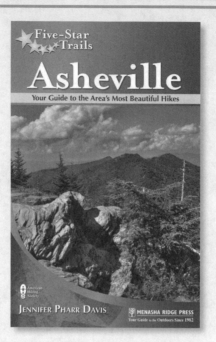

Five-Star Trails: Asheville

Jennifer Pharr Davis
ISBN: 978-0-89732-920-0
$15.95

5 x 8, paperback
264 pages
maps and photos

Five-Star Trails Asheville provides in-depth descriptions, directions, and commentary on what to expect along the way. Each hike features an individual trail map, elevation profile, and at-a-glance information, helping readers quickly find the perfect trip.

Sized to fit in a pocket, the book's detailed trail descriptions will help readers find their way on and off the trail. Driving directions and GPS trailhead coordinates will help with navigating myriad unnamed roads. The trails covered range from those best suited to novices, families, experienced hikers, or backpackers.

MENASHA RIDGE PRESS
www.menasharidge.com
Your Guide to the Outdoors Since 1982